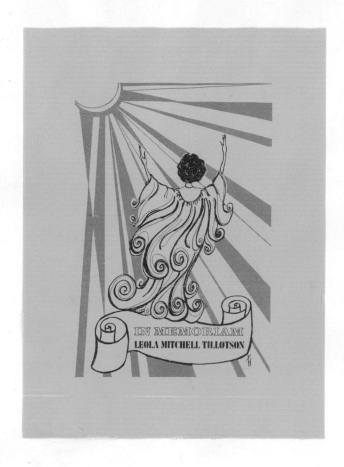

IN MEMORIAM
LEOLA MITCHELL TILLOTSON

JANE AUSTEN
AND SOME CONTEMPORARIES

JANE AUSTEN

AND SOME
CONTEMPORARIES

MONA WILSON

With an introduction by

G. M. YOUNG

KENNIKAT PRESS, INC./PORT WASHINGTON, N. Y.

JANE AUSTEN AND SOME CONTEMPORARIES

Originally published in 1938
Reissued in 1966 by Kennikat Press

Library of Congress Catalog Card No: 66-25953

Analysed in the ESSAY & GENERAL LITERATURE INDEX

For Margaret Llewelyn Davies, in the hope that she may find entertainment in the company of some old friends and some new.

CONTENTS

PREFACE

I APOLOGISE to the shade of Miss Cassandra Austen for what I have written about her sister. Cassandra objected to desultory writing, but Jane will forgive me: she rather liked it; and too much has been said about Miss Austen for any little additions to be other than desultory. But I wanted to express my conviction that her name should be linked with that of the great Vindicator of the Rights of Women, Mary Wollstonecraft, and that the *vis comica* of the one has been as powerful an agency in their vindication as the *saeva indignatio* of the other.

Jane Austen and Mary Wollstonecraft were bent on the destruction of the fair sex, of Keats' "milk-white lamb, that bleats for man's protection", and the evolution of the rational woman. When, about the middle of the Nineteenth Century, Sex became a Cause—an unfortunate but inevitable phase in the movement to establish women's rights—another Jane Austen should have been at hand to sustain their poise.

I recall a little picture in my own childhood, one of those many little pictures which never fade though their significance seems unaccountable: a large elderly lady in a black bonnet and a coat and boots, with a black bag from which she extracted a roll of papers. I saw a petition for the first time, and heard that women had a right to vote. The petition was signed. The small observer approved: naturally she would want to vote just like a man, and, still more important, to play polo just like a man, a desirable woman's right which had not been mentioned. But when the old lady and her bag had gone I saw the signatories smiling, and recognized her afterwards as the female in *Punch* who refused, somewhat unnecessarily, to be the plaything of a man. In the works of that missing novelist that old lady, and others like her, would have evoked only an affectionate smile. Sharper treatment was needed for her opponents, that group of women who, feeling themselves exceptional, stood aloof, and thought to maintain their own position by the sacrifice of their sex. I will not name them; some are dead and some have repented.

In his *Essay on Comedy*, which has, I fear, suffered the eclipse of his novels, Meredith maintains that the Comic Spirit can reign only over a world in which woman takes her share both naturally and equally. The time is ripe. The need for a Cause has gone by, women should become a Sex again; and I look anxiously for a successor to Miss Austen to preside over the transition.

By rights, my first essay should have been devoted to Mary Wollstonecraft, but on her I have already said my say elsewhere (in *From Anne to Victoria*: edited by Bonamy Dobree). For the rest, my choice was guided by my desire to work from records left by the women themselves. Harriet Grote stands somewhat apart from the others, because her life cannot be separated from that of her husband, the only man of genius, I fear, whom any of my women managed to capture. But I have included her because in her life we see the persistence into the full Victorian age and the days of Women's Rights, of a type of mind formed in earlier conditions. She and Mary Somerville are in fact transitional figures, reminding us that the generations, and even the centuries, do not live in mutual exclusiveness.

To Dr. R. W. Chapman I am indebted for permission to quote from his edition of Jane Austen's letters—and for how much more all students of her life and writing will understand. My thanks are also due to Mr. R. J. Mayor for information about the Grotes; to the Earl of Ilchester, and to Earl and Countess Russell, for leave to make use of passages from *Memorials of Holland House,* and from *The Amberley Papers.*

M.W.

INTRODUCTION

IN THESE ESSAYS, Miss Mona Wilson has undertaken
the double task of showing what the pre-Victorian
age felt like to a girl, and how the Victorian girl
came to be what she was. They are, in a sense, studies
in education, and I think the impression left on most
readers will be that, for the lucky ones at any rate,
the education of the late Eighteenth Century was of
a decidedly stimulating and encouraging kind. In
Jane Austen and Eliza Fletcher we have characters
of an achieved and easy balance: the story of Mary
Somerville shows us genius making its way, with
singularly little friction, little fuss, towards its con-
templated end: and no one, I think, will read the
tale of Mary Butt's delightful childhood without
feeling that her conversion to the creed of Human
Depravity was at least a minor calamity for our
literature. In Harriet Grote we see the Eighteenth
Century, stalking, undefeated, in a red flannel
petticoat (there are some still living who can remember that soldierly garment, the hoop-skirt discarded,
marching up and down a muddy lane under the
shocked eyes of the village), far on into the Nineteenth. But if we go from one age to the other, or
more exactly from about 1780 to 1840, it is impossible
not to feel that something chilly, constrictive, censorious has come into the atmosphere. What is it?

Memories of the French Revolution, for one thing, bringing with them the sense that the upper middle classes were, or might find themselves, at bay. It is striking to observe Mary Butt, now Mrs. Sherwood, writing in old age that the "easy and even affectionate relations" between rich and poor of her childhood had now become impossible. For another, the prodigious and unhealthy development of industry and increase of wealth during the Napoleonic wars, which set the stable society of the Eighteenth Century seething and working with new ambitions and new resentments, alarms, jealousies, aspirations, restraints. Finally, imposed on these, but at the same time in curious conformity with the society to which it was applied, Evangelicalism; with its insidious tendency to equate the Respectable and the Regenerate, to extend its moral ascesis over the whole of human life, and yet, in its soul-saving individualism, leaving the sphere of natural human relations almost unexplored.

I believe the discipline was salutary: that thanks to it we were able to accumulate a fund of moral energy which, when once the merely mechanical restraints on opinion and behaviour were relaxed, as they were towards the middle of the nineteenth century, created that "intense and glowing" civilization out of which, really, all the ideas by which we are now living issued. The discipline was hard: it left characters at once impoverished and distorted like Mary Anne Galton (in passing consider the relations

xiv

of the Galtons and their Catholic neighbours in 1780, with Protestant feeling in 1828, in 1843, or 1850). And yet it was the same concentration on Protestant truth and the way of salvation, that makes Charlotte Elizabeth Tonna at once the most intolerant anti-Papist in Ireland, and the fearless and far-sighted champion of the sempstresses and factory children of England.

I have called these essays studies in education, and under education I include that emotional ambient within which the people of any age or class do the necessary things of life, waking up and working, eating, playing, dressing and making love. It is created by the pressure of society, bent, unconsciously and instinctively, on maintaining the way of life which it feels to be satisfactory. By society, I mean nothing abstract or remote, but simply the conversational judgments, whether for approval or disapproval, to which the individual is subjected. The judgments of parents, nurses, governesses, of pastors and masters in all degrees, are the voice of society in equilibrium: the judgments of the younger generation are the voice of society dissident and exploratory. Such is the provision Nature has made for the stability and progress of her human tribes, and to keep these tendencies—the historical and the logical way of thinking, the conformist and the dissident—in healthy equipoise, mutually reacting and progressively diminishing the number, or at least the influence, of die-hards, dug-outs, misfits and cranks, seems to me the prime object which education should set before itself.

A very wise man once said to me when I was young: "If a man starts a sentence with 'I have often noticed that women . . .' listen to him, he may have something to say worth hearing. If he begins: 'Women . . .' he is pretty certainly a fool." Even with this warning in one's ears, one may, I think, say that, being by nature the more stay-at-home animal, girls need more than boys that corrective which Mary Wollstonecraft called "running wild", and which the more fortunate damsels in Miss Wilson's bevy enjoyed. And, looking back, one can now see that our civilization in the Nineteenth Century did suffer from an over-fostering of the conformist element in its women; one can respect the foresight and courage of those who went back and picked up the thread of an older and better tradition, and, unalarmed by the outcries of Aunt Groves and Mrs. Schimmelpenninck, called Beatrice and Sophia and Diana Vernon back from the enchanted woods where they had been waiting. G. M. YOUNG

JANE AUSTEN 1775–1817

TRUTHFULNESS—so I have been told—is my one qualification for scholarship. It is a dismal one. For some ecstatic moments I believed, putting my trust in Dr. Chapman, who had no means of knowing better, that Jane Austen had met Miss Iremonger at the Andover Ball in November 1800. But, when I was indulging in a vision of their meeting, the elder woman languidly tolerant of so provincial an entertainment, the younger sparkling and observant—not a detail wasted—harsh facts broke in. "Facts are such horrid things," as Lady Susan's friend subtly observes. It can only have been a niece. *The* Miss Iremonger, in exuberant enjoyment of particularly bad health, namely an inflammatory spasm, was taking an uninterrupted course of Epsom salts and nitric, with the addition of frequent bleedings, under the direction of her London doctor. Now, reluctantly, I believe that they never knew each other at all: such a personality must have left some trace on the novels, but I have failed to detect a single authentic phrase; and though Miss Iremonger's letters, when she is not dilating on her own dreadful symptoms and those of her family and friends, are chiefly concerned with her literary tastes, there is not a word about Jane Austen. But, if they may never have met, both attended Andover Balls. Here is Miss Iremonger in 1790:

1

The Andover Ball which followed, about which you have interested yourself sufficiently to ask for an account of, had not any other recommendation to me but as an act of Duty indispensable, for I quite hate the sort of thing and was not in my element again till it was over. Could I suppose it could have given you pleasure to have made one of the number I am sure I should have wished you there, but you have raised ideas of it beyond any thing it deserves, for it was confin'd entirely to the two families who support an interest there, Lord Portsmouth's and my Father's, and the Town of Andover. Little indeed, therefore, is there to relate but that the Corporation was gratified and in good humour, and that I was delighted to find myself at full liberty to come home at two in the morning and left my Niece, my elder Brother's daughter, with her Father and Mother to take care of her, dancing till four.

And here is Jane Austen in 1800, writing to her sister, Cassandra:

It was a pleasant evening; Charles found it remarkably so; but I cannot tell why, unless the absence of Miss Terry—towards whom his conscience reproaches him with now being perfect indifferent—was a relief to him. There were only twelve dances, of which I danced nine, and was merely prevented from dancing the rest by the want of a partner. We began at 10, supped at 1, and were at Deane before 5. There were but 50 people in the room; very few families indeed from our side of the Country, and not many more from the other. My partners were the two St. Johns, Hooper Holder—and very prodigious—Mr. Mathew, with whom I called the last, and whom I liked the best of my little stock. There were very few Beauties, and such as there were, were not very handsome. Miss Iremonger did not look well, and Mrs. Blount was the only one much admired. She appeared exactly as she did in September, with the same broad face, diamond bandeaux, white shoes, pink husband, and fat neck. The two Miss Coxes were there; I traced in one the remains of the vulgar, broad-featured girl who danced at Enham eight years ago; the other is refined into a nice, composed-looking girl like Catherine Bigg. I looked at Sir Thomas Champneys and thought of poor Rosalie; I looked at his daughter and thought her a queer animal with a white neck. Mrs. Warren, I was constrained to think a very fine young woman, which I much regret. She has got rid of some part of her child, and danced away with great activity, looking by no means very large. Her husband is ugly enough; uglier even than his cousin John; but he does not look so *very* old. The Miss Maitlands are both prettyish; very like Anne; with brown skins, large dark eyes, and a good deal of nose.

"But," some reader interrupts, "who is this Miss

3

Iremonger? I don't know the woman." The loss is yours, and the remedy in your own hands. She is the most entrancing of Dear Miss Heber's correspondents, and her letters are published among those discovered at Weston by Mr. and Mrs. Sacheverell Sitwell. Some insensitive reviewer, I remember, described *Dear Miss Heber* as "much cry and little wool". Little wool, indeed! Enough can be pulled from those fragrant bushes with which to weave a tapestry of figures savouring as fully of their time as Jane Austen's own. In fact, as household words, their remarks become confounded with hers. After an interrupted morning's work what more bitterly apt than "'Tis a delicious neighbourhood, Mary, hardly a morning but somebody calls in." This is not one of the younger Miss Bennets speaking: it has dropped from the pen of Miss Mary Curzon, a somewhat fast young lady, who addresses Miss Heber by her surname only, and has a masculine love of hunting.

Titles are commoner in the Heber circle than in Miss Austen's, and a London season a more regular part of the programme, but the two overlapped. Lady Banks, wife of the famous botanist and another of Miss Heber's correspondents, remarks in 1791: "It is a most extraordinary Thing that Sir Brook Bridges shou'd marry 3 Daughters at one time and all so well". Now Elizabeth Bridges married Miss Austen's brother, Edward Knight of Godmersham Park, and her sister-in-law's letters, seventeen years later are full of the family's grief at her loss: "but it is sweet to think of her great worth, of her solid principles, her true devotion, her excellence in every relation of Life". Jane's interest in her wardrobe never fails, and we know also that she wore bombazeen and crape on this melancholy occasion: "*One* Miss Baker makes my gown and the other my bonnet, which is to be silk covered with crape", and as her velvet pelisse had already been relined her mourning did not impoverish her.

If someone had read to me Miss Iremonger's letters as excerpts from a newly discovered novel by Miss Austen I should not have doubted their authenticity for a moment. Jane, I should have said, is laughing at a new subject, a professed intellectual, now vulgarly denominated a highbrow, in her day a blue stocking, and a valetudinarian, a female Mr. Woodhouse, to boot. It is the absence of this tempting type which convinces me that Miss Austen and Miss Iremonger could not have had more than a nodding acquaintance. The heroines of the novels are intelligent and clever, but never markedly intellectual or pseudo-intellectual. Books mean something to them: to Fanny Price a resource in her piteous loneliness; to Marianne Dashwood an outlet for her romantic impulses. To be conversant with the literature of the day is eminently respectable. Has any statistically-minded reader, by the way, counted the *respectables* and *respectabilities* in the novels, used either in praise or ironically? They must amount to many score. This decent taste distinguishes the sensible women

from the fools. One of Lady Middleton's reasons for
disliking Elinor and Marianne Dashwood was that
they were fond of reading: "she fancied them satirical:
perhaps without exactly knowing what it was to be
satirical; but *that* did not signify. It was censure in
common use, and easily given." It would be delightful
to entertain any of the heroines, and some of the fools
and semi-fools, but I do not want to discuss books with
any of them over the tea-cups, unless to draw poor
little Fanny out of her shell, or invite Marianne to
share my indignation with the Reverend Mr. Gilpin's
strictures on beech trees. The boring causticity of
Elinor—and I can never make up my mind whether
Miss Austen knows what an odious woman Elinor is,
or whether she is the one failure—would make me
shrink from the subject. Mary Wollstonecroft remarks
significantly that "Most of the women in the circle
of my observation, who have acted like rational
creatures, or shown any vigour of intellect, have
accidentally been allowed to run wild." Running wild
meant, in her case, and in that of most of the women
with whom I am concerned in these pages, adventures
among books. They were in large measure self-educated. In this sense none of Miss Austen's young
ladies ran wild. Like the Austen girls themselves
they learnt enough either at school or at home from
governesses and masters to make reading a pleasant
occupation if they had any natural inclination for it.
The Bennets had visiting masters only: we remember
Lady Catherine's arrogant surprise:

6

"No governess! How was that possible? Five daughters brought up at home without a governness! I never heard of such a thing. Your mother must have been quite a slave to your education."

Elizabeth could hardly help smiling, as she assured her that had not been the case. "Then, who taught you? Who attended to you? Without a governess you must have been neglected." "Compared with some families, I believe we were; but such of us as wished to learn, never wanted the means. We were always encouraged to read, and had all the masters that were necessary. Those who chose to be idle, certainly might."

They could enjoy Pope and Johnson, Crabbe and Cowper: Fanny brings out her quotations easily and, since she, like her creator, has a sailor brother, is interested in travels. Mary Crawford's conversation shows her to be distinctly well-read. Emma is aware that she ought to read, but is too much concerned with practical affairs—her own and other people's—to get beyond good intentions: "Emma," says her critical, middle-aged lover, "has been meaning to read more ever since she was twelve years old. I have seen a great many lists of her drawing up at various times of books that she meant to read regularly through—and very good lists they were—very well chosen, and very neatly arranged—sometimes alphabetically, and sometimes by some other rule. The list she drew up when only fourteen, I remember thinking it did her judgment so much credit, that I preserved it some time; and I dare say she may have made out a very good list now." Jane Fairfax is the best educated, but she had an ulterior motive: the poor creature was compelled to earn her living.

Miss Austen is, indeed, far from regarding education as a mere matter of superficial accomplishments designed to snare husbands, the view taken by her one really wicked woman, Lady Susan Vernon, who says of her daughter:

> She is a stupid girl, and has nothing to recommend her. I want her to play and sing with some portion of taste and a good deal of assurance, as she has my hand and arm and a tolerable voice. I was so much indulged in my infant years that I was never obliged to attend to any thing, and consequently am without the accomplishments which are now necessary to finish a pretty woman. Not that I am an advocate for the prevailing fashion of acquiring a perfect knowledge of all languages, arts and sciences. It is throwing time away to be masters of French, Italian, and German: music, singing, and drawing, &c., will gain a woman some applause, but will not add one lover to her list—grace and manner, after all, are of the greatest importance. I do not mean, therefore, that Frederica's accomplishments should be more than superficial, and I flatter myself that she will not remain long enough at school to understand anything thoroughly.

And when Maria and Julia Bertram, whose vacant minds are a foil to Fanny's, boast that years ago they could repeat the chronological order of the kings of England, with the dates of their accession, and most of the principal events of their reigns, and of the Roman emperors as low as Severus; besides a great deal of the heathen mythology, and all the metals, semi-metals, planets, and distinguished philosophers, they are gently reminded by their obsequious aunt that "much as you know already, there is a great deal more for you to learn". "Yes," answers one of them, "I know there is, till I am seventeen." The Misses Bertram's Mythology was doubtless derived from *The Pantheon, Representing the Fabulous Histories of the Heathen Gods and Most Illustrious Heroes*, translated by Andrew Tooke from the *Pantheum Mysticum* of the Jesuit father, François Antoine Pomey, which reached its thirty-fifth edition in 1824.

Miss Austen did not bother herself about theories. Like Elizabeth she had found a home education with encouragement to read quite satisfactory for a woman of native wit and intelligence. Her little digs at schools and school-mistresses perhaps had their origin in memories of the school at Reading where, little more than a baby, she went as an appendage to her sister, because, as her mother said, "If Cassandra were going to have her head cut off, Jane would insist on sharing her fate." She is finding a place in Bath for a young servant and writes:

9

I hope I have acquitted myself pretty well; but having a very reasonable Lady to deal with, one who only required a *tolerable* temper, my office was not difficult. Were I going to send a girl to school I would send her to this person; to be rational in anything is great praise, especially in the ignorant class of school mistresses, and she keeps the school in the Upper Crescent.

On another occasion she is visiting a young friend at school in London:

She looks very well, and her hair is done up with an elegance to do credit to any education. Her manners are as unaffected and pleasing as ever. I was shewn upstairs into a drawing-room, where she came to me, and the appearance of the room, so totally unschool-like, amused me very much; it was full of all the modern elegancies—and if it had not been for some naked Cupids over the mantelpiece, which must be a fine study for Girls, one would never have smelt instruction.

The feline kindliness of her treatment of the school in *Emma* shews at least her preference for the Reading type to the London finishing school.

Mrs. Goddard was the mistress of a school—not of a seminary, or an establisment, or anything which professed, in long sentences of refined nonsense, to combine liberal acquirements with elegant morality upon new principles and new systems—and where young ladies for enormous pay might

be screwed out of health and into vanity—but a
real, honest, old-fashioned Boarding-school, where
a reasonable quantity of accomplishments were sold
at a reasonable price, and where girls might be
sent to be out of the way, and scramble themselves
into a little education, without any danger of
coming back prodigies.

Miss Austen herself read intensively rather than
widely. She chiefly delighted in—dare I say, or
would it be to speak only for my own generation?—
authors who still delight us—Pope and Johnson, Addison
and Cowper, and, of course, her kindred spirit, Crabbe.
She was familiar with every detail of Richardson's
novels, took her history from Goldsmith and Hume
and Robertson and could, doubtless, have said like
Henry Crawford: "Shakespeare one gets acquainted
with without knowing how. It is part of an Englishman's constitution." Of Scott's poems she does not
seem to have been a great admirer—"Ought I to be
very much pleased with Marmion?—as yet I am not,—
James reads it aloud in the evening," and as early
as 1814 in a letter to her niece she professes resentment at Scott's new departure:

Walter Scott has no business to write novels,
especially good ones. It is not fair—he has Fame and
Profit enough as a Poet, and should not be taking
the bread out of other people's mouths. I do not
like him, and do not mean to like Waverley if
I can help it—but fear I must. I have made up my

11

mind to like no Novels really, but Miss Edgeworth's, yours, and my own.

But she should have excepted Miss Burney, to whose works her letters contain many references, and other figures in that curious outburst in *Northanger Abbey* over the novel reading of Catherine and Isabella.

Yes, novels;—for I will not adopt that ungenerous and impolitic custom so common with novel writers, of degrading by their contemptuous censure the very performances, to the number of which they are themselves adding—joining with their greatest enemies in bestowing the harshest epithets on such works, and scarcely ever permitting them to be read by their own heroine, who, if one accidentally take up a novel, is sure to turn over its insipid pages with disgust. Alas! if the heroine of one novel be not patronized by the heroine of another, from whom can she expect protection and regard? I cannot approve of it. Let us leave it to the Reviewers to abuse such effusions of fancy at their leisure, and over every new novel to talk in threadbare strains of the trash with which the press now groans. Let us not desert one another; we are an injured body. Although our productions have afforded more extensive and unaffected pleasures than those of any other literary corporation in the world, no species of composition has been so much decried. From pride, ignorance, or fashion, our foes are almost as many as our readers. And while the abilities of the

nine-hundredth abridger of the History of England,
or of the man who collects and publishes in a
volume some dozen lines of Milton, Pope, and Prior,
with a paper from the *Spectator*, and a chapter from
Sterne, are eulogized by a thousand pens,—there
seems almost a general wish of decrying the capacity
and undervaluing the labour of the novelist, and
of slighting the performances which have only
genius, wit, and taste to recommend them. "I
am no novel reader—I seldom look into novels—
It is really very well for a novel." Such is the common cant.—"And what are you reading, Miss—?"
"Oh! it is only a novel!" replies the young lady;
while she lays down her book with affected indifference, or momentary shame.—"It is only
Cecilia, or Camilla, or Belinda"; or, in short, only
some work in which the greatest powers of the
mind are displayed, in which the most thorough
knowledge of human nature, the happiest de-
lineation of its varieties, the liveliest effusions
of wit and humour are conveyed to the world
in the best chosen language. Now, had the same
young lady been engaged with a volume of the
Spectator, instead of such a work, how proudly
would she have produced the book, and told its
name; though the chances must be against her
being occupied by any part of that voluminous
publication, of which either the matter or manner
would not disgust a young person of taste: the
substance of its papers so often consisting in the

statement of improbable circumstances, unnatural characters, and topics of conversation, which no longer concern anyone living; and their language, too, frequently so coarse as to give no very favourable idea of the age that could endure it.

This passage has peculiar interest as, perhaps, the first claim for the novel as a serious form of art, and it should be noted that the authors instanced, Miss Burney and Miss Edgeworth, are both women. How we long to overhear more of the conversation with young Mr. Gould—"a very young Man, just entered of Oxford, wears Spectacles, and has heard that *Evelina* was written by Dr. Johnson." Did Miss Austen ask him why Fanny Burney should not have written it herself; did he reply in his Oxford accent that it was obviously too good for a woman; and is her choice of novels an indignant memory of this?

Mrs. Hannah More was too didactic—"You have by no means raised my curiosity after Caleb," writes Jane to her sister. "My disinclination for it before was affected, but now it is real; I do not like the evangelicals —of course I shall be delighted, when I read it, like other people, but till I do I dislike it." Cassandra points out the force of the hero's diphthong, but Jane is impenitent—"the only merit it could have, was in the name of Caleb, which has an honest, unpretending sound; but in Coelebs, there is pedantry and affectation. Is it written only to Classical Scholars?" *Coelebs in Search of a Wife* was looking for Milton's

Eve, Eve in her state of innocence. After turning down several young ladies who did not fill the bill, he found Lucilla, possessed of all Eve's characteristic virtues together with a modern individuality of her own:

"Lucilla Stanley is rather perfectly elegant than perfectly beautiful. I have seen women as striking, but I never saw one so interesting. Her beauty is countenance; it is the stamp of mind intelligibly printed on the face. It is not so much the symmetry of features as the joint triumph of intellect and sweet temper. A fine old poet has well described her:

> Her pure and eloquent blood
> Spoke in her cheeks, and so distinctly wrought
> That one could almost say her body thought.

Her conversation, like her countenance, is compounded of liveliness, sensibility, and delicacy. She does not say things to be quoted, but the effect of her conversation is that it leaves an impression of pleasure on the mind, and a love of goodness on the heart. She enlivens without overpowering. Contented to please, she has no ambition to shine. There is nothing like effort in her expression, or vanity in her manner. She has rather a playful gaiety than a pointed wit. Of repartee she has little and dislikes it in others; yet I have seldom met with a truer taste for inoffensive wit. Taste is, indeed, the predominating quality of her mind; and she may rather be said to be a nice judge of the genius of others than to be a genius herself. She has a

15

quick perception of whatever is beautiful or de-
fective in composition or in character. The same
true taste pervades her writing, her conversation,
her dress, her domestic arrangements, and her
gardening, for which last she has both a passion
and a talent. Though she has a correct ear, she
neither sings nor plays; and her taste is so exact
in drawing, that she really seems to have *le compas
dans l'oeil*; yet I never saw a pencil in her fingers,
except to sketch a seat or bower for the pleasure-
ground. Her notions are too just to allow her to
be satisfied with mediocrity in anything, and for
perfection in many things, she thinks that life is
too short, and its duties too various and important."

If Miss Austen persevered—"pictures of perfection
as you know make me sick and wicked" and her own
Anne Elliot was almost too good for her—her comment
was surely: "give me Eve when she has eaten her
apple". Another novelist is too like Marianne Dashwood
at her worst: "To set against your new novel of which
nobody ever heard before and perhaps never may
again, we have got *Ida of Athens* by Miss Owenson;
which must be very clever, because it was written,
as the Authoress says, in three months. We have only
read the Preface yet; but her *Irish Girl* does not make
me expect much. If the warmth of her Language
could affect the Body it might be worth writing in this
weather." Nevertheless I think that Miss Austen
would have extracted some amusement from the

maturer work of that popular novelist, afterwards Lady Morgan. Parody, perhaps because her own pen never needed that corrective, was her passion. She is enthusiastic over the *Rejected Addresses*, and the *Heroine*, a romance taking off the absurdities of the Terror Novel, by Eaton Stannard Barrett, an Irishman, author of various political satires. The works of Mrs. Radcliffe, Horace Walpole, Monk Lewis and their imitators, which betrayed Catherine Morland into her follies at Northanger Abbey, held much the same place as the modern detective story. Everyone read them: the Isabella Thorpes and the intellectuals alike. Henry Tilney teases Catherine, but is himself well up in her favourite literature.

Then, as now, local culture supported its own little book-club. Mrs. Digweed, to whom it makes little difference which of the twenty-six fortnights in the year books lie in her house, is asked whether *Rejected Addresses* had amused her:

Her answer was, "Oh dear yes, very much, very droll indeed—the opening of the House, and the striking up of the Fiddles." What she meant, poor woman, who shall say? I sought no further.

Other members are omnivorous:

Ladies who read these enormous great stupid thick quarto volumes which one always sees in the Breakfast parlour there, must be acquainted with everything in the world. I detest a quarto. Capt. Pasley's book is too good for their Society. They will

17

not understand a man who condenses his thoughts into an octavo.

Miss Austen has been suffering from a spate of travels. Here at last is a book of the month of which she can heartily approve, "delightfully written and highly entertaining. I am as much in love with the author as ever I was with Clarkson or Buchanan, or even the two Mr. Smiths of the City—the first soldier I ever sighed for—but he does write with extraordinary grace and spirit." Canning had anticipated her in the *Quarterly*, and Sir Charles William Pasley's *Essay on the Military Policy and Institutions of the British Empire* went into four editions. Her old loves are James and Horatio Smith of the *Rejected Addresses*, Thomas Clarkson, of whose *Portraiture of Quakerism* she is probably thinking, and the Rev. Claudius Buchanan, author of *Christian Researches in Asia*.

Let us now hear Miss Iremonger state her literary opinions:

> Have you read *Caroline de Litchfield*, the most charming French novel that ever was written and very much in fashion this last Spring, tho' *I* have but just met with it? It is the best French, has the most charming Sentiments without anything to except against, and hits off in the most natural pleasing manner all those little distinguishing Delicacies of Character that I am so fond of.

Now I can put on a girlish costume of my great

great grandmother's, with soft frills and pale forget-me-not bows, and follow the adventures and changing heart of the exquisite Caroline with something like tears and a heaving breast, but I know that a call from Miss Austen would dissipate the illusion: we should have become "sick and wicked" and gigglesome. What profanity! In spite of the very young gentleman from Oxford there is no reason to think that Dr. Johnson ever offered a fatherly name to *Evelina*, but, if we are to believe her authoress, no less a person than Mr. Gibbon professed himself ready to assume paternity for *Caroline*. In her third edition (1815) Mme. de Montolieu explains that the two former were anonymous, Gibbon's friend M. Georges d' Eyverdun had borrowed her MS. and published it without her knowledge. Gibbon who, be it remarked, admitted later a temporary infidelity to Suzanne in favour of the Baronne, was in the plot. When she complained he replied: "*Je suis si sur du succès de votre roman, que si vous voulez me le donner j'y mettrai mon nom.*" The modest authoress objected that no one would believe that the English Tacitus had written a novel. It would indeed have been a credulous public which could accept *Caroline* as own sister to the *Decline and Fall*, but she might have secured some fluttering new friends for her brother.

Rousseau is never mentioned by Miss Austen, but Miss Iremonger, of course, read *Emile*, and Bernardin de St. Pierre is "*selon mon goût*". She dotes on the studied despair of Charlotte Smith's *Sonnets*—"most beautifully melancholy"—a Bishop had told her "that he thinks they approach nearer to Petrarch's excellence than anything we have." Bowles' *Sonnets* accompany her Walks: "If You are fond of beautiful Strains of Melancholy, Read them by a Stream or over a Rock." Southey is a genius of the Soil, and she is enraptured with Dr. Darwin's *Loves of the Plants*: "*There* is such Poetry surely, and such a new Vein of Imagination, as we have not had to boast of a great while." Like Marianne Dashwood she is a disciple of the Rev. Dr. Gilpin, and also admires Alison's dreary *Essays on Taste*. She is captivated by the erudition of the Abbé Barthélemy, and eagerly follows *Le Voyage du jeune Anacharsis*, "written in the only style that could now recommend History to *me*." "Four most corpulent quartos," says Horace Walpole: I suspect that they were among the enormous great stupid thick quartos which irritated Miss Austen in the Breakfast parlour. Miss Iremonger never travels without Zimmermann on *Solitude*: he "could defy Sickness or a Wet Season." Politically she has strong Whig sympathies, and commends *Vindiciæ Gallicæ*, Mackintosh's reply to Burke; "I do not know any thing of the Author, but in him I meet with most of the Notions I have all along formed with regard to the French Revolution, very cleverly stated and put together. It really contains my Political Creed." Godwin is too much for a devotee of Blair's *Sermons*: "He is a known Democrat and, I believe, Infidel, and the Author of a deep, mischievious, great Work entitled *Political Justice*." But she has a qualified admiration for *Caleb Williams*: "It is written in a masterly superior style, quite a philosophic novel and no love in it. It portrays and analises Character admirably and is wonderfully interesting, but the *perversion* of fine Talents is Conspicuous thro' out." Miss Austen seems also to have found Godwin's novels antipathetic, as she remarks of a Bath acquaintance: "He is as raffish in his appearance as I would wish every Disciple of Godwin to be." On another subject our two ladies see eye to eye: perhaps most women are a little jealous of poor Hester Thrale or of her opportunities. "Mrs. Piozzi has so much affectation that I never could bear her; she surfeits me at once." On another they seem to be also in accord. Miss Iremonger is delighted with Miss Hamilton's "superlative novel, *The Memoirs of Modern Philosophers*, a most uncommonly able performance, replete with humor and good strokes of every sort, and excelling equally also in the pathetic style." Miss Austen was glad to hear that someone had presented Miss Hamilton with a copy of *Sense and Sensibility*: "It is pleasant to have such a respectable writer named."

The *Memoirs of Modern Philosophers* is a satire on Godwin and his followers. The scamps masquerading as philosophers, and the young ladies whom they captivate, talk a jargon derived from *Political Justice* and other of Godwin's writings: perfectibility, general utility and so forth. They inveigh against religion and

21

marriage, and deride the old-fashioned virtues of family affection, gratitude and repentance. The Gonoquais Hottentots, as depicted in Vaillant's travels, are their ideal of a civilized people, and they propose to emigrate to that earthly paradise. The curious reader may still derive some leisurely entertainment from the travesty, but the pathos which appealed to Miss Iremonger, the rescues and conversions finally effected by the virtuous characters, and the edifying death-beds, are heavy going. The wise old men are broad-minded, though wordy, and Harriet Orwell, the foil to the misguided Julia and Bridgetina, a thoroughly sensible young woman. Both here and in her *Letters on Education* Mrs. Hamilton is emphatically on the side of the rational woman as against the lovely trembler, though she stops short of the claim for women of equal opportunities, educational and professional. Her criticism of Rousseau's system of female education is in full accord with Mary Wollstonecraft's. Unlike Hannah More and Horace Walpole, she has read the *Vindication*, and, after a discussion of Rousseau, puts into the mouth of her hero, Harriet's lover, a surprisingly bold defence of it:

The inconsistency and folly of his system was, perhaps, never better exposed than in the very ingenious publication which takes the Rights of Women for its title. Pity that the very sensible authoress has sometimes permitted her zeal to hurry her into expressions which have raised a prejudice against the whole. To superficial readers it appears to be her intention to unsex women entirely.

Miss Austen must have enjoyed a letter from Harriet's rejected lover to the man she had chosen:

Immediately on leaving you, I met with a party of friends who, like myself, were on the wing for India; but as the fleet will not be ready to sail for a few weeks, they resolved to take a dash to Bath in the interim. I liked the thought, and was glad to accompany them; and here we are beating about like so many spaniels in a rabbit-warren. No cessation from amusements. Morning, noon and night, all here are on the scent of pleasure; but for what is called *pleasure* I find I have lost somewhat of my relish, for I now find living in a crowd to be abominably insipid. Poor Dr. Orwell was shocked at the idea of girls of character going to the Indian market; but had he come to Bath, he might have beheld a perpetual fair, where every ball-room may be considered as a booth for the display of beauty to be disposed of to the highest matrimonial bidder. Having been introduced to some very pleasant fellows, all of them men of large fortune and high connexions, I have through them had an opportunity of making what acquaintance I chose. The mothers have all smiled upon me, and I have had no reason to complain of my reception from the daughters. I have admired the beauty of several, and do not know, had it been less pressed upon my observation, what effect it might have had upon my heart. But what one sees morning, noon and night, soon ceases to interest; and in a society where intimacy takes place without any acquaintance, the mind can never rivet the chain which is forged by the senses.

Harriet Orwell would not, I think, like Bath. No; she likes *conversation*, and here is only *talk*. But were Harriet Orwell here, she would, I make no doubt, soon discover some congenial souls who form a more rational society than that which has come within the sphere of my observation. But why do I mention Harriet Orwell? Why, to shew you that I can do it without pain; and to convince you that my heart has been made the better, and not the worse, for its admiration of excellence.

And Mrs. Wollstonecraft would have applauded Dr. Orwell's answer to Bridgetina, when she argued that perfectibility would only be possible for women when they became too enlightened to submit to the slavish task of family cares:

"One philosopher, and only one, has appeared, who, superior to all prejudices, invariably treated the female sex as beings who were to be taught the performance of duty, not by arbitrary regulations confined to particular parts of conduct, but by the knowledge of principles which enlighten the understanding, and improve the heart."

"And pray what was the name of this philo-

24

sopher, sir?" said Bridgetina. "I wonder whether he is an acquaintance of Mr. Myope's. I never heard him speak of him."

"Very probably not," rejoined Dr. Orwell; "his name was *Jesus Christ*. He was the first philosopher who placed the female character in a respectable point of view. Women, we learn from the Gospels, frequently composed a great part of his audience; but to them no particular precepts were addressed; no sexual virtues recommended. He knew that by whomsoever his doctrines were sincerely received, the duties annexed to their situation would be fully and conscientiously fulfilled. His morality was addressed to the judgment without distinction of sex. His laws went not to fix the boundaries of prerogative, and to prescribe the minutiae of behaviour, but to fix purity and humility in the heart. And believe me, my children, the heart that is thus prepared, will not be apt to murmur at its lot in life. It will be ready to perceive, that true dignity consists not in the nature of the duty that is required of us, but in its just performance. The single woman whose mind is embued with these virtues, while she employs her leisure in cultivating her own understanding, and instructing that of others, in seeking for objects on which to exert her charity and benevolence, and in offices of kindness and good-will to her fellow-creatures, will never consider her situation as abject or forlorn. Nor will she who is the mother of a family, consider its humblest duties as mean, or void of dignity and importance. The light of the mind is necessary for the performance of every duty; and great is the mistake of those who think ignorance the guard of innocence and virtue."

Miss Iremonger's views of life and marriage may follow:

After owning myself so much delighted with a Novel and so interested for Caroline, it may be less necessary perhaps for me to reply to your direct Enquiry about my *Tabby Determinations*, and You will have answered Yourself that I am not insensible to the charms of a virtuous attachment and the Comforts of a well-suited Connection. I have always admired Diderot's *Père de Famille*. It has always been a great favourite of mine, and his manner of representing the two States is in many respects very just, tho' I certainly know several *Filles surannées* who are very far from being in the disconsolate, miserable situation that He describes them to be. I make no resolutions, but I take every opportunity of forming and cultivating those sort of valuable female Friendships that are the best substitute for the other kind of Connection, and which will *alone* supply Comforts and Pleasures worth living for, at the same time that I am also fully convinced that no other Happiness on Earth can equal that of the *Lien sacré* to which Diderot does so much justice; but I say with Cécile "*Où sont de telles Femmes, et de telles Epouses?*" With *no right* to be difficult therefore, I profess myself *extremely* difficult, and am clearly of opinion that to be *without* a Companion is far preferable to the being tied to a *disagreeable* one. If ever you see me married, it will be to a Man *out* of what is commonly called *the World*, who has that sort of Taste and Feeling which is reckoned very unfashionable, who knows how to prefer *Employment* to *Ennui*, his *Farm* to *Newmarket*, and a Domestic Life to all others. The Duty of the Wife would then be to endeavour to become every Day more worthy of this distinguished Blessing and to be continually gaining Improvement from his superior mind. How do you like this Picture? and don't You think it will scarcely be met with in these Times?

Miss Austen did not dissipate her mind in desultory up-to-date reading; she also made the greater effort required not to dissipate her time in aimless sociabilities and acquaintanceships which would not ripen into friendships. Family claims she never repudiated, although the relation might sometimes be puzzling and painful. Of a brother she writes:

I am sorry and angry that his Visits should not give one more pleasure; the company of so good and so clever a Man ought to be gratifying in itself; —but his Chat seems all forced, his Opinions on many points too much copied from his Wife's, and his time here is spent I think in walking about the House and banging the doors, or ringing the bell for a glass of water.

These claims increased in later life when nephews
and nieces were dumped upon her for long periods,
and it is clear both from her novels and from her letters, that she was not an indiscriminate child-lover,
one of those universal aunts whose pose strikes even
the children themselves as somewhat forced. I remember apologizing for the horrid noises which had proceeded from my own garden to an aunt of others, who
replied, "Oh, but I love to hear their merry little
voices," and the caustic comment of one of those little
voices: "I suppose you have to pretend to be pleasant if
you live in the country, but no one can really like to
hear other people's children." For the rest she must
maintain some sort of perspective by which as an artist
she could survey the world. She was a satirist, not a
misanthrope: her fellow-creatures amused her: more,
they were the necessary material for her art, but they
must not come too close. "I do not want people to be
very agreeable, as it saves me the trouble of liking
them a great deal." "I cannot anyhow continue to find
people agreeable;—I respect Mrs. Chamberlayne for
doing her hair well, but cannot feel a more tender
sentiment. Miss Langley is like any other short girl
with a broad nose and a wide mouth, fashionable dress,
and exposed bosom. Adm. Stanhope is a gentlemanlike
Man, but then his legs are too short, and his tail too
long." There is the pleasant and commonplace Miss
Armstrong: "like other young ladies she is consider-
ably genteeler than her parents", who must be pla-
cated by a walk, as she "had called on me the day

before, and gently upbraided me in her turn with change of manners since she had been in Bath, or at least of late. Unlucky me! that my notice should be of such consequence and my Manners so bad!—She was so well-disposed, and so reasonable that I soon forgave her, and made this engagement with her in proof of it.—She is really an agreeable girl, so I think I may like her, and her great want of a companion at home, which may well make any tolerable acquaintance important to her, gives her another claim on my attention. I shall endeavour as much as possible to keep my Intimacies in their proper place, and prevent their clashing."

Mrs. Chamberlayne, who did her hair so well, also insisted on co-operative exercise:

> It would have amused you to see our progress;—we went up by Sion Hill, and returned across the fields;—in climbing a hill Mrs. Chamberlayne is very capital; I could with difficulty keep pace with her—yet would not flinch for the world. On plain ground I was quite her equal—and so we posted away under a fine hot sun, *She* without any parosol or any shade to her hat, stopping for nothing, and crossing the Church Yard at Weston with as much expedition as if we were afraid of being buried alive. After seeing what she is equal to, I cannot help feeling a regard for her. As to Agreeableness, she is much like other people.

On another occasion they walked to Lyncombe and Widcombe:

Mrs. Chamberlayne's pace was not quite so magnificent on this second trial as in the first; it was nothing more than I could keep up with, without effort; and for many, many yards together on a raised narrow footpath I led the way. The walk was very beautiful as my companion agreed, whenever I made the observation. And so ends our friendship, for the Chamberlaynes leave Bath in a day or two.

Mr. Evelyn's advances she evidently met half-way:

There is now something like an engagement between us and the Phaeton, which to confess my frailty I have a great desire to go out in;—whether it will come to anything must remain with him,— I really believe he is very harmless; people do not seem afraid of him here, and he gets Groundsel for his birds and all that.

Mr. Evelyn is obviously not the prototype of that fast young man Mr. Thorpe, who gave Catherine Morland such thrills in his curricle: "I am just returned from my airing in the very bewitching Phaeton and four, for which I was prepared by a note from Mr. E. soon after breakfast. We went to the top of Kingsdown and had a very pleasant drive."

Observation without any tiresome consequences she thoroughly enjoyed:

I am proud to say that I have a very good eye at an Adultress, for tho' repeatedly assured that another in the same party was the *She*, I fixed upon the right one from the first. She was highly rouged, and looked rather quietly and contentedly silly than anything else. Mrs. Badcock and two Young Women were of the same party, except when Mrs. Badcock thought herself obliged to leave them to run round the room after her drunken Husband. His avoidance, and her pursuit, with the probable intoxication of both, was an amusing scene.

But I must not forestall Dr. Chapman in the delightful task of anthologizing the letters. He must do it himself if they are to secure the appreciation they deserve.

Miss Austen's acquaintance, was, of course, loth to accept her terms: when she had parted with them with relief they expected, like Dear Miss Heber's friends, that a constant correspondence would follow. In spite of good resolutions I must allow myself another quotation:

A few days ago I had a letter from Miss Irvine, and as I was in her debt, you will guess it to be a remonstrance, not a very severe one, however; the first page is in her usual retrospective, jealous, inconsistent style, but the remainder is chatty and harmless. She supposes my silence may have proceded from resentment of her not having written to inquire particularly after my hooping cough, &c. She is a funny one.

I have answered her letter, and have endeavoured to give something like the truth with as little in--

civility as I could, by placing my silence to the want of subject, in the very quiet way in which we live.

We are told by her nephew, and it is confirmed by the descriptions of people in her letters, that Miss Austen did not photograph the living, and transfer the results to her books. She only took hints, hints the course of which we can sometimes trace: her creations are her own. She knows them—or she usually knows them: I never quite feel that she knows Henry Crawford and his sister. Does not her apologia at the end of *Mansfield Park* suggest that she attributes their vices too much to circumstances and too little to the native badness of their hearts? But it is proof of her own powers that she distrusts her knowledge of real people. "Nobody ever feels or acts, suffers or enjoys, as one expects." And she feels remorse because, her tiresome young nephews having been peculiarly exasperating, they show signs of grace by appearing at the Sacrament. "After having much praised or much blamed anybody, one is generally sensible of something just the reverse soon afterwards."

It may seem a far cry from the husband-hunting butterfly, the aspect which Miss Austen displayed to undesired acquaintance, to Horace Walpole's *Hyena in Petticoats*. Their lots in life could not well have been more different. Jane Austen lived in the midst of an eminently respectable family: her claims and cares were merely those inseparable from ordinary family life: a turned pelisse or retrimmed gown her only approach to deprivation, and her anxieties about her books those of the artist, never of the wage-earner. Mary Wollstonecraft, even as a young girl, assumed responsibility for a wastrel father and a graceless crowd of brothers and sisters. She had to support herself and meet their shark-like demands as a governess, the mistress of an unsuccessful little school, and later—"the first of a new genus"—as a professional journalist. She replied to Burke's *Reflections on the French Revolution* with *A Vindication of the Rights of Men,* followed by her still more provocative *Vindication of the Rights of Women.* She lived for years with a man to whom she was not married and bore him a child: she became— too late for respectability—the wife of Godwin, whose name stank in the nostrils of Whigs and Tories alike. If Jane Austen ever heard her name it must have been as a notorious woman, one of Godwin's raffish crew: there was only one incident in Mary Wollstonecraft's career which could have excited her interest or envy. Dr. Johnson, just before his death, "treated her with particular kindness and attention, had a long conversation with her, and desired her to repeat her visit often". Yet, as I contend, these two, the reformer with a head full of theories, and the artist who never troubled about women's rights or any other cause, used their pens with equal force to the same intent, indeed the younger was for years, perhaps always with one sex, the more effective of the two.

Mary Wollstonecraft, like Jane Austen, had no special interest in the intellectual woman: she could look after herself. Her concern was to deliver the ordinary woman from the false and dishonest ideal which had been imposed upon her by society. The elegant female, whose one object was to capture a man in marriage and keep his affections by guile, must go if women were to take their just place in this world, or the next. Equal education, equal professional opportunities, and equal political rights were only corollaries. Her main contention was that a woman should be allowed to develop "individuality of character, the only fastener of the affections": to which the orthodox subordination, first to parents and afterwards to a husband, was an obstacle. Miss Austen is innocent of any didactic intentions. She does not set out like Hannah More, to improve the minds of addicts of the Terror Novel and the Minerva Press: "I thought there were already good books enough in the world for good people; but that there was a large class of readers whose wants had not been attended to—the subscribers to the circulating library. A little to raise the tone of that mart of mischief, and to counteract its corruptions, I thought was an object worth attempting." She writes because she must create her own world on "the little bit (two inches wide) of ivory": because she is a great artist. But there is another adjective beginning with "r" besides respectable, which she uses—not indeed so often, but with greater intention and emphasis— rational. Woman is, or should be, a rational being. The moral is insidiously conveyed, but Mary Wollstonecraft's polemic is not more subversive of the ideas of the day, preached from the pulpit and the Press—I am sorry to say that even Miss Iremonger calls Dr. Gregory's abominable advice to his daughters "the pretty little elegant Book entitled *A Father's Legacy*"—and inculcated by parents and school-mistresses.

When Catherine Morland becomes heartily ashamed of her ignorance as the result of intercourse with the Tilneys the author comments: "A misplaced shame. When people wish to attach, they should always be ignorant. To come with a well-informed mind is to come with an inability of administering to the vanity of others, which a sensible person would always wish to avoid. A woman especially, if one have the misfortune of knowing anything, should conceal it as well as she can." The words are the words of Dr. Gregory, but it is the Wolf speaking, not Grandmamma.

Did Warren Hastings and other male admirers of Elizabeth Bennet grasp the full purport of the words addressed to the persistent Mr. Collins: "Do not consider me now as an elegant female intending to plague you, but as a rational creature speaking the truth from her heart"? Did they ignore Georgiana's alarm at the insubordinate way in which young Mrs. Darcy teased her husband? Did they realize that Mr. Bennet's fate, without the armour of irony which enabled him sometimes to enjoy his wife's folly, was a common one, and that he and others might pass their youth without once meeting a rational woman?

Did they see the dangerous implications in the

analysis of Charlotte Lucas' feelings after she had accepted Mr. Collins?

> Her reflections were in general satisfactory. Mr. Collins to be sure was neither sensible or agreeable: his society was irksome, and his attachment to her must be imaginary. But still he would be her husband. Without thinking highly either of men or of matrimony, marriage had always been her object; it was the only honourable provision for well-educated young women of small fortune, and however uncertain of giving happiness, must be their pleasantest preservative against want.

Charlotte knew that Elizabeth Bennet would disapprove; might not Miss Austen make some of her women readers discontented with "the pleasantest preservative from want", and incite them to revolutionary desires for economic independence?

Mr. Knightley indeed knows that he wants "a rational companion", and is watching, waiting and reproving Emma in the hope that she may become one. Is it not due to Miss Austen that other men also began to change their ideals? After meeting Miss Tilney whose "manners shewed good sense and good breeding; they were neither shy, nor affectedly open; and she seemed capable of being young, attractive, and at a ball, without wanting to fix the attention of every man near her, and without exaggerated feelings of ecstatic delight or inconceivable vexation on every little trifling occurrence", did they become more wary of some Isabella Thorpe? In her letters her sympathy with women who cannot secure any life of their own leads her into strange places! She says of a young married woman: "Anna has not a chance of escape; her husband called here the other day, and said she was *pretty* well but not *equal* to so long a walk; she *must come in her Donkey Carriage*. Poor animal, she will be worn out before she is thirty. I am very sorry for her. Mrs. Clement too is in that way again. I am quite tired of so many Children—Mrs. Benn has a 13th." And again, of an older woman: "Good Mrs. Deedes!—I hope she will get the better of this Marianne, and then I wd. recommend to her and Mr. D. the simple regimen of separate rooms."

In experience and temperament Mrs. Wollstone-craft and Miss Austen were quite unlike. Wickham and Willoughby, Henry Crawford and Frank Fairfax suggest that Jane's young heart had been fluttered at times by the fascinations of some youth whom she could not rationally approve; but she was too prudent to have committed herself in love letters to Fuseli, neither would she have consented to live with Imlay or Godwin without the respectability of marriage lines. The lover of whom death bereft her was, I feel sure, more like Captain Wentworth or Henry Tilney, or even the sober Brandon or the solid Knightley. For myself, Mr. Bennet is my only fancy. I long to sit in that armchair in the library, opposite his own, where Elizabeth occasionally curled up with a book. What

did he read there? Miss Austen never told: perhaps she
had not made out the list even for herself. She would
not have married Mr. Bennet: she saw his faults
too clearly.

Yet their view of marriage as a fundamental institution of society, "a great Improver", was the same,
although Mrs. Wollstonecraft came late to anchor.
With Imlay she had looked forward in vain "to a
rational prospect of as much felicity as the earth
affords—with a little dash of rapture into the bargain".
And "Bath could hardly contain any other two beings
at once so rationally and so rapturously happy" as
Captain Wentworth and Anne Elliot. Like Marianne,
her creator had no sympathy with second marriages,
but she can make exceptions.

> Lady Sondes' match surprises, but does not offend
> me; had her first marriage been of affection, or had
> there been a grown-up single daughter, I should not
> have forgiven her; but I consider everybody as
> having a right to marry *once* in their lives for love,
> if they can, and provided she will now leave off
> having bad headaches and being pathetic, I can
> allow her, I can *wish* her, to be happy.

Mary Wollstonecraft in her youth courageously delivered her sister from a miserable marriage; some of
Miss Austen's most delightful and self-revealing letters
are written to a niece who fell in and out of love.
Mr. J. P. had been Fanny's first Young Man, and she
had believed herself in love with him. Her aunt

thought so too. Now, having given him every encouragement, she has changed her mind. What is to be done? He is so eligible that Miss Austen at first recommends that she should grow in love with him again:

There *are* such beings in the World perhaps, one in a Thousand, as the Creature You and I should think perfection, Where Grace and Spirit are united to Worth, where the Manners are equal to the Heart and Understanding, but such a person may not come in your way, or if he does, he may not be the eldest son of a Man of Fortune, the Brother of your particular friend, and belonging to your own County. Think of all this Fanny. Mr. J. P. has advantages which do not often meet in one person. His only fault indeed seems Modesty. If he were less modest, he would be more agreeable, speak louder and look impudenter; and is it not a fine Character of which Modesty is the only defect? I have no doubt that he will get more lively and more like yourselves as he is more with you; he will catch your ways if he belongs to you. And as to there being any objection from his *Goodness*, from the danger of his becoming even Evangelical, I cannot admit *that*: I am by no means convinced that we ought not all to be Evangelicals, and am at least persuaded that they who are so from Reason and Feeling, must be happiest and safest.

But later in the letter she changes her tune, and

entreats her niece not to commit herself unless she is sure that she cares for him: "Anything is to be preferred or endured rather than marrying without Affection." Then the comic spirit bobs up in the postscript: "Your trying to excite your own feelings by a visit to his room amused me excessively,—The dirty Shaving Rag was exquisite! Such a circumstance ought to be in print; much too good to be lost."

No doubt it was, but it came too late for other record than this.

Fanny wobbles again, and thinks that perhaps she ought to accept J. P., but her aunt is sure that she will not stand the strain of a very long engagement. "The unpleasantness of appearing fickle is certainly great— but if you think you want Punishment for past Illusions, there it is—and nothing can be compared to the misery of being bound *without* Love, bound to one, and preferring another. *That* is a punishment which you do *not* deserve."

The next letter of the series is written more than two years later:

You are inimitable, irresistable. You are the delight of my Life. Such Letters, such entertaining Letters as you have lately sent! Such a description of your queer little heart! Such a lovely display of what Imagination does. You are worth your weight in Gold, or even in the new Silver coinage. I cannot express to you what I have felt in reading your history of yourself. How full of Pity and Concern and

Admiration and Amusement I have been. You are the Paragon of all that is Silly and Sensible, commonplace and eccentric, Sad and Lively, Provoking and Interesting. Who can keep pace with the fluctuations of your Fancy, the Capprizios of your Taste, the Contradictions of your Feelings? You are so odd!—and all the time, so perfectly natural—so peculiar in yourself, and yet so like everybody else! It is very, very gratifying to me to know you so intimately. You can hardly think what a pleasure it is to me, to have such thorough pictures of your Heart.—Oh! what a loss it will be when you are married. You are too agreeable in your single state, too agreeable as a Neice. I shall hate you when your delicious play of Mind is all settled down into conjugal maternal affections.

Fanny, it appears, cannot bear the idea of J. P.'s consoling himself elsewhere, and her aunt reminds her now, not of points in his favour, but of all the old draw-backs. "Think of his Principles, think of his Father's objection, of want of Money, of a coarse Mother, of Brothers and Sisters like Horses, of sheets sewn across, &c." After this no wonder that the letter ends: "You are *not* in love with him. You never have been really in love with him." Meanwhile another admirer had appeared with a Castle in the background, but he does not persist; perhaps because Fanny obliges him to read certain anonymous novels. The author is much amused by her report of his com-

41

ments, "and I *hope* I am not offended and do not think
the worse of him for having a Brain so very different
from mine," adding, "I particularly respect him for
wishing to think well of all Young Ladies; it shews an
amiable and delicate Mind.—And he deserves better
treatment than to be obliged to read any more of my
Works." Had Fanny, like the wretched Eliza Bishop,
made an unhappy marriage, her aunt, we may be sure,
would have been her most sympathetic friend and her
wisest adviser. As it was, she had to leave her niece
still unmarried:

> Well, I shall say, as I have often said before, Do
> not be in a hurry; depend upon it, the right Man
> will come at last; you will in the course of the next
> two or three years, meet with somebody more
> generally unexceptionable than anyone you have
> yet known, who will love you as warmly as ever
> He did, and who will so completely attach you, that
> you will feel you never really loved before. And
> then, by not beginning the Mothering quite so
> early in life, you will be young in Constitution and
> spirits, figure and countenance.

Most of Mrs. Wollstonecraft's programme has
been carried, and the elegant female has disappeared
from Miss Austen's circles, though she may reappear in
others, distracted by the length of a skirt or the tilt
of a hat. But, were they living, Mary Wollstonecraft
would still find much to deplore, and Jane Austen
much to satirize.

ELIZA FLETCHER 1770-1858

ELIZA FLETCHER'S upbringing would have been in the eyes of Mary Wollstonecraft both desirable and enviable, with just the mixture of intelligent affection, "running wild", happiness and experience, likely to fit her to be a companionable wife, a sympathetic and capable mother, and an active, broad-minded citizen. Some political differences they might have had, but both believed in woman's right to the full development of her personality, and both were democrats.

Eliza Dawson was born at the village of Oxton in Yorkshire in 1770. Her father was a land-surveyor of yeoman descent, and her mother, who died soon after the child's birth, the daughter of neighbouring gentry. The household consisted of Mr. Dawson, his mother, brother and sister, all united in adoring Eliza. Her grandmother's affection took the form of terror lest the father should marry again. Hearing some gossip of the kind, she took the seven-year-old Eliza by the hand, saying, "Child, you and I will beg our bread through the wide world together rather than you shall submit to the cruelty of a stepmother," and they started to trudge away, but were overtaken after a mile or two, while both were still in full enjoyment of the heroic episode. A year or two before, old Mrs. Dawson had effected a more necessary and successful rescue. A

schoolfellow of Eliza's mother, Miss Hebburn, an
heiress, with whom she had travelled as a girl, had
married Edward Brudenell, an ex-soldier, who took
orders for the sake of securing a family living. He was
grossly profligate, and his wife, after the death of two
infant sons, determined to leave him. She wrote to
inform him of her intention, while staying with the
Dawsons, and he pursued her there in order to persuade her to keep up appearances. They retired to
separate bedrooms, and Mrs. Dawson had arranged
that, during the night, the unhappy lady, accompanied
by Miss Dawson, should ride pillion with two gentlemen, also in the secret, to a lonely village nine miles
off, where she could be concealed until her husband
had been forced into agreement by threats of exposure
to his aristocratic connections. The elegant and accomplished Mrs. Brudenell was then established in a
thatched cottage *orné* close to the Dawsons, and devoted herself to Eliza's education. Her tuition was
stimulating, but not altogether judicious: the little
girl spouted Shakespeare and Pope to admiring audi-
ences before she could read, and was inclined to regard herself as an infant prodigy. Pope seems to have
gone to her head, and was responsible later for a
serious check in Mr. Fletcher's courtship. He had objected to some passages as translations, and a cattish
remark of Eliza's was repeated to him about people
who are hard to please and only criticize for the sake
of showing off. Instruction in needlework was less
successful: plain sewing gave Mrs. Brudenell a strange

pain in her thumb, and Eliza refused to learn elaborate
stitches. When able to read she devoured every book
within reach. Her father's library was sound, but not
extensive: Shakespeare and Milton, Pope and Dryden,
the *Spectator*, Shenstone's *Poems* and Hervey's
Meditations among the Tombs. He also possessed
Sherlock's *Sermons*, those of the bishop, or possibly of
the earlier Royalist chaplain, who refused to cut his
beard after the King's execution, and had such a passion for preaching that he seldom gave any of his three
curates a chance. Mrs. Rowe's *Letters* were there too.
Mrs. Elizabeth Rowe was the authoress of *Letters Moral
and Entertaining* and of *Friendship in Death*, written
in the form of letters from the dead to the living. Dr.
Johnson speaks of "the copiousness and luxuriance of
Mrs. Rowe", "her brightness of imagery, her purity of
sentiments". "The attempt to employ the ornaments
of romance in the decoration of religion, was, I think,
first made by Mr. Boyle's *Martyrdom of Theodora*;
but Boyle's philosophical studies did not allow him
time for the cultivation of style; and the completion
of the great design was reserved for Mrs. Rowe."
Bishop Ken sought her society, Dr. Watts admired her
verses, Matthew Prior addressed a love poem to her,
Pope printed her elegy on her husband as appendix to
the second edition of *Eloisa and Abelard*. And now?
Now, when I wished to be moralized and entertained,
even the London Library has failed to provide me with
her *Letters*. History and geography were represented
in Mr. Dawson's library by some text books, to which

Mrs. Brudenell added Robertson's *History of Scotland* and Sully's *Memoirs*.

When she was eleven Eliza exchanged the adoration of her family, and all the freedom of village life, running to the old women with her grandmother's teapot that they might enjoy a second brew of that expensive beverage, and sharing the local country festivals, for the Manor House School at York, where her mother and Mrs. Brudenell had first met. This must have been the school from which *The Runaway* escaped in that delightful book, recently resuscitated and illustrated by Gwen Raverat, which ought to be given to every little girl on her ninth birthday. There deportment reigned supreme: the spoilt girl found that her recitations and erudition counted for nothing, and that she was a totally inelegant female child. Her homesickness was mitigated by some lasting friendships, and by the school library, which consisted of four odd volumes of the *Spectator*, supplemented by contraband literature.

Four years of this school was not a serious interruption of Eliza's education: the stimulating return to freedom compensated for the lapse. When the mornings were light enough she rose at four, and went out into the fields with a book, usually poetry. She wrote verses herself, but judging from the later samples preserved, they were no more than a harmless habit, fashionable in her day. A friend gave her £20 to spend on books, and she records the purchase of Warton's edition of Milton's lesser Poems, the first edition of

46

Cowper, Hayley's works, and Brydone's *Tour through Sicily and Malta*, a popular work which went into seven or eight editions. *The Sorrows of Werther* she borrowed from friends at York, where she was staying for her first ball, and so swollen were her eyes that she could not appear.

A miniature painted when Eliza was fifteen shows a handsome, spirited young creature with a fine forehead and features which would improve with maturity and stand the wear of time. There was no temptation to vanity in such beauty: it was too obvious: the besetting sin against which she struggled prayerfully all her life through, was a craving for admiration and popularity based on her intellectual attainments. Her first admirers, at any rate, probably thought more of her beauty. Their loves and sorrows were taken very seriously: the first of all, an officer, was confidently expected to keep his word and die of a broken heart, when her father insisted on his dismissal. The only one who might have succeeded was too much offended by Mr. Dawson's cold reception to persist in his addresses.

Although Mr. Dawson, no doubt wisely enough, discouraged his youthful daughter's suitors, he gave her extraordinary freedom in other directions. She thought that the milk-woman poetess, Ann Yearsley, had been bullied by Mrs. Hannah More, who first introduced her to the public, so wrote, offering to collect subscriptions for a new volume of her poems. Mr. Dawson advanced £50, and Eliza secured five hundred subscriptions. Another protégée, less worthy, as afterwards appeared, absconded from service in bad company from which they had formerly rescued her. Eliza and a girl friend promptly cantered off to York, had all the slum lodging houses searched till they found her, and made a further vain effort for her salvation.

Mr. Archibald Fletcher made his first appearance when Eliza was seventeen. Author of *The Principles of the Bill for Scottish Borough Reform*, he was on his way to give evidence on the subject before a Parliamentary Committee. Travelling with an old schoolfellow of Eliza's and her husband, he was reluctantly detained by them on a short visit to Oxton. Eliza was flattered by his appreciation of her literary conversation: a present of Ossian's *Poems* followed, with a request that she would write and tell him how she had liked them. This led to correspondence on other books, and the young lady was by no means pleased to hear that he had slept at the neighbouring town of Tadcaster on his way back from London, without calling upon her. The explanation that he had not arrived till midnight and had wandered round and round the house in the dark was some satisfaction to her craving for romance: still she felt that, if really in love, he would have done something more effective. Next year he reappeared: she curled her hair more carefully than usual, was thrilled by his account of the Hastings trial, and resumed the correspondence.

Fletcher was forty-three when he first saw Eliza Dawson, and he had been in love for seven years, in love, not like Coelebs with Milton's Eve in her state of

innocence, but with that more human figure, Fielding's Sophia Western. One of his letters to Eliza tells
the story:

Sophia was too beautiful and too brilliant a figure
not to attract in a most peculiar manner my attention. I was astonished: Sophia, painted by the
inimitable pencil of Fielding, was just the woman I
desired to see. She was in every respect so. Her person, her manners, her sentiments, her disposition,
were such as it was impossible not to admire. She
never uttered a thought of which I did not cordially
approve, nor disclosed a passion with which I did not
instantly sympathize, and her manner of saying and
doing everything was unspeakably graceful; the
more surprising, too, that she never appeared to
have been away from the house of her father, a
country gentleman. In this lady, from almost the
first moment I was introduced to her acquaintance,
I took the warmest interest. I was perfectly uneasy
when she was out of sight. I passed over parts of the
book until I came to those parts where I was to be
introduced to her company. In short I loved Sophia
with sincerity, and although I am ashamed almost
to confess it, as it seems so ridiculously romantic, yet
the truth is that this ideal Sophia made so deep an
impression on my imagination that it never was
effaced till the second or third day of my visit (I know
not yet whether to call it fatal or fortunate visit) at
Oxton, in April 1787; and since you have desired me

to tell why I have given you the name of Sophia, you must excuse me if I relate the time and manner in which you completely erased from my mind every trace and impression of the ideal Sophia, who had been so long the object of my adoration, but whose place you have ever since occupied with additional advantages.

He goes on to explain that for the first few hours he had been captivated by the mature charms of Mrs. Brudenell and had scarcely noticed her young friend, but:

Miss Eliza gradually unfolded herself; she riveted my attention more completely than Mrs. Brudenell had done. I listened with greater surprise and pleasure. I soon discovered in a beautiful form an elegance of mind and sentiment, and an easy gracefulness of manner which I thought were not natural to the little village of Oxton. I began to be interested in Eliza; I felt a very particular desire to sit beside her at supper, and I think I contrived to do it. I was still more and more pleased with her manner and conversation. Her easy affability was such that I think we were tolerably well acquainted before supper was done. Nothing could be more pleasing to me than Eliza's frankness—nothing more delightful than her elegant turn of manner and conversation, and the peculiar intelligence by which it was conducted. "There is," I said to myself, "something very uncommon about this girl."

His irritation at the delay in their journey to London entirely vanished.

My only anxiety now was to see Eliza again in the morning, and I felt an irresistible desire to place myself beside her at breakfast. She appeared still more to advantage; I was indeed charmed. When breakfast was about over and I took a view of Eliza's form, manner, and conversation, the character of Sophia Western flashed on my mind. The resemblance was in every feature striking.

He had at last discovered his Sophia in the flesh.

If I had found brilliants on the wild and rugged mountains among which I first drew my breath, I could not have been more surprised and delighted than I was by meeting such a person as Eliza. "Fielding," said I, "you have drawn your heroine, it must be confessed, with a fine pencil, but there is in real life, at a little country village, a character every way equal; in some respects far superior. Without saying anything of external form, the mental accomplishments of Eliza Dawson are above those of the amiable and intelligent Sophia Western. You seem to think, Fielding, that knowledge of books is no ornament to a woman; but had you known Eliza Dawson, you would have altered your opinion. She would have taught you how compatible literary acquirements are with the most engaging feminine manners, and when so blended you would have seen how much they must contribute both to the ornament and the happiness of life." Such were my sentiments of Eliza Dawson, early adopted, and since confirmed by indubitable experience.

It is not difficult to detect a resemblance between Fielding's warm-hearted, spirited, flesh-and-blood heroine, and the natural, gracious, enthusiastic Eliza. Both were devoted to adoring fathers, though the foul-mouthed choleric Squire was not reproduced in Mr. Dawson. There is something curiously prophetic about Mr. Fletcher's letter, because, though Eliza's experience was less melodramatic than Sophia's, and she did not require so much hartshorn to see her through, Mr. Dawson quite unexpectedly showed himself as uncompromising a parent as Squire Western, and she was to suffer as much from the conflict between love and duty.

Meanwhile Eliza was eagerly seizing her opportunities—the first of many which her beauty and intelligence brought—for becoming acquainted with celebrities. The first lion of all, the poet Mason, then Precentor of York Minster, had been a bitter disappointment.

Many a time had I walked before his door in the Minster Yard, to get a peep of the author of *Elfrida* and *Caractacus*. But to be in the same room with him, to watch his countenance and hear him speak, the anticipation was delightful! I figured him an interesting-looking man worn with deep affliction, for I had read his beautiful "Monody" on his wife, who died at Bristol of consumption. But when he entered Mrs. Forster's drawing-room, what was my surprise to see a little fat old man of hard-favoured countenance squat himself down at a card table, and give his whole attention to a game at whist!

Alas, he had none to spare for Eliza Dawson! Her next venture was happier. The Rev. Edmund Cartwright, better remembered now as the inventor of one of the earliest power-looms than as the poet of *Armine and Elvira*, which ran through several editions and was admired by Scott, brought Crabbe to see her. Together they visited York: Crabbe sent her some of his books, and corresponded with her for years, but, as he was duly accompanied by his amiable wife, Eliza did not, like Jane Austen, aspire to become Mrs. Crabbe. She did, however, reject the widowed Mr. Cartwright with his five children: otherwise she would have become stepmother of the lady who, under the pseudonym of Mrs. Markham, maintained an honoured place in the schoolroom even as late as the eighties.

Two years after Mr. Fletcher's first visit to Oxton, Eliza went to stay with friends at Perth, where he joined her. Matters reached a climax: it was agreed that he should come south in the autumn and approach her father. Though she dutifully showed him all her lover's letters, and, as she remarks, "perhaps a person much versed in the language of the heart might have discovered more in them than the lectures of a philosopher or the epistles of a friend", Mr. Dawson was quite unprepared for the shock of Mr. Fletcher's proposal. Give his brilliant daughter to a middle-aged lawyer, and one who lived in Scotland into the bargain! They offered to wait until Mr. Fletcher's prospects improved, but he was adamant. Eliza, although, as she says, not romantically in love with Mr. Fletcher—the romance was all on his side—announced her intention of remaining single so long as he did. Mr. Dawson refused to accept this impasse. His candidate was a neighbouring nobleman, Lord Grantley, "a man of insinuating address and of cultivated taste and accomplishments", in the later forties. Eliza suspected his morals, but was flattered by his attentions. His intentions never became quite clear as she choked him off by letting him know of her engagement. By the end of two years' clandestine correspondence, which weighed heavily on her conscience, her lover had persuaded her to defy her father and marry him. Mr. Dawson refused to be present at the ceremony, but relented so far as to bid them farewell, saying to his son-in-law, "Be kind to her, Sir, she has been tenderly brought up."

Although her wedding day was one of the most miserable of her life, it was a prelude to thirty-seven years of married happiness. As she justly observes, there was nothing morbid about Eliza. She had perfect confidence in her husband, a profound admiration for his disinterested character, and entire sympathy with his religious and political views: moreover his friends in Edinburgh, where an English visitor was still something of a novelty, gave her a warm welcome. Fletcher was a strong Whig, a reformer rather than a revolutionary: he had refused to belong to the "Friends of the People". But to be a Whig advocate was *ipso facto* to be unemployed, and the Fletchers were often at their last guinea. Scotland as a whole and Edinburgh in particular was completely dominated by a Tory dictator, Henry Dundas, Lord Melville: elections and appointments went as he willed. The small Whig minority, consisting mainly of young lawyers, reinforced by a few University professors, and one notable preacher, Sir Harry Scott Moncrieff, were powerless: they could only stand by and talk and think. Dundas and the Tories had a powerful weapon in their hands, terror of French revolutionary principles. "If the ladies and gentlemen," writes Lord Cockburn of his boyhood, "believed all that they said about the horrors of French bloodshed, and of the anxiety of the people here to imitate them, they must have been wretched indeed. Their talk sent me to bed shuddering. No doubt the intolerance was justified, or at least provoked by fright at first; but this soon became a pretence; and the hourly violence that prevailed was kept up chiefly as a factious engine. I lived in the midst of it. My father's house was one of the places where the leaders, and the ardent followers of the party in power, were in the constant habit of assembling. I can sit yet, in imagination, at the small side table, and overhear the conversation, a few feet off, at the established Wednesday dinner. How they raved! What sentiments! What principles! Not that I differed from them. I thought them quite right; and hated liberty and the people as much as they did. But this drove me into an opposite horror; for I was terrified out of such wits as they left me at the idea of bloodshed, and it never occurred to me that it could be avoided."

And again:

. . . the great Tory object was, to abuse everybody but themselves, and in particular to ascribe a thirst for bloodshed and anarchy, not merely to their avowed public opponents, but to the whole body of the people. It is frightful even to recollect the ferocious bitterness and systematic zeal with which this principle was acted upon; and this under the direct action of government. No one ever heard of a check being given, even by a hint, from head-quarters, with a view to arrest intolerance or to encourage charity. Jacobinism was a term denoting everything alarming and hateful, and every political offender was a Jacobin. No innovation, whether practical or speculative, consequently no political or economic reformer, and no religious dissenter, from the Irish Papist to our own native Protestant Seceder, could escape from this fatal word. This misrepresentation, and the natural tendency of the traduced, to provoke and frighten by rather extenuating some of the French proceedings, might make the reader of an account of those days suppose that the revolutionary infection had spread far enough and deep enough to justify the proscription it met with. But, unquestionably, this was not the fact. The chief object at which our discontented aimed was parliamentary reform. But this and other home-bred ends were hid by a cloud of foreign follies, which the Tories exhibited as demonstrations that the correction of domestic abuses was a pretence, and Jacobinism the truth. On this foundation they represented the whole lower orders as hostile to our institutions; from which the desired and comfortable inference was, that there was no salvation for the country except in the predominance of their own party.

In such a society Fletcher, the borough reformer, and his eager, outspoken young wife were subject to the darkest suspicions and most absurd gossip. It was even said, and believed, that Eliza had purchased a small guillotine, and was keeping her hand in on poultry, rats and so on, that she might be ready for human victims. Their friends were restricted to a small circle chiefly of their own way of thinking, and did not, of course, include any of the fascinating characters of the old Edinburgh world, the deep-drinking judges and glorious old ladies, who, wonderfully apparelled, adorn Lord Cockburn's early pages. Mr. Dawson was soon reconciled to the marriage: he visited the Fletchers, and gave them the very welcome present of a comfortable house. Babies began to arrive, two sons

and four daughters, and Eliza was fully occupied with
domestic interests, and kindness to her poorer neighbours; she also succeeded, despite strong Tory opposi-
tion, in starting a Female Benefit Society, the first in
Scotland. Her old love of poetry was reawakened by
Lyrical Ballads.

> Never shall I forget the charm I found in these
> poems. It was like a new era in my existence. They
> were in my waking thoughts day and night. They
> had to me all the vivid effects of the finest pictures,
> with the enchantment of the sweetest music, and
> they did much to tranquillize and strengthen my
> heart and mind, which bodily indisposition had
> somewhat weakened.

Her appreciation of the *Excursion*, which she read
on its publication in 1814, is comparatively tepid:

> Wordsworth's Poem, of 423 pages quarto, has
> some exquisite passages, but is on the whole far
> too long. It is marked, however, by that high tone of
> moral sensibility and devout aspirations after good-
> ness for which his other works are remarkable. His
> hero is a pedlar, a Scotch pedlar, too, who carries his
> sublime morality as well as his pack to the native
> mountains of the poet, and then holds converse with
> Wordsworth. The critics may sneer, but the lover
> of nature, and of mankind, will find much to love
> in the *Excursion.*

Ten years after her marriage Mrs. Fletcher paid her

first visit to London, armed with introductions to Mrs.
Barbauld and to Joanna Baillie, whose poems she
greatly admired. The *Lyrical Ballads,* yes; but
Joanna's *Plays on the Passions* did not survive her own
long life, and most beautifully she bore the extinction
of her fame.

Mr. Dawson died in 1798, leaving his property to
Mrs. Fletcher and her children, and a few years later
Mrs. Brudenell showed her gratitude to the family
who had rescued her by bequeathing the Hebburn
estate to Eliza. Strict economy was no longer necessary:
the Fletchers bought a country cottage near Edinburgh,
and enjoyed family holidays in various parts of England and Scotland. Edinburgh society was changing:
the terror of Jacobinism had given place to the terror of
invasion. Tories and Whigs played at soldiers together,
Walter Scott charging with his sabre at Frenchmen in
the shape of turnips, muttering, "cut them down, the
villains, cut them down." Intellectually the important
event was the foundation in 1802 of the *Edinburgh
Review.* Several of the contributors were friends or
acquaintances of the Fletchers, and Eliza writes:

I, who knew Edinburgh both before and after the
appearance of the *Edinburgh Review,* can bear witness to the electrical effects of its publication on the
public mind, and to the large and good results in a
political sense that followed its circulation. The
authorship of the different articles was discussed at
every dinner-table, and I recollect a table-talk

occurrence at our house which must have belonged
to this year. Mr. Fletcher, though not himself given
to scientific inquiry or interests, had been so much
struck with the logical and general ability displayed
in an article of the young *Review* on Professor
Black's Chemistry, that in the midst of a few guests,
of whom Henry Brougham was one, he expressed
an opinion (while in entire ignorance as to the
authorship) to the effect that the man who wrote *that*
article might do or be anything he pleases. Mr.
Brougham, who was seated near me at table,
stretched eagerly forward and said, "What, Mr.
Fletcher, be anything? May he be Lord Chancellor?" On which my husband repeated his words
with emphasis, "Yes, Lord Chancellor, or anything
he desires."

So early had that intriguing Jekyll-cum-Hyde
formed his ambition.

The great literary ladies of Edinburgh society, both
intimate friends of Mrs. Fletcher, were Mrs. Elizabeth
Hamilton, and Mrs. Grant of Laggan. I have already
mentioned Mrs. Hamilton's *Modern Philosophers*, as
arousing Miss Iremonger's enthusiasm. After her return to Scotland, actuated by a desire to improve the
condition of the peasantry, she wrote her popular
Cottagers of Glenburnie, which some of her com-
patriots thought would have been better for more
Scotch and less dirt. Mrs. Grant's two best known
books were *Memoirs of an American Lady* and *Letters*

from the Mountains. Miss Austen remarks that she found the *American Lady* rather better as she proceeded. Its main interest lies in the author's account of her own childhood in Albany, where her heroine, Madame Schuyler, was the great lady of the Dutch colony. Her mother's idea of educating the child was to set her long tasks of needlework. Their library consisted of military treatises and the Bible, until a friendly officer presented her at the age of five with a fine copy of Milton. This she studied with a tattered dictionary to such effect that two years later, when they became acquainted with Madame Schuyler, the child suddenly piped up during a discussion on dreams with—

When nature rests,
Oft in her absence mimic fancy wakes,
To imitate her, but misjoining shapes,
Wild work produces oft.

Milton was Madame Schuyler's favourite poet, and this lucky quotation influenced Anne's whole future. Until she was fourteen, when her parents returned to Scotland, much of her time was spent in Madame Schuyler's household, and that remarkable old lady undertook her education and developed her dormant intelligence. In 1779 she married Mr. Grant, minister of Laggan, who died in 1801, leaving her with eight children, and a small pension as widow of an army chaplain. Her friends launched her forthwith on a literary career. Without her knowledge they started a subscription to publish stray verses of which she had not even kept a copy. "My poetical fugitives", she calls them, and they scarcely deserve the adjective. This was followed by *Letters from the Mountains*, also collected by her friends and not written for publication. Though Miss Austen foisted it unread on other members of her book club, it had a great success, due partly to the contemporary rage for *Ossian*, and consequent interest in Highland life, and partly to sympathy for the misfortunes of the author and her family. Its effect was that of a glorified begging letter. Angerstein and two other merchants sent her £300, and she received other gifts of money, and offers of assistance for her children. Reviewers were rather unkind. Her pluck was, in truth, more to be admired than her pen. Her daughters' health was a constant anxiety and expense. All of them died in youth and only one son survived her.

Mrs. Grant was now living in Edinburgh, and admitting a few young ladies into her household as pupils, in the Barbauld fashion. She was a less intellectual woman than Mrs. Hamilton: the *Vindication* shocked her, and she makes silly jokes about female philosophers suckling their babies in the House of Commons, and putting them to sleep on the Woolsack. She writes of Eliza Fletcher in 1810:

She is a very uncommon person, and one that I am certain you would admire. Her beauty is of a kind peculiar to herself: you have not seen such an

ardent, soul-illumined countenance; you think of
a Roman matron, a Cornelia, an Arria, or a Portia.
There is so much energy about her, she is so utterly
engrossed by benevolent exertions for her fellow
creatures and the pure enjoyments of intellect, that
she thinks less about herself than anyone I know;
and though she has been, for her personal graces,
and the charms of her enlightened, animated, and
unaffected conversation, the admiration of all Edinburgh for years past, she is not in the least degree
spoiled by the general attention. I never knew one
of more ardent benevolence, or one who loves virtue
more. I do not discuss politics with Mrs. F., for I
know it would be to no purpose; but I am honest
enough to say, "Such are not my principles"; and she
is candid enough to allow for my *errors* of opinion.

Mrs. Grant, as an authoress and a Tory, had a
footing in both camps, and her account of the economic
advantages of her position is entertaining:

I have this morning the muddiest head you can
suppose, having had a party of friends with me on
the last two evenings. To understand the cause of
all this hospitality, you must know that, being a
very methodical and economic family, every cow of
ours, as we express it in our rustic Highland dialect,
has a calf; that is to say, when we have a party,
which in Edinburgh includes a cold collation, we are
obliged to provide *quantum sufficit* for our guests,
who, being of a description more given to good

talking than good eating, are content to admire and be admired, and have little time to attend to vulgar gratifications; of consequence, the more material food, after contributing, like the guests, to embellish the entertainment, remains little diminished. As our wide acquaintance includes the greatest variety of people imaginable, there are among them a number of good, kind people, that dress finely, laugh heartily, and sing merrily, and have, in some instances, genealogy besides; yet on these good people the lions and lionesses of literature would think their roaring very ill-bestowed. These, however, make a greater noise in their own way, and before their superior prowess the substantials soon vanish: they are in every sense less fastidious, happier because less wise, and more benevolent because less witty: an assemblage of these contented beings, who can amply appreciate the value of a custard, a jelly, or a jest on its second appearance, are convenient successors to the fine pretenders to originality, who prefer what is new to what is true, and would not for the world be caught eating blancmange while Mr. Jeffrey and Dr. Thomas Brown are brandishing wit and philosophy in each other's faces with electric speed and brilliance. These good fat people, who sing and eat like canary-birds, come with alacrity the day after, and esteem themselves too happy to be admitted so soon to consume mere mortal aliment in the very apartment where the delicacies of intellect were so lately shared among superior intelligences.

Mrs. Grant had figured as one of the possible authors of the *Waverley Novels*, and, in contradicting the report, she had authoritatively attributed them to Scott. He writes to Miss Edgeworth:

> As for honest Mrs. Grant, I cannot conceive why the deuce I should have selected her for a mother-confessor; if it had been yourself, or Joanna, there might have been some probability in the report; but good Mrs. Grant is so very cerulean, and surrounded by so many fetch-and-carry mistresses and misses, and the maintainer of such an unmerciful correspondence, that though I would do her any kindness in my power, yet I should be afraid to be intimate with a woman whose tongue and pen are rather overpowering.

Scott did do her a kindness: he secured a civil list pension for her, and gives an amusing description in his diary of his difficulties with the lady, "proud as a Highlandwoman, vain as a poetess, and absurd as a blue-stocking."

Eliza Fletcher herself was fast becoming the great Whig lady of Edinburgh society. A friend who remembered her at this time, and, unlike Mrs. Grant, sympathized with her political views, shall describe her:

> Throughout life I have never known a purer, a more elevated, a more amiable spirit. Her beautiful countenance and majestic air were combined with the most attractive kindliness. Her full and com-

manding voice and faultless speech live, like every other distinguishing feature, in the memory of all who were privileged to know her, and most of all in the memory of those who were permitted to call her a friend. . . . Her enthusiasm in favour of the rights of man, at a period when this country was threatened with despotic rule by an oligarchy, raised up many violent and bitter opponents; but I doubt whether she ever had an enemy. Her disinterestedness and candour disarmed those who might otherwise, in times of the greatest excitement, have yielded themselves up to personal hostility, even against a woman.

Jeffrey, at first, did not succumb to her spell; he liked the skirt to be long enough to hide the bluestockings, and it was some time before he was assured of the adequacy of Eliza's skirt. She writes after his death:

It is about fifty years since I first met him at James Graham's, brilliancy in conversation was then his great attraction, and flippancy his great defect. It was probably the secret ambition of those who conversed with him that made them afraid of him; I know this from experience, he delighted in checking aspiring or ambitious women, as he used to call Mrs. Millar and me—"women that *would* plague him with rational conversation"—and for many years of our early acquaintance I feared more than I liked him. Just as in proportion as I aspired less, I gained more of his esteem and respect; and latterly there was, as you know, a perfectly friendly feeling tacitly established between us.

She goes on to record with pride Jeffrey's reply to her congratulations when he was elected member for Edinburgh in 1832. "Yes, Mrs. Fletcher, but if it had not been for *the indomitable courage* of your husband, in the worst of times, when he and one or two more maintained the independence of the Bar, we younger men would have been trampled on, and the court of Session never would have enjoyed the confidence of the country."

Despite Mrs. Fletcher's increasing social importance at a time when the younger Edinburgh society was at its most brilliant, and English visitors, like the youthful Lord John Russell, increasingly frequent, she by no means neglected her daughters. Her aim was to give them the same degree of freedom and encouragement to pursue their own tastes which she had enjoyed in her youth, but this was to some extent thwarted by a harsh and unsympathetic governess. That lady, of unimpeachable character and industry, had been recommended by the theoretic educationalist Mrs. Hamilton, herself a spinster with brevet rank, and Mrs. Fletcher utters a warning to mothers against tolerating unnecessary discipline in the schoolroom: the children's happiness ought to be the first consideration. Visiting masters, who followed the governess, were a greater success. But she was unhappy about the eldest girl,

Bessy, who, unlike the rest of the family, was cold and reserved. Charmed by Mrs. Barbauld, and much impressed by her essay on *The Education of Circumstances*, she decided that Bessy should spend some months with her at Hampstead, "where a new view of society, and the great advantage of living with that most excellent and highly-gifted woman, might excite her to more energetic aspirations after knowledge and all that was praiseworthy".

Mrs. Barbauld's father, Dr. John Aiken, was a tutor at the famous Warrington Academy, the home of "low Arianism", and numbered among his colleagues, Dr. Priestley, Dr. Taylor, of Norwich, and Dr. Enfield, whose *Speaker, or Miscellaneous Pieces selected from the best English writers*, has had a prolonged popularity. Among the distinguished visitors to Warrington were Howard, the prison reformer, Roscoe, the historian, and Pennant, the naturalist. Miss Aiken began her literary career in 1773 with a volume of poems including "Corsica", which Mrs. Montagu presented to General Paoli. The Warrington atmosphere was strenuous but prosaic. Romance arrived in the person of a young Frenchman, Rochemont Barbauld, and Miss Aiken, captivated by his melodramatic wooing, married him in 1774, despite the warning that he had already been insane. Her Warrington experience was useful in the boys' school started by her husband at Palgrave in Suffolk, which they maintained successfully for eleven years. Among their pupils were the first Lord Denman, "classic Gell" and William Taylor, of Norwich, whose translation of Burger's Leonore, read later by Mrs. Barbauld to an Edinburgh audience, inspired the young Walter Scott. For her own class of little boys, and for her nephew, Charles Aiken, whom she adopted at two years old, Mrs. Barbauld wrote her *Early Lessons*, and her charming and popular *Hymns in Prose*.

Mrs. Montagu, Queen of the Blues, who had maintained her regard for Mrs. Barbauld, tried to persuade her to start a Ladies' College, but she demurred:

"A kind of academy for ladies where they are to be taught in a regular manner the various branches of science, appears to me better calculated to form such characters as the *Precieuses* or *Femmes Savantes* than good wives or agreeable companions. The best way for a woman to acquire knowledge is from conversation with a father, or brother, and by such a course of reading as they may recommend. Perhaps you may think that having myself stepped out of the bounds of female reserve in becoming an author it is with an ill grace that I offer these sentiments— but my situation has been peculiar, and would be no rule for others. I should likewise object to the age proposed—geography, languages, &c. are best learned from about nine to thirteen. I should have little hopes of cultivating a love of knowledge in a young lady of fifteen who came to me ignorant and uncultivated: it is too late then to begin to learn.

The empire of the passions is coming on—those attachments begin to be formed, which influence the happiness of future life—the care of a mother alone can give suitable attention to this important period. The ease and grace of society; the duties in their own family, to their friends; the detail of domestic economy—lastly their behaviour to the other half of their species, who then begin to court their notice—these are the accomplishments which a young woman has to learn till she is married or fit to be so; and surely these are not to be learned in a school: my next reason is that I am not at all fit for the task. I have seen a good deal of the Education of boys, but in a girls' school I should be quite a novice. I never was at one myself, I have not even the advantage of sisters; indeed for the early part of my life, I conversed little with my own sex. In the village where I was there were none to converse with; and this I am sensible has given me an awkwardness about common things which would make me peculiarly unfit for the education of girls. I could not judge of their music, their dancing; and if I pretended to correct their air, they might be tempted to smile at my own; for I know myself to be remarkably deficient in gracefulness of person, in my air and manner. I am sensible the common schools are upon a very bad plan, and believe I could project a better—but I could not execute it."

Maria Edgeworth made another proposal: a woman's

paper with all the eminent literary women of the day as contributors—one of old Mr. Edgeworth's bright ideas—which Mrs. Barbauld rejected with some humour: "All the literary ladies! Mercy on us! Have you ever reckoned up how many there are, or computed how much truth, and how many discordant materials would be poured in from such a general invitation? I feel also doubtful of the propriety of making it declaredly a *lady's paper*. There is no bond of union among literary women, any more than among literary men; different sentiments and different connections separate them much more than the joint interest of their sex would unite them. Mrs. Hannah More would not write along with you or me, and we should probably hesitate at joining Miss Hays, or if she were living, Mrs. Godwin."

Mrs. Barbauld herself stands half-way between Mary Wollstonecraft and Hannah More, and she had a more direct personal influence on women's education in her day than either. Mrs. Wollstonecraft respected her intellectual attainments, but laughed at her sentimental verses about flower-like girls: Mrs. More also found her a truly intellectual woman, although the difference in their views, political and religious, destroyed her pleasure in intercourse. But her essays on "Education" and "Prejudice", sensible and well-written, to us nothing more, had a profound effect on the minds of anxious parents. Mothers felt that a few weeks of Mrs. Barbauld's influence and example was the perfect completion of a daughter's education, and her approval an order to be proudly worn on confronting the world. Mrs. John Taylor sent her vain and bouncing Sally at fourteen for a visit to Mrs. Barbauld, where she compared Pope and Boileau under her hostess' tuition, construed Horace and was introduced to Miss Joanna Baillie. Sally bounced and flirted a little longer after she went home. Then came the grave and scholarly John Austin, and she "passed five years feeding only on love, and severe study, in order to become worthy of being a wife". Austin was taken to see Mrs. Barbauld, and after "some very pleasant argumentation on moral and metaphysical subjects" the engagement received her august sanction. Alas! Mr. Gordon Waterhouse's recent revelations show that the conversion of Sally Taylor, which had so startled Norwich society, was less radical than it appeared. Even Mary Wollstonecraft, I fancy, would have felt that Sarah Austin's correspondence with the charlatan Prince Pückler-Muskau, like Anne Gilchrist's pursuit of Walt Whitman, was a deplorable debauch of personality: Jane Austen, a little shocked, would have found their sentimental capers exquisitely funny. Mrs. Galton hoped that her queer Mary Ann might become more like other girls after a course of Mrs. Barbauld, but the future Mrs. Schimmelpenninck needed a surer anchor for her soul: Mrs. Barbauld's high thinking was devoid of any mystic tendency. Perhaps the nearest modern analogy to her educational influence is—*longo intervallo*—the insight into Greek literature and Greek thought, which Janet Case and Melian Stawell managed to impart to

their pupils without insistence upon grammar, or even
in some instances any knowledge of the language.

In her own day Mrs. Barbauld's verse was as famous
as her prose. Landor at a Bath dinner-party "spoke of
her as the first writer of the day, and became so
eloquent in praise of some of her poems that he fixed
the attention of the entire party. His good memory
enabled him to repeat the passages he most admired.
One was from the 'Summer Evening's Meditation',
and after repeating it, he asked in the manner which
those who ever heard him can well remember, 'Can
you show me anything finer in the English
language?' "

But her literary labours came to a tragic end with
her poem, "Eighteen Hundred and Eleven". The
theme is the impending destruction of England as a result of the Orders in Council which, framed as a reply
to Napoleon's attempted blockade, were gradually
irritating the United States into war:

Thy baseless wealth dissolves in air away,
Like mists that melt before the morning ray:
No more on crowded mart or busy street
Friends meeting friends, with cheerful hurry greet;
Sad, on the ground thy princely merchants bend
Their altered looks, and evil days portend,
And fold their arms, and watch with anxious breast
The tempest blackening in the distant West.
Yes, thou must droop; thy Midas dream is o'er;
The golden tide of commerce leaves thy shore,

73

Leaves thee to prove th' alternate ills that haunt
Enfeebling Luxury and ghastly Want;
Leaves thee, perhaps, to visit distant lands,
And deal the gifts of Heaven with equal hands.

"Yet, O my Country", there are compensations.
American boys will continue to be instructed by Locke
and Paley: enamoured American virgins will dream of
Hagley's Woods: Joanna Baillie and William Shakespeare will be acted on alternate nights in every
American town. The desolate island will be visited by a
better-informed class of tourist than so far seems to
have reached its shores: ingenuous youth after doing
the round of Oxford, Runnymede, Cambridge and
Stratford will:

Anxious inquire where Clarkson, friend of man,
Or all-accomplished Jones his race began;

and resume its journey by way of Olney, Chatmoss (in
memory of Roscoe), the lakes,

Feast with Dun Edin's classic brow their sight,
And "visit Melrose by the pale moonlight".

But who their mingled feelings shall pursue
When London's faded glories rise to new?

*   *   *

Pensive and thoughtful shall the wanderers greet

Each splendid square, and still, untrodden street;
Or of some crumbling turret, ruined by time,
The broken stairs with perilous steps shall climb,
Thence stretch their view the wide horizon round,
By scattered hamlets trace its ancient bound,
And choked no more with fleets, fair Thames survey
Through reeds and sedge pursue his idle way.

While civilization retires to South America,

And pours through feeble souls a higher life,
Shouts to the mingled tribes from sea to sea,
And swears—Thy world, Columbus, shall be free.

This manifesto was too much for the *Quarterly*.
Miss Edgeworth and her father snatched up their pens
to answer—"so ungentlemanlike, so unjust, so insolent
a review I never read," but they settled on silent
contempt. "It is not their criticism on your poem
which incenses me, it is the odious tone in which they
dare to speak of the most respectable and elegant
female writer that England can boast. The public, the
public will do you justice." But the public remained
unmoved, and the *Quarterly* was too much for Mrs.
Barbauld: she lived another thirteen years and published no more.

Though only one of her poems has survived, "Life,
we've been long together", which Wordsworth envied, and Mme. D'Arblay repeated to herself every
night, she has added vicariously a phrase to the language: Mrs. Barbauld will always be remembered

75

as the Mother of Macaulay's New Zealander.*
Mrs. Barbauld certainly had a way with girls. She
writes of the difficult Bessy:

I cannot let Miss Fletcher make up her *pacquet*
without adding a line to say—in truth, what I said
before, yet a mother, I fancy, will allow me to repeat—that her child is well and lovely, and the darling of every one who sees her. I am every day more
and more pleased with her intelligence and the just-
ness of her taste, as well as with the sweetness of her
manners. You would have been amused with a
dialogue that passed between us the other day. We
were reading Paley. "But," says she, "I do not want
all this evidence, for it never entered into my mind
to doubt of any of these truths." I observed to her,
that there were those who had made objections and
had written books against them, and that it might
occur to her, at some time of her life, to be asked for
a reason of the hope that was in her: "But," replied
she, with great *naïveté*, "I think it would be the best
way, then, to read first one of these books that are
written against Christianity." You may believe I did

* An earlier version will be found in an essay on Mitford's
History of Greece, written at twenty-four, which Macaulay did
not think worth republishing: "when, perhaps, travellers from
distant regions shall in vain labour to decipher on some moulder-
ing pedestal the name of our proudest chief; shall hear some
savage hymns chanted to some misshapen idol over the ruined
dome of our proudest temple; and shall see a single naked
fisherman wash his nets in the river of the ten thousand masts."

76

not recommend one, but I felt the conviction that we do not even wish our children to inquire without a bias on their minds. Nor ought we; if we think ourselves to be in possession of important truths, it is both right and kind to impress them on the mind of youth without waiting for the uncertain process of their own crude reasonings. There is a great deal of unjust prejudice against prejudice.

Was Bessy so naïve, or had she, perchance, a sense of humour, in which I suspect her earnest, high-principled and energetic family were somewhat deficient? It is a relief to find that they could enjoy Jane Austen's novels, and even nicknamed Eliza "Miss Bates" from her incorrigible habit of seeing good in everybody. Yes, but there is a touch of spiritual pride, quite unknown to dear Miss Bates, in Mrs. Fletcher's exultation in her own breadth of mind: she could actually love some Tories.

Bessy married three years later, and is henceforth referred to as Mrs. Taylor, with affection, but with less enthusiasm than Mrs. Fletcher felt for her other daughters. Grace, who combined her own passions for poetry and philanthropy and freely expressed her fine feelings, her own favourite and generally beloved of her friends, died young. As Mrs. Barbauld puts it in her letter of condolence: "Like Young's Narcissa, 'she sparkled, was exhaled, and went to heaven'." Her mother has left a short memoir of her.

After Grace's death Mrs. Fletcher withdrew to

some extent from Edinburgh society, and devoted still
more of her time and energy to her various philan-
thropic interests. In 1819 she and her younger daughters paid a visit to London, where they spent some impressive hours in Newgate with Mrs. Fry. They were
accompanied by Robert Owen, "the notorious soci-
alist", but not yet a declared secularist. As a reformer
he had been esteemed by the Fletchers, but his later
views were too much even for the broad-minded
Eliza:

> It would be unfair perhaps to refuse him credit
> for wishing to promote the present good of man-
> kind, but when he cannot but perceive that a con-
> sideration for present good, even when accompanied
> by a belief in a Divine judge, is not sufficient to
> enable man to regulate his passions and abstain
> from evil, how is it likely that when these restraints
> are removed, as Owen desires, the sovereignty of
> reason alone, a vegetable diet, and one loose gar-
> ment, will transform the human race, as he expects,
> from misery to happiness.

Owen took Mrs. Fletcher to see William Godwin:

> Godwin, then an interesting-looking old man,
> lived at a small bookseller's shop on Ludgate Hill,
> with a figure of Aesop over the door. We sat half an
> hour with this mild philosopher. His countenance
> was benevolent, as were his writings. Thirty years
> before the time we saw him, his *Political Justice* was

thought to have allayed the insurrectionary fever produced, as some imagined, by the writings of Thomas Paine; but now that the days of alarm were over, Godwin was more known as the author of "Caleb Williams" and "St. Leon" than as a political writer. He had a beautiful portrait of Mary Wollstonecraft, by Opie, above the chimney-piece of his little parlour. We were pleased with our interview with this distinguished man and very eloquent writer.

She renewed her friendship with Mrs. Barbauld and Joanna Baillie, but refers briefly to other literary society, as though it were losing its glamour: "Mrs. Opie and Jane Porter also passed before us, as dissolving views; along with the Smiths of 'The Rejected Addresses', the Miss Berrys and Sir Lumley Skeffingtons of the day." James and Horace Smith could never have been names with which to allure the earnest Eliza Fletcher, as they did their fellow-satirist, Jane Austen.

Although he retained his political interests to the end, Archibald Fletcher was becoming old and infirm, and during his last years they lived nine miles from Edinburgh at Auchindinny House, formerly the home of Mackenzie, the Man of Feeling. In 1828 the long sympathy of their married life came to a close.

Mrs. Barbauld had set a high standard of intellectual and moral perfection for girls: who could do the same for a grandson? There was only one answer. Mrs. Fletcher had read Dr. Arnold's pamphlet on *The*

Christian Duty of Conceding the Roman Catholic Claims: Rugby was the school for *us*. She took a cottage at Bilton, and the warm friendship began with Dr. and Mrs. Arnold which lasted the rest of their lives. Other congenial neighbours were the Rector of Rugby and his wife. Mrs. Fletcher speaks of the accomplished scholar and poet, but to one who can just recall a dim picture of a frail old gentleman with a long white beard, it is a proud memory to have seen, not the Rev. John Moultrie, whose verses have long been forgotten, but that Johnny Moultrie, who still lives in the letters of his friend. Did he ever speak to her of Keats?

Mrs. Fletcher also renewed relations with Mrs. Arnold's sister-in-law, Mrs. Penrose, better known as Mrs. Markham, the daughter of her old friend, Mr. Cartwright. Mrs. Penrose writes:

We had the great gratification of a visit of two days from Mrs. Fletcher. Her appearance is so engaging, that the mere looking at her is itself a pleasure. In her youth she was brilliantly beautiful (she is about sixty); she retains so much symmetry of feature, so much fine expression of countenance, and so much grace of deportment, such a gentle-womanliness of manner, with such an expression of goodness, as make her absolutely lovely. She is rather fat than thin, and her beauty is matured more than faded. Her conversation is delightful, full of variety and anecdote. She is an enthusiast in politics, and on what is called the Liberal side, but

80

there is such a feminineness in all she says and does, that even her politics could not allay the charm of her agreeableness. She has a most extensive acquaintance with literary persons, and her conversation is a stream of lively anecdote continually flowing.

Another twenty years can have made little change, as George Richmond's lovely drawing of Mrs. Fletcher at eighty shows. Her youngest daughter married Dr. John Davy, brother and biographer of Sir Humphry: she is remembered for her sympathetic account of Sir Walter Scott at Malta, quoted in full by Lockhart. Mrs. Fletcher and her daughter Mary spent a few years in travelling, visiting, and looking after the old aunts in Yorkshire, till, in 1839, she established herself permanently at Lancrigg. The Lake country had attracted her ever since a holiday spent there early in her married life: now Fox Howe provided the society most congenial to her. Mary, who edited her mother's *Autobiography*, married Sir John Richardson, but both the Richardsons and the Davys had houses in the neighbourhood, so she had the constant care and companionship of her own family. The Wordsworths were old friends: Tory friends be it noted, but the real affection on both sides survived the strain of political and religious differences. It was the aggressive Harriet Martineau who deplored Mrs. Fletcher's intolerance. They fell out on the subject of mesmerism, and agreed that it must never be mentioned if they were to remain friends, but the publication of *Man's Nature and Development* was too much for Mrs. Fletcher, and she wrote that all intimacy must cease. One constant visitor at Rydal Mount found it a relief to walk the four miles to Lancrigg for breakfast and unguarded conversation with Mrs. Fletcher. "Mrs. F. calls herself a *very old* woman, a title which no one admits to be correct," wrote Crabb Robinson in 1852—"and retains all her youthful attachments while she allows herself to form others—Lord Brougham may be considered her first Love and Lord John Russell her second. Mazzini is her passion and Kossuth the object of her *temperate* attachment." She had maintained relations with her "first love", the enigmatic Brougham, who wrote most affectionately during her last illness, and refers to her as "one of the most accomplished of her sex, who, with the utmost purity of life that can dignify and enhance female charms, combined the inflexible principles and deep political feeling of a Hutchison or a Roland". Mrs. Fletcher's vigour of mind and enjoyment of life did not flag until a few months before her death. In the autumn of 1857 she wrote to an old friend: "My own bodily health is good, and I pray against despondency; for in my eighty-eighth year I can make little effort. You would not know me, I am so changed in mind and temperament." Three months later Wordsworth's grandson, William, described her condition to Crabb Robinson:

My late visit to Rydal was among other things

much saddened by the melancholy state in which I found dear Mrs. Fletcher. For many Years, I have been accustomed to consider calling for a talk with her as almost the first duty before me after my arrival: in essentials we pretty much agreed, tho I could never, I fear, work myself up to what in her eyes was the proper pitch of enthusiasm for certain members of the Whig Aristocracy. At her age it would be idle and presumptuous to speculate on her chances of recovery; one might rather pray for a speedy release—and yet the very brightness and serenity of her past life makes so dark and cheerless a close by contrast all the more painful.

Love, as her daughter says, never failed her, but she, who had seemed to Arthur Stanley "a personification beyond any other I had ever seen of Christian Hope" was no longer sustained by her old hopefulness. She died in February, 1858, at the age of eighty-eight.

ANNE WOODROOFFE 1766-1830

IN THE CHURCHYARD of the still peaceful village of Somerford Keynes, formerly in Wiltshire, now ceded to Gloucestershire, is a large rectangular tomb, a memorial to a former vicar, the Reverend Nathaniel George Woodrooffe, and his wife, Anne. Mrs. Woodrooffe, whose maiden name was Cox, was born in 1766 and died in 1830. Her memory is also preserved in *Shades of Character: or, Mental and Moral Delineations; Designed to Promote the Formation of the Female Character on the Basis of Christian Principle*, which went into seven editions between 1824 and 1855. The beautiful old church is little changed since the Woodrooffe's time, but the vicarage, now in private hands, has been enlarged beyond recognition. There Mrs. Woodrooffe received a few young ladies for purposes of education. She was not concerned, like her contemporary Mrs. Barbauld, with girls who would have to play their part in intellectual and political circles, but with the daughters of country gentlemen, who might inherit estates of their own, and would eventually marry men like their fathers. Among her pupils were the daughters of the Lord of the Manor and patron of the living, the Misses Foyle, the elder of whom inherited the manor house. The famous evangelical, Daniel Wilson, Bishop of Calcutta, also entrusted one of his daughters to Mrs. Woodrooffe. Her system was "to individualize—to scrutinize character, and even 'shades' of character"; and then to suit her instructions to each particular mind that came under her plastic influence. "In order to educate a child rightly, you must descend into the character; and, to those who know they share the same nature, this descent will be the most easy and natural." Although Mrs. Woodrooffe lays as much stress on individuality as Mary Wollstonecraft, whose name she would have abhorred, there was no running wild, no freedom for self-development at Somerford Keynes, and as little room as possible left for experience, but guidance at every turn in the path, and warnings against every snare.

Her book describes her method and her pupils and neighbours under the guise of fiction, and we are told that she has "insensibly" drawn her own portrait in the saintly Mrs. E. Groves.

The definition of Christian will always be a matter of controversy. I have heard an elderly Colonel declare with vigour that, though not a Christian, he was a Protestant, and I have been told of a lady speaking on behalf of missions, who began by dividing society into three classes, Christians, Roman Catholics and Pagans. In Mrs. Woodrooffe's day the question was of even greater moment. Mrs. Gilbert, better known as Ann Taylor, one of the *Several Young Persons* who wrote those delightful verses *Original Poems for Infant Minds*, taxes that popular prophetess, Mrs. Hannah More, with laxity:

She frequently writes as if the two classes which divide society—"the children of the kingdom", and "the men of this world"—were amalgamated in a third—natives of some country midway of those distant regions: Christians who are not *Christian*. We admit that there are many who present such an appearance to the eye of man—many whom charity would fain regard as brethren, although they do not "come out" and "separate" with such entire consistency as to render their character indubitable. But this uncertainty exists, not in the subject, but in the observer, to whom the heart is inscrutable; and while it suspends his judgment, it must not confuse his language. Amidst endless diversities of situation, temper, and knowledge, every individual is, or is not, a *Christian*; and he that is not must not be flattered with the name.

Upon what ground, therefore, does Mrs. More bestow the name of *Christians* upon such as are destitute, according to her own account, of the "vital spirit of Christianity"? "The good sort of people" she is exhibiting are well described as "contractors for heaven, who bring their merit as their purchase-money, who intend to be saved at their own expense", and "do not always take care to be provided with a very exorbitant sum, though they expect so large a return in exchange of it".

Mrs. Woodrooffe is as sound as Mrs. Gilbert could wish on the subject of vital religion, but she also has her three classes: those who have acquired it by rebirth, those who, whatever their virtues, graces and aspirations, are not decided Christians for lack of it, and the worldly.

The Egg's no Chick by falling from the Hen;
Nor man a Christian, till he's born agen.

When the story opens Mr. and Mrs. Deane have decided to send their daughter, an only child, to Mrs. Delany's boarding-school. Mrs. Deane would have preferred a governess, but Mr. Deane considers governesses so badly treated that few of them are worth having: "they are," he says, "suspended between parlour and kitchen, as unworthy of either. I once knew a very competent governess: she was sensible of her own value, though not in the least conceited; and she stipulated, before she entered the house of a certain friend of mine, that if she undertook the education of their children, she *should* have a suite of apartments to herself, and her own servants." The same lady also made it a condition that the children should not go down and guzzle dessert and admiration while she sat above neglected.

Both Mr. and Mrs. Deane are vital Christians; Mrs. Deane of the most aggressive type: she loses no opportunity of expressing her opinions in and, as at any rate most of her modern hearers must feel, out of season. Elizabeth is aged eleven, but, though not intended to be a case of arrested development, she asks so many artless questions and maintains such an unshaken belief in the infallibility of her Mamma, that her mentality throughout the book appears to be four or five years behind-hand. When, finally, a suitor of unimpeachable character is produced at the normal age by her parents, she is so much surprised that any-one should think of marrying her—so are we—that it is a relief to find that the long letter of advice about her future state, which her Mamma presses into her hand as she leaves home, enjoins her on no account to economize in her personal washing bill.

Elizabeth has been reading the *Pilgrim's Progress* with her Mamma, and she is fired with the desire to set out at once on a pilgrimage. Her Mamma says she may go, but has much difficulty in explaining the allegorical nature of the proposition. She is very anxious to meet Evangelist, and when told that Evangelist is any clergyman who preaches the Gospel, enquires whether Mr. Smith, the local incumbent, is Evangelist, and is met with the evasive reply: "Mr. Smith is a very amiable man, my love; very kind to the poor, and very obliging to your Papa." Mrs. Deane, we feel, might have made an Evangelist of the young Edmund Bertram, but never of Henry Tilney. Several clergy appear in the book, and the Shades of Religion which constitute their characters are carefully de-picted. The Infant Pilgrim goes to school, armed with a red morocco diary in which to record the events of each day that her Mamma may give a spiritual explanation of her worldly adventures. Her habit of quoting her Mamma and Bunyan at every turn naturally makes for

trouble: the mean girl steals her diary, and the clever
girl, who, though good at heart, is a quiz, and therefore
fails eventually to obtain a husband, teases her. But
she finds a kindred spirit in Agnes Groves, three
years her senior, and their relation throughout the
book is a foretaste of the friendship between the two
girls in Mrs. Ewing's *Six to Sixteen*. The great event of
the school year is a ball at which Mrs. Delany's pupils
perform. Agnes's widowed mother, the fashionable
Mrs. Groves (she must not be confused with her
saintly aunt by marriage, Mrs. E. Groves, who enjoys
brevet rank), is present, as her daughter is to make a
brilliant appearance. Mrs. Deane, on the other hand,
swoops down and removes her innocent child from the
contaminating atmosphere of worldly excitement.
Miss Forbes, the assistant mistress, is indignant, but
Mrs. Delany, who has exquisite manners, dresses
rather too well, and is competent in all educational
matters except vital religion, has learnt to tolerate the
caprices of parents. When Elizabeth returns to school
after the holidays there is no Agnes. Although the dear
girl only went to the ball to please her mother, she
caught cold, and is hovering between life and death.
She wants to see her little friend: the doctor says it may
be fatal to thwart any of her wishes, and the agonized
Mrs. Groves entreats Mrs. Deane to allow Elizabeth to
visit them. Agnes's mother is placed for us by the
following description:

Mrs. Groves was a fashionable woman; the

fashionable world was all to her; to be unfashionable was the acme of everything contemptible. She' had one principle that it would be well if characters of a higher kind could practise: in writing, in speaking, in acting, she had always an eye to her own character. She had what the artists call a beau ideal; and to that standard she endeavoured to conform. She never spoke without considering that it was Mrs. Groves, the elegant Mrs. Groves, who was speaking. I do not censure the regard Mrs. Groves had to consistency. Consistency is perfection. I censure the meanness of her object—the sole approbation of dying mortals, like herself.

This lady was surprised, not unnaturally, at Mrs. Deane's reply to her invitation to Elizabeth:

MADAM,

I so deeply enter into your present anxiety, that I am anxious to relieve it. My little girl is not yet thirteen, and I think her too young to visit without me. If you really think her presence necessary to Miss Groves's recovery, I will bring her; and if you will have the goodness to assign us a sitting and sleeping apartment, with another for my own maid, I shall be very happy to be of any use to you. In a house situated as yours is at present, I should be very sorry to add any care: I shall immediately become one of your family, and my own servant will attend me. I am moderate from inclination and principle: one dish is sufficient for me; so I trust

I shall give no trouble. My own menservants and carriage will be in your village, as I shall wish occasionally to take Elizabeth short airings. Should no unforeseen event happen, I shall be with you on Friday.

Mrs. Groves could only suppose that Mrs. Deane wished to worm herself as well as her child into really good society. She had not grasped, neither, so far, had we, that Mrs. Deane, apparently an ordinary country lady, though very genteel, was the youngest daughter of the Russian Envoy (*i.e.* the English Ambassador to Russia), and had behind her a magnificent cosmopolitan past. She is not, therefore, discomposed by the grandeur of Abberley Park and its attendant lackeys:

They entered the marble hall; and Elizabeth, who had seen her Mamma only at home, was surprised by the coldness with which she received the attentions of these men, and to hear her say, without any ceremony, to a very genteel-looking woman, who stood at the bottom of the stairs ready to conduct them up, "You will be so good as to show my maid her apartment."

They are received by their hostess, who takes Elizabeth at once to see Agnes. Mrs. Groves, with fashionable ease, took a chair, and drew Elizabeth towards her: "And now, my little friend, I expect your visit will be of the greatest use to Agnes; and I shall leave you quite free to do everything you like. I only ask one favour of you; and that is, that you will not talk about religion." Elizabeth, scarlet with surprise, asks whether she may not speak of God on Sundays, as they talk about Him every day at home, and she is afraid of not being able to keep such a promise. Mrs. Groves explains: "My dear Miss Deane, Agnes is so weak at present, that these subjects are too much for her. You see how ill she looks: the very mention of these things has quite flurried her. My dear love, shall I ring for Joss?" "No, it is not speaking of God that flurries me; it is, that you should wish me not to speak of Him." "Dear child, you are only too good!" exclaims Mrs. Groves, with ready hypocrisy, and leaves the room in a passion.

Reader! would you like to follow Mrs. Groves to her apartment, to see her in her moments of unmarked spleen? Behold her stretched on her bergère. "I thought how it would be; and that Mother walking every step by rule, canting and whining." Joss came in. "I beg pardon, my lady; I did not know you were here." "Joss, give me a cordial." "Are you not well, my lady?" "I am over fatigued, Joss." She took the cordial, remembered she had left Mrs. Deane in the morning-room, composed her ruffled features, and was again the soft and lovely Mrs. Groves.

Mrs. Groves's house-party consisted of Mrs. E. Groves, cultivated in spite of the relentless expression of her piety, in the hope that she might leave her property to Agnes; the light-hearted parasite and gambler, Colonel Stanley, whom Mrs. Groves afterwards married; Lady Emily Grey, who is under the spell of Aunt Groves (everyone's aunt, real or adopted), but has not quite broken with the world of fashion; and Mr. James. This gentleman is a bachelor, on the right side of forty, handsome, rich, generous, warm-hearted and outspoken, but the victim of constant persecution by all the true Christians, because he resists vital religion. I shall return later to some of their more virulent attacks on the most attractive character in the book as essential to the understanding of Mrs. Woodrooffe's point of view. James was the devoted friend of the late Groves, and is the guardian of Agnes, for whose sake he continues to visit Abberley, much as he dislikes the widow and her ways. Mr. Groves had been a model Lord of the Manor, but Mrs. Groves hated the country and the poor, and would not allow her daughter to visit the villagers lest she should catch some complaint: the girl's illness is regarded by them as retributive: "they as puffs at the poor never comes to no good". One old man remarked: "It was a bad day for our village when the Squire went to his grave; he knew us all; and there wasn't a child born in this parish but went down in his pocket-book; and a three-shilling piece, caudle for the first fortnight; and after that, for the next fortnight, meat and pudding from his table. The meat ate sweet—it was given from his willing heart."

Mrs. Groves also managed to convey the living to a

"drowsy doctor" instead of retaining the excellent Mr. Wilton, an Evangelist in Mrs. Deane's sense and loved by the whole parish. His offence was that he had insisted on Agnes being christened in church, just like a poor child, instead of suitably in the drawing-room, and because in his sermons, as the old clerk said, "he *laid* it down so *plain*".

Mr. James is on the war-path: he has already dealt faithfully and publicly with Mrs. Groves about her dismissal of the former clergyman, and has spent the morning in visiting and chaffing the villagers, old servants and others valued by the late Mr. Groves and neglected by his widow, and in entertaining Agnes and Elizabeth, now also adopted as his niece. After serious reflection Mrs. Deane has consented to emerge from her seclusion and join the company at dinner: "she thought it was for the honour of God's cause that she should not quite absent herself, lest they should suppose she resigned the world because she was unable to enjoy it". But, although the bell has been rung twice, Mr. James does not appear. His hostess supposes that he is somewhere in the village: "he has a number of acquaintances there: he is not very select. I believe he visits his washerwoman as frequently as anybody."

At that moment he entered, in complete undress, boots, his hair in the rough state of the morning; "I beg your pardon; I hope I have not kept you waiting; but I have had so much to do, for you have not a single manservant in your house." Mrs.

Groves stared: "What can you mean, Mr. James?"
"It is a fact; you have none but gentlemen. I walked
through your servants' hall: some were reading the
newspaper; some at back-gammon; and one sleek
fellow was drinking chocolate. I looked for one to
carry my niece's chocolate to the summer-house, but
Joss informed me that no one could go; it was the
chambermaid's place to carry slops." "Is this a
time?" said Mrs. Groves; "is this a time, Mr.
James." "Really, Madam, I am obliged to seize this
opportunity, to apologize for my appearance. I have
literally been employed in carrying Agnes the refreshment she needed; for, among all these gentlemen (glancing his eye sternly on the lackeys who
were in waiting), not one could be found to carry the
heiress of this house the refreshment of which she
was in want. Oh, for the return of the Harry's and
the George's of old time, to whom every service was
delightful which could prove their honest faith and
zeal!" He kept it up during the whole of dinner:
he rose for everything he wanted. Lady Emily
enjoyed it; it was precisely the thing she would have
done herself. Mrs. E. Groves thought they deserved
as much. Mrs. Deane was secretly amused.

It does not seem to occur to anyone but the reader
that such manners are singular in a guest.

Mrs. Deane finds a kindred spirit in Aunt Groves:
they drive and converse together. Mrs. Deane considers talking about others in a censorious spirit a con-

stant snare, though it will be observed that she manages to enjoy a good deal of it, in order, of course, to protect Elizabeth from dangerous intimacies, or from some other high motive. Aunt Groves values astronomy, botany, and visiting all the wonders of creation, as a means of distracting the mind from personalities: she also thinks experimental philosophy a very pleasing, and a very profitable, study for youth. Their taste in literature is the same. "There is one book," says Mrs. Groves, "which is universally laid aside, from a peculiarity in the style, being too much adorned for correct taste. I cannot help wishing it were allowable for some judicious hands to pass over these works, lop some of their redundancies and render them once more objects of our attention. The well bred, though flowery conversations, tinctured with such real piety, might prove a safe Christian guide; and——" Mrs. Deane instantly guesses Hervey's *Theron and Aspasio*. As it is a dialogue in three volumes on Imputed Righteousness I am still waiting for it to be lopped, and may, even then, make Wesley's strong disapproval an excuse for not reading it.

Meanwhile Agnes is recovering: she and Elizabeth walk and read together, books carefully selected by their elders, of course—there are no adventures, like the large Dante propped on the kitchen table by the two friends in *Six to Sixteen*—Mrs. Sherwood's *Hedge of Thorns*, a less lively work than her *Fairchild Family*, Bowdler's *Life*, not that of Thomas, who was still purifying Shakespeare and Gibbon, but an equally virtuous John, the *Life of Henry Martyn*, and other books on India, an echo, no doubt, of Mrs. Woodrooffe's friendship with the Bishop of Calcutta. But there was one dreadful lapse: in the absence of Mrs. Deane, Mr. James brought from the circulating library, his name for an old woman who peddled books, *Jack and the Bean-Stalk*. He read it aloud to them, and they laughed so much that Elizabeth was afraid, as she reported to her Mamma, that Agnes would be ill again. "Well, my dear," said Mrs. Deane, "do you think you have gained much by this story?" "No, Mamma; but I really was very much entertained; Mr. James is uncommonly good-natured." Her Mamma is so abrupt that she inquires anxiously: "Mamma, do you think there was any harm in Mr. James reading *Jack and the Bean-Stalk*?" Mrs. Deane replies:

Not the slightest: but I think *this*, Elizabeth, that lightness of character, and a constitutional gaiety of heart, are very great snares, and especially to young people. A child well brought up would be terrified at wicked conversation; she would shudder to hear the name of the great and glorious God profaned: but this wild playfulness, which it seems hard to censure, and which steals even on sober minds—to this, if a child were constantly exposed, I should think her in danger of losing that placid, equal disposition so favourable to a listening state, which every day imbibes some gathered strength from the life of wisdom, and the word of God. I should be sorry to give up Mr. James as an acquaintance, because I feel a love and respect for his character; and a great deal of this gaiety is the effect of habit, arising from the assurance that he is everywhere liked, and free to say and do as he pleases. But, I hope, under all this folly there is some settled principle; and I really believe, if he could always be kept in rational society, he would soon drop his frivolous conversation, and become all his friends could wish him. But I should be sorry, Elizabeth, if you very much admired this nonsense.

In short Mrs. Deane has joined the hue and cry after the soul of the unfortunate James. It transpires that Mr. Deane, in his unchastened youth, had been a college friend, which facilitates further intercourse.

Agnes goes off for her convalescence with Aunt Groves, and Elizabeth returns to school. But a great change is at hand: Mrs. Delany's clerical brother had married a worldly West Indian of large fortune: she has now died, leaving three little girls, and Dr. Delany has persuaded his sister to live with him, handing over her school to the assistant mistress, Miss Forbes. This lady is always described as "correct"; year in, year out, she reads Miss Talbot's *Reflections on the Seven Days of the Week*, a moral and religious work, published after the author's death by Dr. Johnson's learned friend, Mrs. Elizabeth Carter. Her lack of humour is underlined, a necessary precaution where the standard is not high, and her conscientiousness is eventually rewarded by marriage with a country gentleman, a widower with nine children, two of whom she has already correctly trained. Elizabeth is not confided to Miss Forbes: Agnes Groves is to complete her education under the care of Dr. Delany and his sister, and they have agreed to receive her little friend also. Mrs. Delany, who, like Aunt Groves, has assumed brevet rank, had been obliged hitherto to support herself by running a boarding-school on the ordinary lines, but the methods now adopted were, no doubt, those of Mrs. Woodrooffe's own establishment at Somerford Keynes.

Dr. Delany is a scholar, and is advancing more ponderously along the Higher Path than the genial and impetuous Mr. Wilton, who had been so offensive to the widow Groves. Hitherto his course has been impeded by his unfortunate marriage.

While Mrs. Delany lived, his house was a shelter, but it was not a home: his spirit rested not except in his quiet study: and even there, when his lady entered, it was "Well, Doctor, and what parties am I to invite? We are so rusticated, that we shall soon be unfit for society; we really must not live thus, or our existence will be forgotten." "Not by our friends, Lucretia." "While we have property we shall not want friends, Dr. Delany," was the low, mercenary reply. The Doctor gave one upcast look of involuntary concern; and his lady continued,

"Well, I do not take high flights: I never was very poetical: I have no great heights to descend from; but I certainly wish to keep up connexions for the sake of my family." Silence was the Doctor's refuge; and he more than once heard this chosen friend of his retirement regret that she had thrown herself away upon a man of narrow views, whose children would probably disgrace themselves. How unlike the tender and excellent Mrs. Walker, of Truro, who would enter her husband's study, and when asked what she wanted there, would reply, "Nothing, my dear, but to ask thee how thou dost, and to see if thou wantest anything," and then, with an endearing smile, would say, "Dost thou love me, my dear?" and when her husband replied "Most truly," she would answer, "I know it, I know it abundantly! but I love to hear thee tell me so."

This dialogue is obviously the prototype of Mr. Punch's "Nothing, darling, only darling, darling."

Mr. Deane's conscience had always reproached him because he had sent Elizabeth to a school not professedly religious, and he is still rather perturbed about Mrs. Delany's faith, as she has not the Vital Christian habit of constant profession, but her brother assures him that she is silently progressing. Mrs. Delany, however, is not to be bullied: she can hold her own even with the saintly Aunt Groves, who congratulates her because, now she has given up her school, she is no longer obliged to take her pupils to dances:

"There is such an inconsistency in pressing upon them religious principle, in leading them to prayer, and the reading of the Scriptures, and at the same time encouraging all the gaieties of fashionable life."

"I think, Madam," said Mrs. Delany, "persons are very often censured for doing that which they cannot avoid, the difficulties of a situation such as mine are hardly to be conceived: and, indeed, I will not deceive you: at the time I resided at S. I was never convinced of the wrong of public dancing; I thought it an innocent amusement, and a pretty sight, equally gratifying to myself and to their parents."

Mrs. E. Groves: And by the warmth with which you defend it, my dear Madam, perhaps you still think me unnecessarily strict.

Mrs. Delany: I believe I do not view the subject so strongly as you do. I can allow that it dissipates and unsettles; but, in seeing a number of happy little beings dancing about, for the mere pleasure of dancing, I really cannot see any harm.

Mrs. E. Groves: I doubt that position, my dear Madam. Take from them the admiration and the finery, and I believe, most of them would prefer sitting still. No! Vanity is the spring which sets the whole business in motion: the vanity of the dancing-master to exhibit his pupils, and the vanity of the governess to the same end; the vanity of the parents to share the admiration their children excite; and the vanity of the poor little beings themselves, living for weeks upon this breath, and inhaling at every exhibition the same poison. No, my dear Madam, depend upon it, if this air were withdrawn, the fire would go out; each party would cease to desire anything so vapid as dancing about a room for the mere pleasure of dancing. And then it is so anti-scriptural.

Mrs. Delany: I never could find anything in Scripture that went directly to this point.

Mrs. E. Groves: The quotations concerning vanity would be endless; but our Saviour cuts it up by the root, when he says, "Ye cannot serve God and Mammon"; and I believe it is the opinion of all those who *study* the subject, that a dancing Christian is a very incongruous character.

Mrs. Delany: I am not about further to defend this custom; but I must say that persons of fortune who become religious, and sit at home in their large mansions, who choose their own plans, and are unaccountable to any but God, have very inadequate ideas of the difficulties which await a humble path.

Dr. Delany: And can give less noble proofs, my dear, of the perfect disinterestedness of their attachment to the sacred cause. Had you remained, my beloved Harriet, I should have expected, from the natural independence of your mind, and from your increased view of Christian duty; I should have expected, I say, to have seen you make a noble stand, reforming all that was anti-scriptural, and risking everything rather than to walk inconsistently in the Christian path.

Mrs. Delany: I fear, my dear brother, you over-rate both the strength of my mind and of my principles.

Agnes Groves will come into possession of a large estate, and her responsibilities have already been impressed upon her: her mother had wished to convert some of the beautiful old trees into ready money, but by her father's will timber could not be felled without the heir's consent, and both the old steward and Mr. James had persuaded Agnes to veto the desecration. Elizabeth will eventually inherit Mr. Deane's property, and both girls are intended by their elders to marry suitable country gentlemen. Their education should therefore be solid and useful, not such as would make them hanker after a gay life like the widow Groves and the late Mrs. Delany. The Doctor questions Elizabeth about her past schooling:

"Have you read much with Mrs. Delany?" "Not much, Sir; we have so many pursuits, practising music, drawing, French, and various lessons. . . ." "Do you learn with facility?" "I believe not, Sir. There are others who learn much quicker." "But you remember what you have learnt?" "Yes: it takes me considerable time; but when I have learnt it, I hardly ever forget." "That is what I should suppose: Everything worth knowing must be acquired with labour, if we would retain it. Have you gone through a course of History?" "No, Sir; I have read an abridgment of England, Rome, and Greece."

"Well, abridgments are very good things in their places, but a mind of any depth is not satisfied with abridgments."

Elizabeth was now given Sharpe's *Introduction to History* and Le Sage's *Chronology:* and the Doctor pointed out a plan for their connecting dates and events; first, by writing the date, then finding what happened, and then exercising herself in writing what happened, and connecting the date. He said, in all historical recollection, clearness was very material. As a relaxation she was permitted to compare some botanical plates with dried specimens.

Agnes, as befits her years, can give a more satisfactory reply to the Doctor's question.

"I have read Littleton's *England;* Goldsmith's *Rome and Greece;* and the lives of many of the Poets, from which I first began to esteem Johnson; at my aunt's I found Hawkesworth's *Life,* and I had read Boswell's at home; and I met with Piozzi's as we started, and we brought it as our travelling companion. I have read Rollin's *Ancient History,* but I really do not remember much of it." "Well, we have Sharpe and the Abbé Bossuet; and I think we shall do well to begin again. Well, now then for the Abbé Bossuet. Let us have the ten epochs: Adam, Creation; Noah, Deluge; the Call of Abraham, or the renewal of God's covenant with men; Moses, or the Written Law; taking of Troy; Solo-

mon's Temple; Romulus, or the foundation of the
Roman Empire; Cyrus, or the deliverance of the
people of God from the Babylonish captivity; Scipio,
or the conquest of Carthage; the birth of Christ;
Constantine, or the peace of the Church; Charle-
magne, or the establishment of a new empire. Now
these steps in the history of the world are very useful. Get these thoroughly settled in your memory,
and then sit down steadily to read; and consider the
history connected with the first epoch, and then
write it and exchange your observations; but observe one thing—do not copy, but read readily, with
so fixed a mind as to recall events; and observe the
moral consequences. Let this be our first lesson in
history; and always keep the map of that country
you study under your eye. I shall be very happy to
walk over this old ground again; and by associating
myself with you, as Miss Edgeworth observes, to
diminish the pain of attention, we shall find *method*
more useful to us, and I have no doubt, that what
at first appears very dry will, ere long, deeply
interest us."

Let us here interrupt the learned doctor to inquire
whether his system or something less cumbrous and
compendious produced the mature and intelligent
interest in history of a contemporary of Agnes's and
Elizabeth's, destined to a more exalted marriage than
either. You will remember the conversation. That
deplorably half-educated girl, Catherine Morland, says:

"I can read poetry and plays, and things of that
sort, and do not dislike travels. But history, real
solemn history, I cannot be interested in. Can you?"

"Yes, I am fond of history."

"I wish I were, too. I read it a little as a duty, but
it tells me nothing that does not either vex or weary
me. The quarrels of popes and kings, with wars or
pestilences, in every page; the men are all so good
for nothing, and hardly any women at all—it is very
tiresome: and yet I often think it odd that it should
be so dull, for a good deal of it must be invention.
The speeches that are put into the heroes' mouths,
their thoughts and designs—the chief of all this
must be invention, and invention is what delights
me in other books."

"Historians, you think," said Miss Tilney, "are
not happy in their flights of fancy. They display
imagination without raising interest. I am fond of
history, and am very well contented to take the
false with the true. In the principal facts they have
sources of intelligence in former histories and records, which may be as much depended on, I conclude, as anything that does not pass under one's
own observation; and as for the little embellishments
you speak of, they are embellishments, and I like
them as such. If a speech be well drawn up, I read
it with pleasure, by whomsoever it may be made—
and probably with much greater, if the production
of Mr. Hume or Mr. Robertson, than if the genuine
words of Caractacus, Agricola, or Alfred the Great."

Appreciation of style Dr. Delany probably thought superfluous for his young charges. To return to them:

Mrs. Delany suggests that Agnes and Elizabeth should gradually initiate his three small daughters into sacred history after Sharpe's manner, which will help them to get it into their own heads: at the same time they can read that admirable little work, Miss Neale's *Sacred History*. Dr. Delany agrees.

Now then for the four principal Monarchies: the Assyrian, Persian, Grecian, and Roman. The Assyrian, 2059 years before Christ; the Persian, 561 before Christ; the Grecian, 331 before Christ; the Roman, 758 before Christ. Now every day I shall expect a clear account of one of these monarchies; and I shall not busy myself with the account of what occurred in other countries, till each is completely established in your minds. We must follow one plan of chronology, for I am sorry to inform you that the learned are divided sometimes upon these subjects. Therefore I shall take Blair whom I esteem highly: and I was thinking we might make some very entertaining plays for the children; and make their forfeits consist of work for vagrants, such as very common worsted stockings; so many rows for such a forfeit.

Mrs. Delany: But, my dear brother, should you do right, as a magistrate, to encourage these people?

Dr. Delany: I would not establish them, Harriet; but there is a text, "Turn not thy face from any

107

poor man." I think we should have two evenings in the week to work for poor. By work, I mean to fit and prepare work for others; and then I will read to you the Papers of the Society for bettering the Conditions of the Poor, and the Missionary Register. These are transactions with which we ought to be acquainted; and if we have not a settled time, they will escape our notice. I could wish you to have a map of Europe upon a large scale, that we may occasionally refer, and accurately mark the place of which we are reading. It is an excellent saying (he is quoting Hakluyt's *Preface*) that geography and chronology are the eyes of history.

Mrs. Delany: I think, my dear, we should have a little poetry.

Dr. Delany: I am quite of your opinion, Harriet, if I may be allowed to select it; and, I think, we will begin with Thomson's "Seasons", and take some of the pieces of my favourite Goldsmith; and, when we have a mind for a higher flight, there are Milton and Young; and, when we wish for amusement, we will bring down Walter Scott, to whom I think we are all indebted, for very spirited descriptions of the olden time. Yet these must not be meat and drink, but dessert.

Scott, it should be observed, comes under the head of poetry: the novels would probably have been considered inflammatory.

At a later stage they pursued some secret studies

with Dr. Delany, but, as he remarked slyly to his fellow clergyman: "You know, Sir, we never talk of ladies learning Latin, lest it should frighten the gentlemen." "I am quite on your side. I have taught my quiet girl; and I find it a great advantage to her. Her taste in literature is very correct, and I do not think I shall ever have reason to regret it: though my dear wife strongly opposed it at first." "Upon what ground could Mrs. Wilton object?" "The old ground, Sir. She thought it would spoil her domestic habits; and I promised that if I perceived it the least likely to spoil her for stitching wristbands, I would give it up immediately. But as yet no ill consequences have ensued; and she is likely to be very useful to her mother in this way, and is kept in pretty good practice."

The two girls visited the village school every Monday morning, examined the children's work, and heard them read aloud: on Saturday they went again to note the week's progress. Assisted by the small Lucretia Delany in the capacity of pupil teacher, they also conducted a third degree Sunday class with a background of espionage.

Lucretia: Mary West, where were you this morning before church?

Mary: Miss?

Lucretia: Were you up in good time?

Mary: Oh yes, Miss; I was up at six o'clock.

Lucretia: And where did you go after you had your breakfast?

Mary: Miss, I was at the Sunday-school.

Lucretia: Yes, that is true; but who was seen nutting in the wood this morning?

Mary: Miss, my father lives not far from the wood.

Elizabeth: True; but you know very well that we do not allow little girls to go nutting on a Sunday.

Mary: No, Miss.

Elizabeth: Did you not ask Jane Jones to go along with you?

Mary looked, and began to mutter, and to call Jane tell-tale.

Elizabeth: Now, that is very wrong, Mary; for Jane did not tell me anything. I was behind you at the very moment, and was exceedingly sorry to find that you not only do wrong yourself, but turn tempter. And now for you, little Jane. It is true you did not listen, but you went home to your mother full of vanity; and when she asked you to assist in dressing your little sister, and fitting her for the school, you pretended that you had a lesson to learn, and could not do it; whereas, you know, much as we love to have perfect lessons, the end of all lessons is obedience, and especially obedience to parents.

Their visits to the village poor anticipate the methods of the Charity Organization Society. Dr. Delany's three children had a fortune of £3,000 each, inherited from their West Indian mother, from which he set aside £150 a year, to be administered by his sister with the help of the two girls. In passing, one wonders what the Court of Chancery would have said to this arrangement.

The particular objects of our consideration should be, bedding, lying-in women, and the providing of those necessary articles, fuel and potatoes; and prizes to the cleanest children in the village. We cannot interfere with their fathers and mothers. One cannot say to persons advanced in life, that their appearance disgusts you; but you may create a taste in the young mind for order and cleanliness, and it is very desirable to do so.

Mrs. Delany gave them note-books to be used in their district visiting: "Now, observe me, you must divide your book into five; the first must contain the names of the poor, and their characters, with the numbers in their family; the second, their actual wants: and this must always be drawn from observation, not inquiry; the third must mark what you give, and to whom, that you may not deal unequally by them; the fourth must contain an account of small sums lent for the purchase of pigs, or coal, or potatoes, or barley; and a fifth for the nursery-man. And we must consult the housekeeper upon the best mode of going to market, and employ her in these things; still, regularly settling the account every Saturday morning."

Aunt Groves was well-satisfied with her niece's education.

The Doctor is an excellent man; she is in train for improvement; and Mrs. Delany, though not a prominent character, is steadily and quietly pursuing every plan most likely to fit Agnes for the station appointed her. I was extremely pleased, when I was at Langley, to see how every study was suited to the sphere in which they were to move; and though, I suppose, it might be the Doctor's thought, it was certainly a good one, and the execution of it rested with Mrs. Delany. Agnes was learning everything necessary for a land proprietress, and has a pretty comprehensive view of the relative value of landed and funded property; and one thing is deeply rooted, for which I feel more than thankful to Dr. Delany—a sense of her complete responsibility; and the whole of the evening I spent there, while they sat talking to me, they were cutting out for the poor of Langley. Now, this is exactly the training I wished.

She suggested that they should index parts of Scripture suitable for the various descriptions of persons visited, but we are not favoured with specimens of this production. The pet innovation of the more practical Mrs. Deane is a system of contributory insurance, which she has instituted in her own village. She rings the bell on an icy morning for her maid, who acts as her almoner:

I have been thinking, Hiblet, that, this exceedingly cold weather, some of the cottagers must want help.

Hiblet: Yes, Ma'am; they have all had the soup every day, and you know, Ma'am, the slater, the plasterer, and the glazier, went about in the autumn, and I do not think there is a crack in any of my master's cottages.

Mrs. Deane: Do you remember if there was a door put to that staircase of Nalbro's? they complained of the cold wind rushing up the staircase when they were in bed.

Hiblet: Yes, Ma'am, that was done in the summer. I don't think that any of my master's cottages wants anything done to it.

Mrs. Deane: Well, so far it is well: but I think, Hiblet, if you will step to the store-room, and bring me word of what stock of blankets we have, and what flannel, and whether there are any cloaks, we must see about these things; and, in the meantime, I will look to my book, and see who has paid the winter five shillings. Oh, I see Jamieson's family have not paid this year; Smith's have only paid half-a-crown.

It was a law that Mrs. Deane had made, that every poor person who expected help at Christmas should bring five shillings after harvest. She relieved them according to the numbers in their families: but she expected from all this providence.

Hiblet explains that a Jamieson boy was ill, and Mrs. Smith had a young baby, and the defaulters are dealt with leniently by Mrs. Deane.

It is the duty of landed gentry to look after their poor, body and soul, but the poor, even when Vital Christians, must not be permitted to step above the rank in which it has pleased Divine Providence to place them. What is sauce for the goose is sauce from the gander. The question is raised whether religious families should seek religious servants. It is agreed that servants should be conformable but not reborn: if there is a rebirth it is safer that it should take place in the employer's house and under his guidance. The curate had recently engaged a religious servant with most unfortunate consequences.

The other evening, after church, Mr. Morrison and his daughter walked to the Castle, round the grounds, and returned to tea. This servant opened the door: "Oh, Sir! how can you expect I can preserve any order in the kitchen, on the Sabbath-day, if Master himself goes a-walking? Oh! Sir!" and she turned her head away in holy indignation. The good man's humility was such, that he replied, "Sarah, if I have done wrong, I hope God will pardon me; more especially I desire it may never lead my servants astray." "*If* you have done wrong, Sir. Oh, Sir, I must be faithful. Can you think it right to lead Miss abroad, when she should be thinking over what she has heard?" Ellen Morrison was exceedingly hurt at this freedom in Sarah. She is the only person in her father's house who, I think, views the matter correctly. She replied, "Sarah, were it

114

necessary to account to *you*, as our servant, for our conduct, my father and myself might satisfactorily answer this charge. But, 'all things are open to the eyes of Him with whom we have to do'; and 'we are not careful to answer *you* in the matter'"; and she said, "My dear father, do not stand—let us go into the parlour directly."

Mrs. Morrison was told of the incident, and Ellen said that Sarah ought to be dismissed.

"My dear," said Mrs. Morrison, "Sarah is a good woman, but an uneducated woman; and . . ." "Oh, Mamma!" and "Oh, my love!" said Morrison and Ellen both at once: but "if she reads her Bible". "Very true (thoughtfully). I have often felt the pressure of this woman's conduct; and have considered it as a cross which I was called to bear." Mr. Morrison, whose temper is really very good, and the warmth of it under great religious restraint, had been moved by his daughter to see the thing in a new light; and he said "Really, my dear, I think we have carried this cross long enough; and, to-morrow morning, it is my desire you would dismiss Sarah." "Very well, my dear—if you are of the same opinion to-morrow morning, I certainly will." When the bell rang for prayers, this woman attended with a sorrowful, almost a grieved countenance, that seemed to mourn over the sin of her master; and this was so evident, that the whole family perceived it; and Mrs. Morrison was strength-

ened in the opinion, that to part was best. So, the
following morning, she sent the children into the
garden, and rang for Sarah—"As you seem to have
forgotten the place you hold in my family, I think
it is best to part, Sarah, this day month." "Very
well, Madam; very well, Madam. I have delivered
my testimony. I have delivered my conscience; and
shall deliver it while I remain." "If that is the
case, Sarah; if you are determined to persevere,
and to fancy you do God service; we are so convinced of your error, and the impropriety of your
behaviour, that we think it will be best to give you
a month's wages, that you may depart to-day."
"What! turn me out like a thief, because I am
faithful to your evil doings; because I set before
you the things ye have done?" "It is enough,
Sarah—go": and Mrs. Morrison took a book while
Sarah, muttering, left the room, and, in two hours,
the house.

When Mrs. Woodrooffe was writing her story the
questions of enclosures and of the lease of land to small
farmers were agitating the public mind. She expresses
her own view that, when commons near villages were
enclosed, one-tenth should be reserved for the poor,
and that the lord of the manor should pay all legal ex-
penses in order that small freeholders might not be
obliged, as was often the case, to sell the shares allotted
to them in order to pay the lawyers. The gentlemen
discuss politics at a party at the Farquhars. The worthy

Farquhar, by his ability in commerce, had acquired a
mansion with "the finest Grecian figures in different
parts of the hall, holding lights", and some very unpleasant daughters, who, as Mr. Deane explains to
Mr. James, look down upon their father. 'You will
hear Miss Julia say, "Pa understands business and all
that sort of thing; but Pa knows no more what is doing
in the world than Noah did in his ark." "Dear me,"
said Elizabeth, "how could she tell what Noah did in
his ark? that's very presumptuous, I think." "I think
so too, my dear," said her mother.' Mr. Deane intro-
duces the subject by saying to Mr. Farquhar: "I think,
Sir, it would be very desirable if we could let our land
to the poor at modest rents": but he is interrupted at
once: ' "Oh, dear," said Julia, "there's Mr. Deane beginning money business and the poor: now there's to
be no peace." "Let me tell you, Miss Julia," said Mr.
Deane, "that if something is not done for the poor,
you will have no peace; for if you do not help them,
they will shortly help themselves; and you may expect
them in your parlour ere long." "Dear, how shocking!" "It is very shocking; and I feel for them very
much." "Oh, but I mean how shocking it would be
to have them come here!" "I suppose their wants
may bring them." "I am sure we hear of nothing else
but their wants," said the elder Miss Farquhar. "We
cannot eat a meal in peace now. It really seems a sin to
satisfy one's hunger." ' The rest of Mr. Deane's views
are lost to us in the young ladies' grumbles, "I never
knew Papa stay so long in the country at this time of

year; it is these stupid poor people who brought him down. One of these M.P.'s, whose goodness is always running over, made a fine speech in the House, about the absolute necessity for every man to think of his tenants and his poor dependents, so that now we are always thinking of them." And we only return to the gentlemen in time to hear Mr. James, "looking warm", declare: "I tell you, Sir, and I speak the sense of all the country gentlemen round, I believe: we may be persuaded, but we cannot be driven. If the measure is necessary, prove its necessity." Mr. James, no doubt, feels that people ought to behave decently without compulsion: he manages his own estate with generosity and good-humoured banter: indeed it is to be feared that in his relations to the poor he forgets the dictum of Hannah More's milk-woman poetess, quoted with approbation by Dr. Delany: "True friendship can never exist but in equality." And the beauty of his garden is rather startling to a Vital Christian. Gardens, according to Mrs. Deane, are a snare. The ingenuous Elizabeth objects that dear Papa is constantly beautifying his. This might be thought to be what the authoress terms a "closer", but Mamma is ready for her. Papa is no æsthetic follower of Capability Brown: his improvements are undertaken solely in order to give employment to the poor, and himself opportunities for exhortation while they are at work. Mr. and Mrs. Wilton, though truly Christian, are less rigid. They are walking in Mr. James's garden: "Why, Charles, I never saw anything more lovely." "I knew

you would say so: I knew it was exactly to your taste."
"I fear you think I am romantic, my dear." "Oh, by
no means. I do not esteem a love of rural beauty as
romance. When God had finished his most perfect
work, where did he place man? In a garden." They
are joined by the unconverted James who has no
qualms on the subject.

There are a vast number of stupid people in the
world, my dear Mrs. Wilton, who think everything
that is very dull and very dowdy very good. Had
they had a hand in creation, no leaf would have been
allowed to have a point, they would all have been
cut off square. Uniformity, dull uniformity in life, in
pursuit, and in manners, is natural to them, and
that Nature being their medium of sight, every
variation from it is error. I remember once hearing
a lady make a great merit of resigning the theatre,
and I am certain, if you had read ten lines of
Shakespeare to her, she would not have been able
to comprehend them: yet she took great credit to
herself for the resignation; when, in fact, I can conceive nothing more dull than to sit for an hour
listening to that which one cannot understand: and
many a person who has no taste for rural beauty
censures, I doubt not, the interest I take in my
garden. They would think me a better man if I had
square edge-rows, encompassing turnips and potatoes. Now there is a chance, that if I sold my potatoes I might not give all the money away, and if so,

and I like to have a garden like the Garden of Eden,
I come back to old times; and if I put my Aunt
Groves in it, you will allow her to be a better woman
than Grandmother Eve.

Drink, oddly enough, is not included among the
snares: the temperance movement had not yet set in.
Wine is consumed and mentioned comfortably, and
when the little girls of the village are entertained on
Elizabeth's birthday beer is provided with their vic-
tuals. But Mrs. Deane, with her usual shrewdness, had
not ignored the possibilities: she instructed the inn-
keeper at Abberley to give her the bill for her men-
servants' keep at the end of the fortnight, but they
must pay ready-money for their beer: she would
refund it, but to provide them with unlimited credit
would put temptation in the path.

James is not only the most delightful character in
the book, though the reticent Mrs. Delany, and Charlotte Shepherd, the clever girl of the school, the quiz,
and "the deadly foe to monotony, the destroyer of all
set speeches", have their charms; he is also the most
effective. It is James who prevents Mrs. Stanley from
preying on her daughter, and restores Agnes's estate
to its former idyllic condition in the lifetime of his
friend, Groves: it is James who copes with Elizabeth's
calf-lover with brutal, though kindly, common sense:
it is James who teases the little Lucretia out of her
greediness, so that Elizabeth feels justified in assuring
the terrified child on her death-bed that she really has

been reborn. There can be no doubt about Mrs. Woodrooffe's Vital Christianity: are we not told that she was herself the original of Aunt Groves? Otherwise we might suspect a sneaking sympathy with James, and jealousy of his superiority in the concerted attack of the Vital Christians. Aunt Groves gives him no peace either in public or in private, and she is reinforced by Mr. and Mrs. Deane. James himself only begs to be let alone. When Mrs. Deane calls him a coward the poor man replies: "If I am so, observe what has produced it: I am watched; and it is Mr. James here, and Mr. James there. Ah! you will soon be of our mind, says one good lady, and sighs and lifts up her eyes. Ah! I remember his dear mother, says another; the child of so many prayers will never be lost: and then the history of St. Austin comes up, and his good mother." Mr. Deane, who follows up with an independent attack suggests that he is a "waiting character" like Nathaniel, and James answers that it may be so but—"I *cannot, must not* talk; I must stand upright before my God: no human being can ever be a witness of my internal feelings. I have no desire to communicate any of my thoughts on these subjects; I have heard and seen too much of these gospel gossipings, where half that was uttered was untrue, and the other half wilfully mysterious." When Mr. Deane persists, James corners him with a direct question:

"I was brought up under the eye of a father, a man, Sir, of unblemished honour; a man who hated the sickly whinings of modern religionists; he read his Bible, reverenced the established authorities of the Church, loved his King and his country, lived respectably, and died peacefully. He brought me up in dread of innovations (which had begun in his early day); and the regularity of his life equally silenced the tongue of censure, and established his empire over my mind. Is the happiness of such an one *doubtful*, Sir?"

The question was tremendously pronounced. Thus a low murmuring thunderclap comes quickly on, increasing and increasing, till the peal breaks frightfully loud in the ear. Mr. Deane sustained the shock, and replied, with the calmness with which he began, "There is a sacred feeling connected with the memory of a departed friend, which, even had the life been intemperate and vicious, should preserve the memory from violations. It does not become us, Sir, to limit or direct the Most High; and what passed between your departed father and God in the momentous hour—what passed, I say, during the peaceful interview you have described, must be left.

"There's but a word between; and, that word given,
   Yon suffering soul shall be a saint in heaven."

Mr. James: To the point, Mr. Deane. Do you suppose, if my life should pass as my father's life passed, and my eye close as his closed, do you suppose that I should reach the port in safety?

Mr. Deane paused. "I do not know, Sir, that you

have any right to exact from me an answer to such a question; but I do not hesitate to assure you, that my opinion is, 'except a man be born again, he cannot enter the kingdom of heaven'."

Mr. James: Very good; very correct. Pray, Sir, how am I to know that I am born again?

Mr. Deane: When you feel that those things which were your gain, you count but loss,—when you count all things but dross for the excellency of the knowledge of Christ Jesus,—I think, Sir, you may safely conclude you are born again.

Mr. James: There are so many shades that go to this full colouring, Mr. Deane; I hope you do not think I doubt one word of the Scriptures?

This was just what Mr. Deane wished. "I think, Sir, we differ at the first step; I think the doctrine of human depravity is not agreeable to you."

Mr. James: I do not know that it can be agreeable to any person; I believe no man of common sense is fond of a dirty house.

Mr. Deane: I certainly was incorrect in saying, agreeable to you; I meant to say, you do not admit that doctrine.

Mr. James: I can handle a guinea, Sir; but, if you choose to beat it out into halfpenny sheets, I cannot breathe but it escapes me. You say that the whole head is sick, and the whole heart faint; that we are all gone out of the way, and altogether become abominable; that we are full of wounds and bruises —and I am disgusted, Sir.

Mr. Deane: Then, Sir, you are disgusted with the word of God.

Mr. James: By no means; I am only disgusted by the application. I do not feel that it applies to me, Sir.

Mr. Deane: That I must leave; the Spirit of God can alone apply the word to any conscience. Remember what our Lord says: "The whole need not a physician, but they that are sick." Now, if you are whole, Sir,—if you really are satisfied completely with yourself—you have no need of a sacrifice. I would not say that I envy you; but, I must say, I am surprised.

Mr. James: I do not deny that there is much in me for which I am concerned, and from which I would gladly escape. But to say that I have no whole part in me, that I am altogether depraved, and that I am the vilest of sinners, while I do not think it, Sir, I will not say it. There are some sins that, so far from my being disposed to, I have an aversion to them.

Mr. Deane: He that offendeth in one point is guilty of all. The law is a perfect circle; if you break it, it is broken.

Mr. James: I do not understand this.

Mr. Deane: Nevertheless, it is the word of God.

Mr. James: Well, I shall go to my namesake: "Pure religion and undefiled before God," &c.

Mr. Deane: And I, Sir, shall turn to the Galatians: "He that thinketh himself to be something, when he is nothing, deceiveth himself."

This was a closer. James thought so. He rose and lit his candle. "Well, Sir, we must agree to differ, till we agree to agree."

When the conversation was reported, Mrs. Deane was not quite satisfied with her husband's effort. "I think, my dear, there were one or two things in which you were short. I should, first, have told him that our business is with ourselves; and entreated that he would bring forward no human authority or example. And again, when he objected to your quoting Scripture, and applying it to yourself, I should have reminded him how this is continually done in the Bible; and, in order to have enforced its propriety, I would have referred him to Jones's *Figurative Language*, where the right application of the different parts of Scripture is methodically arranged under five heads."

Poor James! At any rate he was lucky in escaping Jones. His fate is left in the air: Mrs. Woodrooffe was too good a psychologist to effect his conversion: she knew that he was incapable of talking Vital Christianity, and Vital Christians must talk. In this lies the interest of Mrs. Woodrooffe's book. Here in this shadow picture we have the actual conversation of a large and powerful class, the country gentry touched by the evangelical revival. This is the world of Wilberforce in one generation, and of Shaftesbury in the next. In 1834, 161 of them voted in favour of Sir Andrew Agnew's Bill for depriving the poor of their Sunday joint and their Sunday jaunt. They compelled the

Great Western Railway to keep separate accounts of Sunday takings. They forbade the first great ocean liner to bear the Scriptural name of *Leviathan*. This atmosphere we must learn to breathe if we are to understand how the successive crises of the century, Catholic emancipation, the Tractarian movement, and Papal Aggression were really felt by the world on which they burst. Indeed in Mr. James's conversation with Mr. Deane on the eternal destiny of his excellent father we hear the mutterings of a controversy which some day was to produce a schism. If Mr. James had been a better instructed Churchman he would have downed Mr. Deane with a phrase from the Baptismal Service, "seeing that this child is regenerate," and left him to square it with Galatians as best he might.

MARY MARTHA BUTT 1775-1795

I SENT for a book called *The Lady of the Manor*, thinking that it might throw further light on the education of young ladies in the country, and prove a useful supplement to Mrs. Woodrooffe's *Shades of Character*. It arrived in four closely-printed volumes. The Lady presided over an ideal village, the inhabitants of which belonged chiefly to the genteel ranks of society. So much so that the clergyman was unequal to dealing with confirmation classes for both sexes. He therefore requested the Lady of the Manor to prepare the young ladies for that ceremony. Her classes began with tea and cakes, followed by a few words on one of the clauses of the catechism, then a moral tale, illustrating the said clause, and closed with a lengthy prayer of the Lady's own composition. I struggled through half the first volume. No. Though her stories were respectably written, she was the spit of the saintly Aunt Groves, and, what with Mrs. Woodrooffe and Charlotte Elizabeth Tonna, I had had a surfeit of Vital Christianity. Wearily I glanced at the autobiography of the author, which had arrived in the same parcel. There I found, to my surprise, a delightful account of the happiest and most wholesome childhood I had yet struck. True it was written in the author's regenerate old age, but she did not, like Charlotte Elizabeth, look back on the pleasures and pastimes of "the little wild

127

girl who was educated in the woods of Stanford" as
Satan's snares. Neither her father nor her mother had
"any distinct ideas of human depravity", and she was
obviously grateful to Providence for giving her such a
jolly time before revealing the vileness of her un-
regenerate nature.

Mary Martha Butt was a granddaughter of Dr.
Carey Butt of Lichfield, who reproved his children
for calling the uncouth young Samuel Johnson
"the great boy": "Take my word for it you will
live to call him 'the great man'." Her father,
George Butt, was educated at Westminster and Christ
Church, and then took orders. The natural purity of
his disposition had protected him against the wiles of
infidel Lichfield, Dr. Darwin, Miss Seward and their
circle, although in the opinion of his daughter, his
religion was always a matter of the heart rather than
the head. He afterwards returned to Christ Church in
the capacity of private tutor, and in 1771, four years
before Mary's birth, his pupil's father, Sir Edward
Winnington, presented him with the living of Stanford in Worcestershire. Meanwhile, heart-broken after
the death of an early love, he had married, at his
father's behest, the plain and pock-marked daughter
of a rich silk merchant. From her came another family
story of Johnson. Before her marriage she was living in
Lichfield, and, walking one day in the Close, she met
the great man:

My mother happened to have a volume of *The*

Rambler, or of *Rasselas*, I forget which, in her hand. Johnson seeing the book, took it from her, looked into it, and, without saying a word, threw it among the graves, from which my mother had to recover it. This was probably done in a fit of awkward vanity by the great Doctor, who, finding a young lady with one of his own volumes in her hand, could neither let the circumstance pass unheeded, as a man of less vanity would have done, nor make some polite speech, which a man with more address would have thought of; but he must needs act the bear and do the rudest thing he could do.

There was no rectory at Stanford. Mr. Butt chose a perfect site, and on it built a perfect home. In front of the house, lawns and orchards sloped down to the Teme with the Abberley hills beyond: to the south lay Stanford Park and a distant view of Bredon and Malvern. The sitting-rooms were hung with paintings and prints, a text for the rector's stories; notable among them was a Raphael cartoon of the martyrdom of St. Stephen with the heavens opening to his gaze, afterwards given as an altar-piece to the old church at Kidderminster.

Marten Butt was a year older than his sister. Both were fine healthy children, Mary placid to a fault. When she was two they were taken to Lichfield for exhibition. Dr. Darwin took up Marten by one leg, as though he were a frog, and exclaimed "What a fine animal! what a noble animal!" Mr. Edgeworth, after

129

like compliment to Mary's physique, tapped his fore-head significantly, "But you may depend upon it, Mr. Butt, you may depend upon it she wants it here."

Mary's intelligence developed slowly. Until she was six her parents were inclined to accept Mr. Edgeworth's view, but they wisely put no pressure upon her. She absorbed the surrounding beauty, peopling the woods and fields with creatures of her own imagining. Mrs. Butt taught them to read from a book with a picture of a white horse feeding by starlight. Religious instruc-tion they had none. But Marten had a dream of heaven and hell, heaven above the highest tree in Stanford Park. This and the cartoon of St. Stephen determined their preference for heaven.

Mr. Butt also held the living of another village in the neighbourhood, Clifton-on-Teme, which he left in charge of a curate, a distant relative. This fascinating gentleman had unfortunately married an old, ill-tempered wife. To escape from her he often came on a visit to Stanford:

Oh! it was a happy day when he was seen coming across the park, in his great bushy wig, his shovel hat, his cravat tied like a King William's bib, his great drab coat, and his worsted spatterdashes. When this figure rose above our horizon, however remote, my joy, and that of my brother, was excessive; for he was the man of all others to delight children. As soon as it was dusk, in a winter evening, I took my place on his knee, and calling him Uncle Robert, begged for a story. Again and again I heard the same, but the old tale never tired. He told of dogs which were supposed to have been spirits, and which were always seen in certain rooms when any of the family were about to die, and other marvels of the like description; added to which, he could bark like a dog, grunt like a pig, play tricks with cards like a conjurer; and was very successful in numerous performances of the same kind; but as to his knowledge of religion, I cannot suppose that it was of any depth.

When Marten was five he tried to follow their dog, Cæsar, who had bounded over a five-barred gate. Climbing up with difficulty, he stood, flapping his little arms like wings, and then fell, striking his head on a stone. The result was a dangerous wound with painful dressings. Mr. Butt promised him a bagful of blue beans if he would be a good boy, but Marten preferred mountain ash berries. It was late in the season, and the fond father rode for miles before he could find a tree on which the berries had not yet shrivelled. On this occasion Mrs. Butt was moved to an observation, all the more impressive to her children because she was usually so sparing of religious reflections. "Marten," she said, "you see that when your dear papa makes a promise, he will take the greatest pains in the world to keep that promise, and this is the reason wherefore he desires it. He is a follower of that perfect Saviour whose ways he dearly loves; and that

Saviour never departs from his holy word, but per-
forms everything which he has promised to his redeemed ones." In consequence of this accident the
little pair were allowed greater freedom than ever.
Marten was indulged in every whim, including
gloriously rowdy games.

My brother, no doubt, had heard of the unique,
but certainly undignified, amusement that was in
fashion in my mother's early days. This fashion
consisted of spreading a large strong table-cloth on
the upper steps of any wide, old-fashioned staircase,
and this being done, all the ladies present, who were
disposed for merriment, seated themselves on this
table-cloth, in rows upon the steps. Then the gentlemen seized hold of the cloth and pulled it down the
stairs, and a struggle would ensue, which usually
ended with the tumbling down of the ladies, table-
cloth and all, to the bottom of the stairs, to the utter
confusion of all order and decorum.

As my brother had no table-cloth at his command, he used to put me into a drawer and kick me
down the nursery stairs. He also used to heap chairs
and tables one on the other, and set me at the top of
them, and then throw them all down. He used to
put a bridle round my neck, and drive me about
with a whip; but being a very hardy child, and not
easily hurt, I suppose I had myself to blame for
some of his excesses; for, with all this, he was the
kindest of brothers to me, and I loved him very, very,

much. Many of his thoughts and expressions were singularly sweet; and I remember once when we had climbed up a high bank among the woods at Stanford, which overlooked the pleasure-grounds, he showed me my mother walking along a path shaded by filbert trees, and he made me look till I cried to think how much I loved her.

For some years Marten's education was taken very lightly: he was never obliged to do more than he liked. Mary began to learn Latin with him, and made far more rapid progress. Mr. Edgeworth's gloomy prognostication no longer troubled her parents. In her case the discipline was severe. From six to thirteen she had to wear a back-board with an iron collar, and did her lessons standing in stocks. Her food was of the plainest, and she was never allowed to sit in her mother's presence. But nothing seems to have affected her spirits. She was intelligent enough to enjoy the conversation of the grown-ups, her father, his visitors, and the pupils whom he took for a while to defray the debt on their house. She had begun to compose stories, and her mother encouraged her by acting as her amanuensis until she could write them down for herself. Later on, Mr. Butt, who believed both his children to be geniuses, shut them up day after day in his study to see which could produce the best tale. The children's library consisted of two books of *Fairy Tales*, *The Little Female Academy*, *Æsop's Fables*, and, Marten's favourite, *Robinson Crusoe*. He used to sit on the bottom step of the stairs, and both children moved up a step whenever he turned over a page. Another of their curious customs was to hide notched sticks secretly in a hollow tree in the wood on the first of every month. A boy four years older than Marten became for some time part of the household, and a second brother to Mary. Together they played in the woods, acting fairy tales with a dragon, an enchanter and a queen, making huts and ships, collecting snail shells, and adorning Mary with garlands of flowers.

In 1784 Mr. Butt was appointed Chaplain in Ordinary to George III. He had to be always in residence at St. James's during the month of November, returning with anecdotes of the Court and the interesting men he had met. Fuseli wished to paint his portrait as "a countenance which was compounded of the features of Sterne and Lavater". A cloud came when Mary was nine. Marten was sent to the Reading School, where the famous Dr. Valpy wielded his birch and taught his own Latin and Greek grammars for fifty years. She consoled herself in the enchanted woods, reading, and listening to the cooing of the doves, the blackbirds' song, and the rush of waterfalls. Latin was her chief lesson: even before she was twelve she had to translate fifty lines of Virgil daily, standing in the stocks with the iron collar pressing on her throat. This was no grievance as she believed iron collars to be the ordinary lot of the female child. Gigantic for her age, the girl was still dressed by her mother in a long pinafore, beneath which she concealed a huge wooden doll, slung round her waist with string.

About this time the library at Abberley Lodge, home of William Walsh, Pope's friend and Addison's, came on the market. Mr. Butt, to the disgust of his orderly wife, purchased a waggon-load of dirty old books for a guinea. The litter in his study already passed all bounds, and Mrs. Butt ordained that this cargo of moth and dust and black calf-skin should be dumped in an empty room over the pantry, known henceforth as the Black Library. There Mary spent many radiant hours, helping her father arrange his treasures. He taught her to discriminate between the various priceless editions of the classics, Elzevirs and the rest, and gave her for her very own Sidney's *Arcadia* and other romances, and a precious *Travels of George Sandy's*, full of prints. Henceforth the wild woods of Stanford were more than ever an enchanted region.

Wherever I saw a few ashes in a glade, left by those who burnt sticks to sell the ashes, to assist in the coarse washings in farm houses, I fixed a horde of gypsies, and made long stories. If I could discern fairy rings, which abounded in those woods, they gave me another set of images; and I had imaginary hermits in every hollow of the rocky rides of the dingle, and imaginary castles on every height, whilst the church and churchyard supplied me with more ghosts and apparitions than I dared tell of.

Mr. Butt became Vicar of Kidderminster when Mary was twelve. He welcomed the increase of income and prestige, but Mrs. Butt wept in the woods and could never accustom herself to the low society of a manufacturing town. How, indeed, could a lady of refinement tolerate neighbours who called washing-day their "execution day"? Or the linen-draper's family, considered the pink of Kidderminster society? The elegant Mr. Dicky, plump and round and forty, always wore a light chintz dressing-gown in the morning with a rose-coloured ribbon round the waist, and his three sisters sat in order of seniority on three chairs in the parlour window. The youngest had long ago accepted the addresses of a young surgeon, who was permitted to visit her daily. When Mary was in Kidderminster some forty years later the situation was unchanged. The old lady lived alone in the old house, which had been presented to her by the faithful lover, who still paid his evening call.

At first acquaintance the S.'s appeared respectable, but when it transpired that Dr. S. was an infidel all intercourse ceased. Not, however, before a seven year old S. had remarked to Lucy Butt, Mary's little sister, aged eight, "that some persons thought that there had once been one Jesus Christ, but that *he* did not believe it. 'Don't you,' said my sister, and she struck him with all her little might, rolled him down on the carpet, and beat him with all her strength, at which, I must confess, I did not interfere, as, being older, I ought to have done."

The heroic Lucy was now Mary's companion. They were two sister queens, mothers of large families, with friends among the fairies. The magic of those Stanford woods still worked even in the sordid streets of Kidderminster. One day Mr. Butt took them in his gig to Hartlebury, where George III and his family were breakfasting on their way from Cheltenham to Worcester. For a curious reason the children were specially noticed by the royal party:

> When they came to where we were, they made a full stop and spoke to us, or rather of us—the Queen using a courtly phrase touching our appearance, and smiling, whilst the King and the Princesses looked at us with encouraging looks. We, of course, blushed, and bridled, and could not imagine how this could be; but they knew my father, and yet were not to know him, according to court etiquette, because he wore not his gown and cassock. The compliment to our *beaux yeux* was simply to express that they knew their chaplain, though restrained by form from addressing him.

During a visit to Dr. Valpy at Reading, Mr. Butt witnessed an entertainment given by the young ladies of the Abbey School. It suddenly occurred to him that his gawky fifteen-year-old daughter would be the better for a little polish. The school had been in the hands of a Mrs. Latournelle. Then one of her former parlour-boarders, whose expectations of a large inheritance had been disappointed, became a partner. Soon afterwards appeared Monsieur St.Q., the son of an Alsatian nobleman, reduced to earning his living by teaching French in Dr. Valpy's school. He extended his attentions to the young ladies, and married the junior partner. When Mary arrived the St.Q.'s had not returned from a London holiday, and she was welcomed by Mrs. Latournelle.

Mrs. Latournelle was a person of the old school, a stout woman, hardly under seventy, but very active, although she had a cork leg. But how she had lost its predecessor she never told. She was only fit for giving out clothes for the wash and mending them, making tea, ordering dinner, and, in fact, doing the work of a housekeeper. Hers was only an everyday, common mind, but a very useful one; for tea must be made, and dinners ordered, and a house would soon tumble to pieces without these very useful everyday kind of people.

Mrs. Latournelle never had been seen or known to have changed the fashion of her dress: her white muslin handkerchief was always pinned with the same number of pins, her muslin apron always hung in the same form; she always wore the same short sleeves, cuffs, and ruffles, with a breast bow to answer the bow on her cap, both being flat with two notched ends.

She received me in a wainscoated parlour, the wainscot a little varnished, whilst the room was hung round with chenille pieces representing tombs and weeping willows. I was cordially received, and made to sit down by a good fire to warm myself before I went to bed.

It was not light when I was called. We were to breakfast in the parlour, and when I came down I found in addition to Mrs. Latournelle, who was making tea almost by fire-light, three teachers, of whose existence I had not even dreamed. I have the scene before me more plainly far than if I had seen it last year. The old lady was, as I said, making tea, and she was seated at a small table, having before her some small cups placed on a small tea-board. She had on a gown which always appeared at packing and unpacking times, a sort of brown or gray stripe, and she was moving quickly, though by no means expediting business. The three teachers sat on three chairs round the fire; each had on what was called in those days a close cap, that is, a large muslin rather blowsy cap, which was to hide black pins, curl-papers, &c., &c., the rest of their dresses being equally indicative of some domestic bustle. To describe these ladies, however, would be no easy matter. Notwithstanding the humility and bashfulness I so lately boasted, I made up my mind on the very first sight of these teachers that I would learn nothing of them. The first was a little simpering English woman, very like a second-rate milliner of those days; she taught spelling and needlework. The second was a dashing, slovenly, rather handsome French girl, who ran away with some low man

a few months afterwards. The third was, I think, a
Swiss, and though plain and pock-marked with the
small-pox, had some good in her, I apprehend; but I
had not the wit then to find it out. There was an
ebony cat standing before the fire, supporting a huge
plate of toast and butter, and, silly as it may seem, I
who had never whilst at home been allowed to eat
toast and butter, nor to come near a fire, thought myself supremely happy under this new order of things.

Mary's description of Mrs. Latournelle and her satel-
lites, has been quoted at length, because some ten
years earlier another small child and her elder sister
had been committed to her care, with the help, no
doubt, of teachers of a similar type. As I have already
suggested, Jane Austen's account of Mrs. Goddard's
school at Highbury is probably reminiscent of her own
experience at Reading.

The St.Q.'s themselves were persons of a different
calibre and social standing. They had made a success of
the school, and had, at this time, about sixty pupils.
Madame was a handsome young woman of fine
presence, whose generosity and delightful manners
had captivated Mr. Butt, though his daughter hints
that she had her failings as an ideal preceptress for
young girls. Accomplishments were her department, while her husband imparted and supervised the
more solid instruction. Mary shall record her first
interview with him:

Full well I remember the morning when he called

me into his study to feel the pulse of my intellect, as he said, in order that he might know in what class to place me. All the girls whom he particularly instructed were standing by, all of them being superior to me in the knowledge of those things normally taught in schools. Behold me, then, in imagination, tall as I am now, standing before my master, and blushing till my blushes made me ashamed to look up. "Eh bien, Mademoiselle," he said, "have you any knowledge of French?" "No, sir," I answered. "Are you much acquainted with history?" And he went on from one thing to another, asking me questions and always receiving a nega- tive. At length, smiling, he said, "Tell me Mademoiselle, then, what do you know?" I stam- mered, "Latin," "Virgil," and finished off with a regular flood of tears. At this he laughed outright, and immediately set me down in his class and gave me lessons for every day.

M. St.Q.'s teaching was lively and interesting. He was assisted by a fine young Frenchman, much ad- mired by the elder girls. M. Malrone, however, was so dignified and well-conducted, and the young ladies, for the most part, so simple and genteel, that no impro- priety resulted. A few bad girls there were, whose coarse conversation in the dormitory Mary, after re- monstrance, thought it her duty to report. Mme. St.Q. put them on bread and water for a day or two, and Mary, at least, heard no more of it.

The elder girls, after a couple of hours' tutoring in
the morning, were free to talk and read and stroll in
the Abbey garden. M. St.Q. being a Roman Catholic,
there was no religious teaching. Morning prayers were
read by a niece of Mrs. Latournelle's, and the old lady
knelt on a chair beside her, whispering, "Make haste,
make haste," when she heard the arrival of the
washerwoman in the next room. It was considered
sufficient if the elder girls put in an appearance before
prayers were over. Mary had been furnished with a
Bible by her mother, and brought it down to read in
the schoolroom her first Sunday, but the practice
aroused such clamorous comment that she soon gave
it up. It was the only Bible she ever saw in the building. As a parlour boarder she had a jovial supper with
the St.Q.'s, their staff and visitors. French was spoken
—except by Mrs. Latournelle, who retailed old stories
of the stage in English, when anyone would listen to
her—and the topics were politics, literature and
society gossip, London and Paris. A holiday was spent
with Mrs. Valpy. Mr. Butt joined them. He bought
Mary a blond cap with pink ribbons and a white
ostrich feather, and they paid a round of visits to the
Nabobs and other elegant residents of Reading. Next
term brought an addition to the staff, Pictet Père, a
wrinkled, white-haired old gentleman, over six feet in
height, who had been secretary to the Empress
Catherine. He wore a large silk wrapper, slippers, and
an open collar, and was very flowery with the ladies,
though he never addressed Mary "in any other way

142

than as a father or a tutor should". It was his habit to
sit with his feet on the mantelpiece, and, when
M. St.Q. reproved him for this impropriety in the
presence of ladies, he used to say, "Bah! bah! have I
not often seen the Imperatrice in her cabinet, sitting
with her Prime Minister, when he had his feet at the
top of the stove, higher than his head?" He took great
pains with Mary's French, and also gave her some
instruction on the nature of the human mind, with
never a reference to revealed religion. These lessons
she found tiresome and crabbed, but, as he was less
blatant than Lucy's little victim and did not dispute
the existence of a God, she did not suspect their
dangerous tendency till later in life.

At the end of a year she left school reluctantly, not
expecting to return, but, after she had been at home
for a few months, it was decided that she should go
back to the Abbey, taking Lucy with her. She found
M. Pictet now installed in a little study of his own,
where he could sit with his feet on the chimney-piece
to his heart's content. Mary and two other girls, Miss
Rowden, Fanny Kemble's future schoolmistress, and a
brilliant Maria Reinagle, daughter of the artist, were
allowed to use this room, whether he were there or not.
In his absence Maria tried to add smoking to her other
accomplishments, but it made her very sick. The great
business of the term was rehearsing for Mme. de
Genlis's play, *La Bonne Mère*, in which Mary took a
leading part, and for a ball given by the dancing master
in the Town Hall. The play was performed twice. Dr.

Valpy brought all his young gentlemen, and Mme. la Fite, one of Princess Amelia's governesses, came over from Windsor. The ball, for Mary, was less pleasant. She led in the quadrille, and danced the rest of the evening with a very pleasant gentleman, whose compliments she enjoyed, but she felt strangely tired. Next day she was down with measles. After her recovery Mme. St.Q. took her for a fortnight to London, where she had a gay time, theatres and dances and visits to her schoolfellows. Soon after their return news came of the execution of Louis XVI. This brought a large number of *émigrés* to Reading; many of them were friends of the St.Q.'s, and half lived at the Abbey. For the elder girls school life was transformed into a Vie de Château: they talked with the ladies, and danced with the gentlemen under the trees in the garden to the music of the harp.

Mary was no longer an awkward girl. She had profited by her social advantages, and was now, in her own estimation and that of her friends, a polished and fascinating young woman. She went home to more gaieties and more high life. Viscount Valentia, that Master Annesley who had been their playmate in the Stanford woods, entertained them at Arley Hall, where an impressive German princess had taken refuge. There were balls innumerable and she "often danced with a Baronet, a very gay widower, who was more than six feet high, and accounted singularly handsome". This gentleman gave a fancy dress dance in honour of forty chosen beauties, and himself as a

Grand Signor led off with Mary in shepherdess attire. Her heart was untouched, but the gratification to her vanity most exquisite.

In spite of all these distractions she was working steadily at her first book, *The Traditions*, acclaimed by her father a work of genius. To her great distress he insisted that it should be published for the benefit of an old friend in financial straits. Since the age of eight her bugbear had been Miss Jenny Bickerstaff, the blue-stocking of the *Tatler*. A literary lady must needs be an eccentric and disagreeable creature: she shrank from such notoriety. *The Traditions* appeared anonymously, but there was no secret about the authorship. Sub-scribers were enrolled to such effect that their friend was rescued from his difficulties. This friend she calls "Mr. Smith", but hints that only a dull reader can fail to identify him. He is obviously her old school-master, M. St.Q., who was thus enabled to start the school in Hans Place, where Mary Mitford, Lady Caroline Lamb, and the unhappy poetess, Letitia Landon, were pupils. And those naked cupids which amused Miss Austen? Did not they adorn the drawing-room at Hans Place?

The Butts now went back to live at Stanford. Soon afterwards Mr. Butt had a stroke, and in the autumn of 1795, when Mary was twenty, he died. With the loss of her genial, admiring father ended the happy youth of Mary Martha Butt. She married a soldier cousin, went to India, was instructed by the regimental chap-lain in the blessed doctrine of human depravity, and became the fleshly mother of many children, and the spiritual mother of *The Fairchild Family*. Far be it from me to deny the merits of that inimitable work, but yet I cannot help feeling that Vital Christianity may have deprived us of a great novelist.

MARY ANNE SCHIMMELPENNINCK 1778-1856

MRS. SCHIMMELPENNINCK dictated in old age a full autobiography of her childhood and youth till her fifteenth year. A morbid child is apt to be an unpleasing and irritating object, but this document comes from the pen of an experienced writer; her upbringing was unusual, and the names of the people among whom she lived—some of them still famous—are redolent of their times.

Mary Anne Galton was born in Birmingham on the 25th of November, 1778. Her father, Samuel Galton, a Quaker by birth, had been educated at the famous Warrington Academy. He returned to his father's business, spending his leisure in scientific research. A friend of Dr. Priestley and Sir Joseph Banks, he became a member of the Royal Society and of the Linnean Society. His appetite for exact information on every possible subject was insatiable, and new items were entered in a folio notebook. "Information on diet, on training, on pugilism, on horses, on building, the various resistances of timber, &c., he noted in this book, which was entitled the 'Book of Knowledge'; it was alphabetically arranged, and formed many volumes." An apter and less magniloquent title would have been "A Prig's Pastime".

Mrs. Galton had been a Barclay. When she was five, her grandfather, as a city magnate, had received

George III. The King perched the pretty child on his knee, and asked how she liked him. "I love the King," she answered, "but I should love him better without his fine clothes." She retained the Quaker speech, and Quaker dress in its most sumptuous form, but selected her friends, irrespective of creed, for their congenial tastes. Mary Anne, a delicate child, was kept apart from noisy younger brothers and sisters, who were handed over to a Swiss *bonne*. While her father packed the little girl's mind with facts, her mother, whom she idolized, played on her emotions. Where, the child asked, did the sun and the sea come from?

She told me to think for a day, and endeavour to find out, but that if I could not, at the end of that time she would tell me. The day seemed interminable; and failing in my endeavour, the next morning I renewed my enquiry. She answered very solemnly that she would take me into a room where we should be alone, and there she would tell me. She took me upstairs, through her bedroom, into a little dressing-room, into which I was not habitually allowed to enter, but which from that time I distinctly remember as though I now saw everything in it. She shut the door, and said she was now going to answer my question;—that that answer would be the most important thing I should ever hear in my life, for that it would involve everything I should hereafter feel, or think, or do;—that if I made a good use of it, I should have such happiness, that

148

nothing whatever could make me completely miserable; but if, on the contrary, I made a bad use of this knowledge, nothing could make me happy.

She then spoke to me of God; of His omnipotence; of His great wisdom shown in all he had made; of His great love to all His creatures, whether human beings or animals. She told me that God had given to every person a voice in the interior of their hearts, and that this voice was called Conscience; that it had spoken to me the other day, when I had been obstinate in spelling my lesson and had made me feel I had done wrong. She then said, that God had invited all His creatures to speak to Him, and to tell him their wants and that this was called Prayer; and to thank Him for all His goodness, and that this was called Thanksgiving; and that we should never begin nor end the day without both the one and the other. She said, also, that when she saw I was going to be naughty, she should give me five minutes to sit still and recollect myself, before she proceeded to punish my disobedience.

From that time, on Sundays she always taught me one of the Commandments, a clause of the Lord's Prayer, or one of the texts from the Sermon on the Mount and explained it to me; as also a question or two in Dr. Priestley's Scripture Catechism. She made me read to her one of Mrs. Barbauld's Prose Hymns for Children; and sometimes she would make me sit still with her, after the manner of Friends.

Sandford and Merton was Mary Anne's favourite book, and Henry Sandford and Sabrina Sidney, the author's pupil, her ideals. She was herself required to rival Sabrina's stoicism with pistols and sealing-wax by slowly carrying some cotton which had caught fire on her hand down a long room, and, when the dentist offered her sweets after extracting four front teeth, she proudly replied: "Do you think Regulus, and Epictetus, and Seneca would take a reward for bearing pain; or the little Spartan boys?"

When Mary Anne was about seven, the family moved to a large country house with beautiful grounds at Barr, a few miles from Birmingham. Old Barr House, which had been added to at different times, was a rambling structure, with four or five staircases. This suited Mrs. Galton's views: servants and children must never meet, and visitors were relegated to their own quarters except at meal times. Mary Anne had a bedroom to herself in the wing occupied by her parents, and shared a schoolroom and a young half-educated governess with a sister. They only met the other children with their attendant governess occasionally out of doors. Fairy tales were forbidden, and Mrs. Galton supplemented lessons by herself reading aloud parts of Stretche's *Beauties of History*, Plutarch's *Lives*, and the *History of the Barmecides*. "This kind of reading," her daughter comments, "whilst it inculcated an abhorrence of much evil, likewise fostered the pride and self-esteem of the natural heart, strengthened the false idea of the dignity and excellence of unassisted human nature, and tended to develop a presumptuous self-confidence, which afterwards expanded in most evil and unhappy fruits." Another practice of her mother's she considers wholly beneficial. Like Mrs. Deane of Mrs. Woodrooffe's *Shades of Character*, she discussed all her little daughter's faults in detail, and instituted a regular Sunday confessional—"I poured out my mind to her as in the presence of God, or as a Catholic to his confessor. She often told me that none could be without faults but that she wished her child to be like Elzevir, who, as fast as he printed a sheet, put it up at his window, offering a reward to any one who could find one mistake."

Visitors were constantly entertained, many and various: old Lord Monboddo, whom the child took to be an escaped dromedary, when he first appeared on horseback with his pack, and Miss de Luc, daughter of Queen Charlotte's reader, who brought so many anecdotes of the Court, that, later on, Mme. D'Arblay's *Memoirs* seemed familiar ground. Then there were all the members of the learned Lunar Society and their friends, dubbed Lunatics by the butler—among them Dr. Priestley and Dr. Parr, Richard Lovell Edgeworth and Day of her admired *Sandford and Merton*, Sir William Herschell and Sir Joseph Banks. Can the Society have been responsible for the title of William Blake's youthful satire, *An Island in the Moon*? One of his philosophers, Inflammable Gass the Wind-Finder, has been identified with Dr. Priestley, and he may well

have heard of, or even met, some of the others, though
not Dr. Stoke, who must have proved irresistible. At
one Lunar dinner a large yellow and black snake
rushed hissing about the room. The calm and omniscient Mrs. Galton, perceiving it to be harmless, told
Mary Anne to catch it, but with a display of parental
power did not impart her knowledge. The absent-
minded doctor had put the frozen snake in his pocket
on the way to the meeting, meaning to dissect it, and
had forgotten all about it. The two members who seem
to have impressed the child most, in their different
ways, were Watt of the steam engine, and Joseph
Berrington the historian. Of Watt she writes—"When
Mr. Watt entered a room, men of letters, men of
science, nay, military men, artists, ladies, even little
children thronged round him. I remember a celebrated Swedish artist having been instructed by him
that rats' whiskers make the most pliant and elastic
painting-brush; ladies would appeal to him on the best
means of devising grates, curing smoking chimneys,
warming their houses, and obtaining fast colours. I can
speak from experience of his teaching me how to
make a dulcimer and improve a jew's harp." And she
tells how a housemaid at the Tuileries, confronted
with English stoves which she did not know how to
clean, appealed to a visitor. It was Charles James Fox,
quite ignorant of the subject, who at once handed her
over to Mr. Watt, to whom he happened to be speaking.
Berrington, then priest at Oscott, became the most
intimate of their neighbours, and brought over his

Roman Catholic associates so frequently that fish was always provided on Wednesdays, Fridays and Saturdays, lest any of them should drop in: there was even a "Catholic quarter" of the house for guests. She says of him—"His conversation abounded in intellectual pleasantry; he was a finished gentleman of the old school, and a model of the ecclesiastical decorum of the church of ancient monuments and memories; his cold, stern eye instantly silenced any unbecoming levity either on religion or morality; his bearing was that of a prince among his people, not from worldly position, but from his sacerdotal office, while his ancient and high family seemed but a slight appendage to the dignity of his character. His voice was deep and majestic, like the baying of a bloodhound; and when he intoned Mass, every action seemed to thrill through the soul."

When Mary Anne was nine years old the tenor of life at Barr was interrupted by her mother's illness. Mrs. Galton disappeared suddenly and cruelly without bidding good-bye, leaving a letter saying that she expected never to see her daughter again, and exhorting her to cleave to the path of virtue in which she had been brought up. The emotional, dependent child was completely overwhelmed by this catastrophe. For two months she had no tidings of her mother, and her inquiries were put aside with the injunction to mind her lessons. The temporary controller of the household was Miss P., a blend of *dame de compagnie* and housekeeper to Mrs. Galton. She was a Quaker, of humble extraction, a family protégée, who had been appren-

tice in a Friends' millinery business. This trade, we
are told, was insidiously destructive of a high moral
standard, because Friends, though they condemned
worldly apparel, substituted the expression of their
precise shades of religious strictness or laxity, involving
subtle distinctions and discussions and compromises—
in short they betrayed their professions by paying as
much or more attention to their hats and bonnets than
the ordinary woman of fashion. Be that as it may, the
child was thrown back violently into her own shell:
there were no more Sunday confessions.

Then one joyful morning came the news that Dr.
Darwin had ordered Mrs. Galton to use the waters at
Bath, and the elder children were to join her there at
once. While they were waiting for dinner on the way
at the Corselawn Inn, a carriage with outriders and
four horses drew up at the door. Mary Anne recognized
Hector and Xanthus, Balius and Podargus. Her mother
had overtaken them, and she was allowed to gaze at her
for a moment through her tears.

Bath was enchanting. It was the centenary of the
arrival of King William:

> Not a lady was to be seen without streaming
> orange-coloured ribbons, or gentlemen without
> rosettes of the same in their button-holes. Besides
> this, balloons were at that time just come into vogue,
> and everybody wore huge balloon bonnets with
> magnificent ostrich feathers; and what appeared to
> me indescribably beautiful, were the ample muffs

and long tippets, and fur linings, of the silken angora goats' hair. It is remarkable that while in each individual person ornament in dress appeared so contemptible, yet this vast moving assemblage only struck me with enchantment, like a bed of beautiful flowers; the whole scene became to me a thing—I thought not of the persons composing it. I felt it was not like the incongruity of an individual in a quiet circle adorned amongst the unadorned; but it was as a brilliant picture in which the whole tone of colouring was raised, and glowing with rich and varied tints. The music, too, I felt most heart-stirring; then the beauty of the shops, which I was never tired of looking at! I could not conceive how it was possible to invent all the wants which here were professed to be supplied.

Mrs. Priestley was in charge of the invalid, and the child was allowed to sit quietly with them, playing at dominoes and listening to their conversation. Mrs. Priestley told how Lord Shelburne had given her a ticket for the Duchess of Kingston's trial, where "the rush for places, the tumult, the trampling, the tearing of clothes, were attended not only with great inconvenience but danger. On her return Lord Shelburne asked how she had enjoyed it. 'Indeed, my lord,' she replied, 'I find the conduct of the upper so exactly like that of the lower classes, that I was thankful I was born in middle life.' " Dr. Priestley had been librarian at Bowood. One day he was summoned by young Petty:

When the doctor entered, Mr. Petty told him he had passed a very restless night, and had been much disturbed by uncomfortable dreams, which he wished to relate to Dr. Priestley, hoping that, by so doing, the painful impression would pass away. He then said he dreamed he had been very unwell, when suddenly the whole house was in preparation for a journey; he was then too ill to sit up, but was carried lying down into the carriage; his surprise was extreme in seeing carriage after carriage in an almost interminable procession. He was alone, and could not speak; he could only gaze in astonishment. The procession at last wound slowly off. After pursuing the road for many hours towards London, it at last appeared to stop at the door of a church. It was the church of High Wycombe, which is the burial place of the Shelburne family. It seemed, in Mr. Petty's dream, that he entered, or rather, was carried into, the church: he looked back; he saw the procession which followed him was in black, and that the carriage from which he had been taken bore the semblance of a hearse. Here the dream ended, and he awoke. Dr. Priestley told him that his dream was the result of a feverish cold, and that the impression would soon pass off. Nevertheless, he thought it best to send for the family medical attendant. The next day Mr. Petty was much better; on the third day he was completely convalescent, so that the doctor permitted him to leave his room; but, as it was in January, and illness was prevalent, he desired him on no account to leave the house, and, with that precaution took his leave. Late the next afternoon the medical man was returning from his other patients; his road lay by the gates of Bowood, and, as Lord Shelburne was away, he thought he might as well call to see Mr. Petty, and enforce his directions. What was his surprise, when he had passed the lodge, to see the youth himself, without his hat, playfully running to meet him! The doctor was much astonished, as it was bitterly cold, and the ground covered with snow. He rode towards Mr. Petty to rebuke him for his imprudence, when suddenly he disappeared; whither, he knew not, but he seemed instantaneously to vanish. The doctor thought it very extraordinary, but that probably the youth had not wished to be found transgressing orders, and he rode on to the house; there he learnt that Mr. Petty had just expired.

When Mrs. Galton was well enough to visit the Pump Room she had stories to tell of people whom she had known during a visit to Bath in her childhood, when old Lord Chesterfield had made a pet of her. On one occasion a woman in the strictest Quaker garb had suddenly addressed the assembled rank and fashion, exhorting them to abandon the world and its pleasures, and seek the spiritual life. She was interrupted by cries of "Down", hisses and groans and beatings of sticks. But one lady had been listening intently. She rose and thanked the speaker for the faithfulness with which she had borne testimony to the truth, adding, "I am not of your persuasion, nor has it been my belief that our sex are generally deputed to be public teachers; but God who gives the rule can make the exception, and He has indeed put it in the hearts of all His children to honour and venerate fidelity to His commission. Again I gratefully thank you." She walked with the Quaker to the door of the Pump Room, and then went back to her seat. It was the Countess of Huntingdon.

Mrs. Galton graced the Assemblies in a French grey satin pelisse with mother-of-pearl buttons and a lining of Angora goats' fur. But her friend, Miss Berrington, sister of their Oscott neighbour, bowed to the fashions. This unfortunate lady, after taking her turn of two hours with the hair-dresser, who covered her superstructure of powdered curls with a Bouffante, a large projecting handkerchief, surmounted with an enormous nosegay of artificial flowers, was unable to dine, or even lift a cup of tea to her lips, before she went to a ball. Mary Anne's own costume is not described, but no doubt her austere mother ordained that it should be simple, if not deliberately unbecoming.

One of their many Bath acquaintances was Dr. Hastings, Archdeacon of Dublin, who endeavoured to convert Mrs. Galton to the Anglican Church. One day, meeting her with Mrs. Priestley and Miss Berrington, he spoke of a book on the Liturgy, which he had given her:

My mother thanked him for the book, but said she feared he would think very badly of her, when she declared how entirely she differed from his view of the Liturgy, he bowed, and politely answered, "Well, my dear Madam, I do indeed wish that you belonged to the Church of England; however, I will not make myself uneasy, as I should were you an Unitarian." My mother, interrupting him, said, "Dr. Hastings, I have omitted introducing to you my friend Mrs. Priestley,"—"or," Dr. Hastings then resumed, "what is so much worse, a Roman Catholic." My mother replied: "This lady is Miss Berrington. I am afraid you will think very badly of my condition." Dr. Hastings courteously answered: "Nay, madam, you are in just the position which the Church of England occupies—the true medium between those who hold too much and those who hold too little."

Baron Dimsdale was another friend. He had been invited to Russia by Catherine the Great that he might explain the new practice of vaccinating recently introduced in England by Lady Mary Wortley Montagu. She had insisted on being inoculated herself before instituting it for her subjects:

On his arrival, Catherine had an interview with him, fixing that he should come at midnight and inoculate her, unknown to all but two or three confidential friends; if she recovered, she proposed to remunerate him handsomely; if not, she explained all the arrangements she had made for conveying him safely out of the Empire, unknown to the public, before her death should be announced. He spoke with deep feeling of her noble nature; he had many portraits of her, which he was fond of showing, and of marking the dignity of her countenance, which, as he was wont to say, was as of a majestic lion, a grand and noble royalty, with deep traces of the impress of an animal nature. Many were the descriptions he gave of her habits and manners, from the faithful exactness with which she imitated the crowing of a cock, or the purring and spitting and hissing of a cat, to the imperial dignity with which, as an autocrat, she ruled the mighty Russias and all her dependencies. He spoke of her wit and delightful kindness, and amenity and charm in domestic society; of her wisdom, intellectual stories, and varied powers, displayed in reunions of the first literary and scientific names; and of the admirable tact with which she was equally able to serve her friends or to baffle their rivalry. When the Princess Dashkoff, whose masculine and enterprising spirit had helped in the conspiracy which placed Catherine on the throne, asked as a reward to be made Colonel of the most influential regiment of Horse Guards, Catherine, well knowing the turbulent spirit she had to deal with, adroitly replied, "That were far too vulgar a reward for so elevated a genius", and, instead of it, made her President of the Royal Philosophical Institution, an

160

honour which, as Catherine observed, "no other woman had ever received, and no other could ever deserve".

Then came another of Mrs. Galton's mysterious illnesses, and the children were left under the care of her sister, Lady Watson. Mrs. Schimmelpenninck ascribes, at great length, much of her future mental misery to the difference in moral tone between the two households. Her aunt was a brilliant and delightful woman, a notable hostess, who frankly enjoyed her wealth, whereas Mrs. Galton, living, it would seem in equal comfort, was constantly denouncing luxury. Lady Watson gave her own children and her little nieces what would have been to an ordinary child a thoroughly jolly time, but Mary Anne's conscience was so distended and her intelligence so spoon-fed that she was lost without her mother to tell her if a thing was noble, and her father if it was useful. Her life at Dawlish was, she writes, "wasted, except so far as health was concerned, in wandering about by the sea, the streams, the woods, and the breezy common, without once tasting the stores of knowledge with which all these things overflowed. Liberty and amusement abounded more and more, but as amusement and liberty increased, unhappiness and the weight of a conscience ill at ease increased likewise. I had felt sorely miserable at Bath, during my mother's illness, but it was unhappiness without the sting of conscience; but now I seemed to have neither conscience nor standard of right left. How often I felt a dull and heavy conviction, which lay as a weight upon my heart, that I was forgetting God; that I was not even seeking to do right; and how did it come like a dagger, the feeling of the deep pain my mother would have felt, could she have looked into my heart, and seen how it went on. Yet I did not know what was right, whom to take as my guide, or whither to turn for help. I felt as enveloped in a dark fog; truly, I thought, 'no man cared for my soul', and I did not even care for it myself."

Another cause of offence was the "pestilential literature" freely exposed in her uncle's library: Fielding and Smollett, French memoirs, plays and novels. The day of the young girl was still to come.

The great increase of literary taste amongst women has wrought a wonderful change, not only in collections of books, but in their composition. Books were then written only for men; now they are written so that women can participate in them: and no man would think of forming a library in his house, without a thought that its volumes must be the companions of his wife and daughters in many a lonely hour, when their influence must sink in the heart, and tend to modify the taste and character. Thus, in literature, as in other things, and especially in domestic life, has the mercy of God bestowed on woman the especial and distinguishing blessing of upholding the moral and religious influence, that

spirit of truth and love by which man can alone be
redeemed from the fall she brought upon him.

Luckily a son of Dr. Priestley's appeared with the
Arabian Nights, her first fairy tales, which she found
both recreative and instructive: "their very extrava-
gance prevented their having that semblance of truth
which would lead to false expectations".

In the autumn of 1788 the Galton family went
home again, to Mary Anne's great relief. Her mother
gave her elaborate scripture lessons, providing her
with a manuscript arrangement of the Prophecies and
Gospels, with the historic circumstances of their fulfil-
ment. Father Berrington read *The Task* aloud, and
told them about Cowper and his lady friends. She
enjoyed Virgil and Tacitus with a visiting Latin master, and read by herself Rollin's *Arts and Sciences of
the Ancients*. The Lunar brethren came again, mysteri-
ously preoccupied: her ears caught the words "Marie
Antoinette", "the Cardinal de Rohan", "diamond
necklace", "Famine", "discontent among the people",
"sullen silence, instead of shouts of *Vive le Roi!*" The
most important event—she calls it "an era in my life"
—was Dr. Darwin's first visit to Barr:

It was in the latter part of the morning that a
carriage drove up to our door, of that description
then called a "Sulky", because calculated to hold
one person only. The carriage was worn, and be-
spattered with mud. Lashed on the place appro-
priated to the boot in ordinary carriages was a large

pail for the purpose of watering the horses, together
with some hay and oats beside it. In the top of the
carriage was a skylight, with an awning which
could at pleasure be drawn over; this was for the
purpose of giving light to the doctor, who wrote
most of his works on scraps of paper with a pencil as
he travelled.

The front of the carriage within was occupied by
a receptacle for writing-paper and pencils, likewise
for a knife, fork, and spoon; on one side was a pile
of books reaching from the floor to nearly the front
window of the carriage; on the other, a hamper containing fruit and sweetmeats, cream and sugar,
great part of which, however, was demolished during
the time the carriage traversed the forty miles
which separated Derby from Barr. We all hastened
to the parlour window to see Dr. Darwin, of whom
we had heard so much, and whom I was prepared to
honour and venerate, in no common degree, as the
restorer of my mother's health. What then was my
astonishment at beholding him as he slowly got out
of the carriage. His figure was vast and massive, his
head was almost buried on his shoulders, and he
wore a scratch wig, as it was then called, tied up in a
little bob-tail behind. A habit of stammering made
the closest attention necessary, in order to understand what he said. Meanwhile, amidst all this, the
doctor's eye was deeply sagacious, the most so I
think of any eye I ever remember to have seen;
and I can conceive that no patient consulted Dr.

Darwin who, so far as intelligence was concerned, was not inspired with confidence in beholding him: his observation was most keen; he constantly detected disease, from his sagacious observation of symptoms apparently so slight as to be unobserved by other doctors. His horror of fermented liquors, and his belief in the advantages both of eating largely and eating an almost immeasurable abundance of sweet things, was well known to all his friends; and we had on this occasion, as indeed was the custom whenever he came, a luncheon-table set out with hothouse fruit, and West India sweetmeats, clotted cream, Stilton cheese, &c. When the whole party were settled at table, and I had lost the fear that the Doctor would speak to me, and when, by dint of attention, I could manage to understand what he said, I was astonished at his wit, his anecdotes, and most entertaining conversation. I was particularly amused by anecdotes he told us of his patients. There was one lady, the Duchess of D——, whom he had recently been called to attend, who was perishing, he said, under the effect of the white enamel paint which some ladies were then very fond of applying. The doctor at once perceived the cause of her malady, but he knew it would be tender ground to touch upon, since her use of this cosmetic was kept a profound secret, even from her family; he therefore put on a very grave face, and said she was certainly poisoned, asked if she had had her servants long, and if she had reason to think

165

they owed her ill-will, he then said he should make the strictest examination of all the kitchen utensils, which he did; no satisfaction could be obtained. He then informed her Grace that poison might be absorbed by the skin as well as received by the stomach; had she observed the dyes of her gloves? &c., &c. At last the Duchess of D——, after a great struggle, confessed she used the white lead enamel. It was soon removed. Dr. Darwin's ingenuity furnished her with some vegetable cosmetic in its stead; and her Grace completely recovered.

With this, and various other anecdotes, did Dr. Darwin beguile the time whilst the dishes in his vicinity were rapidly emptied; but what was my astonishment when, at the end of the three hours during which the meal had lasted, he expressed his joy at hearing the dressing-bell, and hoped dinner would soon be announced. At last, to my sorrow, he discovered me, and said, "I will now see if you are a clever and industrious little girl; translate me these lines of Virgil," on which he began, no doubt, to repeat them, but to me, who could not even understand his English, they were wholly unintelligible. He then quoted some Greek lines, of which language I knew not a word, so that I got into great disgrace with him. This is the recollection of my first childish impressions of Dr. Darwin; an eventful day, not only for myself, was that which first introduced him to our family circle.

On this occasion gluttony appears to have been the Doctor's worst failing, but other visits followed when he entertained the company unchecked with his materialistic views. Mr. Galton probably sympathized, and the dispassionate Mrs. Galton was amused by his wit, while Mary Anne sat in horror at his stuttering sneers. She feels it her duty to dwell at length on his iniquities as the chief villain and corrupter of the society in which she grew up, and the disturber of her childish faith. The wicked old man, consulted about the health of a strict and ethereal Quaker cousin, actually said: "My dear Madam, you have but one complaint; it is one ladies are very subject to, and it is the worst of all complaints; and that is, having a conscience. Do get rid of it with all speed; few people have health or strength enough to keep such a luxury, for utility I cannot call it." Worse still, when asked whether Priscilla might not go on reading her religious books, his reply was: "My dear Madam, toss them every one into the fire. I cannot permit one of them, excepting Quarles' *Emblems*, which may make her laugh."

To the hope expressed that some day he might become a Christian, he replied with a look which Mary Anne could never forget: "Before I do that you Christians must be all agreed. The other morning I received two parcels; one containing a work of Dr. Priestley's, proving there is no spirit, the other a work by Berkeley, Bishop of Cloyne, proving there is no matter. What am I to believe amongst you all?"

About this time Mary Anne came across Lavater's *Physiognomy* in a French translation. She pored over it, hour after hour, finding it a blessed antidote to the poisonous levity of Dr. Darwin. To-day the works of the worthy Swiss retain even less of their savour than the Doctor's verses, but it must be counted to his honour that William Blake, though more critical of his philosophy than Mary Anne, found in the *Aphorisms* a stimulus to his *Songs of Innocence*. He wrote his name below Lavater's, drawing the outline of a heart round the two names, and his annotations were said by his friend Fuseli to be a key to his own character. "Damn sneerers!" wrote Blake after Lavater's: "a sneer is often the sign of heartless malignity." Mary Anne must have recalled that dreadful look of Dr. Darwin's, and, if she read the next, "Who courts the intimacy of a professed sneerer, is a professed knave", would have dreaded still more his "baleful and ominous visits". "Humility and love, whatever obscurities may involve religious tenets, constitute the essence of true religion. The humble is formed to adore; the loving to associate with eternal love." "Sweet!" wrote Blake, and such mild pieties were balm to Mary Anne. From Lavater she learnt to study faces and their expressions, and tried to believe that even Dr. Darwin's face might have been created in the Divine image.

Just as the unfortunate child was gaining some peace of mind from Lavater and her lessons, it was discovered that she had curvature of the spine, and she was condemned to wear an instrument of torture from the age of eleven to eighteen. Dr. Darwin, who, we may be sure, would have sent it flying into the dust-bin and ordered a pony instead, was not consulted, and her mother's only answer to her complaints was "What is that character worth which cannot bear a little pain?" Proper exercise was impossible; too nervous to stand the company of her rampageous juniors, she could only read and learn more and more. To make matters worse her father now took her education in hand, and prescribed those books written for men whose existence she had deplored in her uncle's library. "Shaftesbury's *Characteristics*, Voltaire's Works, of which we had the fine edition in about seventy volumes, Molière's plays, *Gil Blas*, Bolingbroke and Swift succeeded each other, and mingled their evil influences with the large and varied mass of scientific, historic, and classical reading which also occupied me." Lessons became a misery, because her father terrified her by his impatience, saying openly that such brilliant parents had not deserved so stupid and obstinate a child. Her mother, whose luxurious invalidism gave her constant leisure to pursue her own literary tastes, tried Milton, but Mary Anne was "wearied and repelled by the incongruous mixture of classical and sacred allusions". Then Pope's *Iliad*, by which, like other children of her day, she was completely fascinated, until she compared its morals with the Sermon on the Mount, when conscience pestered her again. An attempt to study the works of Dr.

Priestley on her own account brought further trouble: if that was Christianity it was not what she wanted.

Here the *Autobiography* breaks off. My readers must have shared my own impatience with Mary Anne, and her cramming, propping parents. Mary Wollstonecraft would have fled from such surroundings to make a life of her own: Eliza Fletcher would have eloped with her first young man, and Mary Somerville quietly pursued the dictates of her genius. But this unhappy girl, diseased in body and mind, had not developed the necessary independence of character. Her later experiences can only be gathered from the somewhat fulsome *Life* by an adoring relative, and such letters and fragments of diary as are quoted in it.

She first visited her cousins at Earlham when she was eighteen. There she found a kindred spirit and lifelong friend in Catherine Gurney, to whom she afterwards addressed a series of letters on the "Evidences and Importance of Christianity". At twenty she was sent for a month to Mrs. Barbauld, armed with minute written instructions from her mother as to her behaviour there, and the composition of an adequate Collins after she left.

Do not let these acknowledgments be contained in a *note*, nor let the coldness of the manner undo the effect of the thanks you mean to express. Write a letter, therefore, and not a note, and write a *sheet full.* A *note* of thanks, whatever the words may be, can express only this—"I have obtained from you all the advantages I hoped; I have acquitted myself according to the rules of etiquette; and so now I have done with you." Write a letter, therefore, upon different subjects, and so expressed that she may perceive your heart, as well as your head, to have been interested by her attentions; and that you not only think, but that you feel, justly.

Relations were kindly, but Mary Anne was scarcely a case for Mrs. Barbauld's clinique, and the visit was not repeated. Mrs. Galton's injunctions pursued her when she went to stay with some relatives at Bath:

I hope that, if a great many young gentlemen resort to the house in the Crescent, you will learn how to behave on such occasions; not to do too much or too little; not to lay aside established forms, or to practise the starched prude. If young men are present, talk to them as much as you please, but always sit in the circle with the ladies.

Above all things, enter into no investigations with any body; no abstruse speculations, no referring to principles in common conversation, unless your opinion be asked; and then give it clearly *once;* but make no effort to maintain or enforce it, unless some wise and older person lead the way to an argument; and then put an end to it as soon as you can with a jest. Say, "I must beg to be excused from going on, lest you should be convinced by my reasons, which I see you don't like to adopt"; or say, "I am afraid of going on, lest I should be convinced by yours, and so give up the triumph to my adversary". Talk about matters of fact. Surely there are follies enough in the world to supply conversation without referring to reason on every occasion. Expatiate upon the weather, upon the journey, upon the fashions, upon the faces of people you see; in short, upon all you see and hear, but say very little about what you think, and take care to *think* as little as you can help. To quote Dr. Darwin upon *thinking*, who quotes Sancho upon weeping, "Take as little of it as you can, to go through the world decently". And I really believe that the regulation of the heart will do more for us than the reasonings of the head. Do lay yours by for a little while, and let it rest.

The next winter was spent with a Mrs. Beaver, of Dover Street, Piccadilly, who introduced young ladies of good family into society. There she enjoyed the companionship and music of girls of her own age. A winter at Bath with that "respectable writer", Mrs. Elizabeth Hamilton, seems to have been less successful. Mary Anne—and no wonder, if she was conscientiously trying to follow her mother's precepts—was too shy and self-conscious to enjoy Mrs. Hamilton's crowded receptions of the fashionable and literary world. She was a striking young person, none the less. Here she is at a concert:

She was dressed with perfect simplicity; and, as

was the fashion of that day, she wore a gold band round her head, her dark brown hair clustering in rich profusion over and around it: the colour on her clear cheek heightened by the scene, she looked beautiful, her simple dress in perfect keeping with her countenance of rare intellectual beauty. As they entered the room, every eye was attracted by her appearance; and the young Mary Anne, with the unfeigned modesty which then as ever characterised her, was probably the only one in that large assembly who was unconscious of the sensation she occasioned.

Mary Butt met her at this time, and describes her as "a simple, agreeable person, without the smallest display". The acquaintance secured for Mary an invitation to one of Mrs. Hamilton's evenings, where she met the "Child of Nature", who appeared to be "playing a part". I have failed to identify this histrionic sensation of the moment, but Miss Butt gives an amusing account of the rout in her novel, *Caroline Mordaunt or the Governess*. Caroline, who was dismissed by a former employer for being too clever, has just entered the household of Mrs. Delaney (Mrs. Hamilton). The maid is helping her to dress:

"This is my lady's evening," she said: "*belle assemblée* evening; it takes place every Thursday, when all the literary persons in Bath are here. They are already nearly all assembled. There is the Abbé Reynard, and Monsieur le Comte, and the Marquis, and Signior Figaro, and the poet Laureate, and

173

Madame Blarny, and the author of the new novel,
I think they call it—but I have forgot the name—it
is of no consequence, but he is a wonderful man;
and the celebrated writer of sonnets and elegies, I
think my lady calls them; and the great tragedian,
Malpas, and many others; but the Child of Nature
is not come yet. My lady told me to tell you that
you must, if possible, see his *entrée*."

Caroline hurries down to the drawing-room door,
which is opened for her by a footman.

And now what a stage burst upon my eyes!—
what a scene of noise and confusion! The room was
filled, and everybody talking at once. The figures,
too, were all so new—so grotesque—at least my
unpractised eyes thought them so. Half the company were evidently foreign: most of them of a
certain age; and all marked in their deportment and
physiognomy. I heard nothing, for a moment, but a
mingled jargon of exclamations in English, French
and Italian; the French predominating: whilst the
speakers used so much action and such emphasis,
with such contortions of countenance, that I could
almost have thought myself suddenly ushered upon
a stage where a numerous company were acting
pantomimes.

It was more than a minute before I could dis-
tinguish Mrs. Delaney. When my eye, at length,
rested upon her, she was standing at the very far-
thest end of the room, conversing with an exceed-

ingly short gentleman, in spectacles; I made my way to her, and was watching a moment to address her, when she extended one finger to me, nodded, and smiled, adding these words, *"Ne m'interrompez pas à présent"*; and turning again to the little gentleman, said *"Continuez, mon ami, je respire à peine"*.

"Mark me, observe me," continued the small man, evidently carrying on some recital which I had interrupted, "In that crisis, just in that particular moment, I arose. I elevated myself to my utmost height, and I uttered these words, 'Ah, Maria! can it be?' Now, Mrs. Delaney, in that 'can it be?'—those few simple words, those words which, out of unlettered lips"—he was proceeding, when a whisper ran round the circle: "The Child of Nature", —"the Child of Nature!" All was instantly still: many who were standing sat down. I drew myself close up to the wall, and a tall, handsome young man, of Herculean limbs, entered the apartment. He advanced towards one part of the room, with a sort of run, which would have well suited a child just going without leading-strings, and, coming close up to Mrs. Delaney, he said, "I dare say you were thinking I should not come at all. Should you have been sorry if I had not come?" "Should I not," replied my patroness, in her gentlest accents, "Has Nature lost its charms in this sophisticated age?" But her words seem to have been thrown away, for the "Child of Nature" had extended his arm—drawn a chair into the middle of the circle—and was already sitting down, with his back half turned to the company, strumming with his fingers as if playing on the keys of a harpsichord, on his own knee. "What naïveté!" said Mrs. Delaney to a lady who stood between herself and me; " he has already forgotten that any one is present".

The "Child of Nature" began to hum a tune, howing even by this small specimen that he had an uncommonly fine voice; then making a false note—then correcting himself, and finishing off by going to an instrument at the farther end of the room, and accompanying his voice in the same air which he had been humming. In the meantime all was silent in the room, excepting when the ladies whispered, "Unequalled! unrivalled! excellent!" But the "Child of Nature" stopped again at the same note, at which he had hesitated before, and struck the keys like a petted miss, as if they were to blame for his pretended want of memory; and, not seeming to heed the entreaties of the company that he would continue to charm their ears with his unrivalled melody, he took a little book from his pocket, threw himself on the corner of a couch, and read as determinately as if he were reading for a first class at Oxford. "There now," said Mrs. Delaney with a mortified air, "there he is and there he will be to the end of the night. We should not have noticed his singing; he would then have gone on for an hour; and, perhaps, have come amongst us afterwards, and delighted us as much by the charms of his

176

conversation as he has done by his singing; but we have nothing more to expect from him to-night. We are thrown upon our own resources"; and she sighed as she uttered these words.

"Our own resources!" said the small man in spectacles; "and can any company want resources, rich resources, when a Delaney is present?" "When a Christopher Malpas is present?" returned the lady, and then, as if with one accord, the haranguing, reciting, criticizing and complimenting, which had been interrupted by the "Child of Nature", recommenced in every corner of the room; and as I thought it rather tiresome to seem a mere auditor in such a scene, I ventured to try my own powers, and found myself presently drawn into a very animated discourse with a deeply wrinkled French Count, who avoided the ceremony of an introduction by picking up my glove and returning it to me.

Years passed. Mary Anne was still seeking in vain for some assurance which should bring inward peace. Her father's learned friends did not seem to her to have found any true happiness. Members of the Society of Friends, she thought, had obtained something the others lacked. But their words were vague and indefinite: they could not impart it to her. One day, lingering wretchedly in a book-shop at Bath, she burst into tears. A stranger asked whether she could help her. "Oh!" she replied, "can you do anything for a wounded spirit, who knows not where nor how to

obtain peace?" The young woman, a Labouress of the
Moravian Church, comforted her, and suggested that
they should read the Bible together. Their talk was
interrupted, but Mrs. Galton was looking for rooms
where she could leave Mary Anne and her maid, and
the Moravian family with whom the Labouress lived
was fortunately recommended to her. There Mary
Anne spent a happy six months. Theirs was the strong
and simple faith she needed, and, although still distressed about the state of her soul, she clung to what
she had learnt from them when she went home again.

Health was made the excuse for Mary Anne's frequent and prolonged absences from Barr, but it is not
unfair to surmise that she was a misfit in the family
life. In 1806, when she was twenty-eight, the situation
was relieved by the appearance of Mr. Schimmelpenninck, a Dutch gentleman of noble family whose
connection with the shipping trade had located him in
Bristol. The Galtons consulted Mrs. Hannah More.
He was pronounced to be amiable, religious, and well-
read, though not brilliant. Mary Anne now had for the
first time an independent life of her own, and something definite to do: housekeeping, work among the
Bristol poor, classes to whom she taught natural history
and other subjects.

Soon after her marriage a quarrel about the settle-
ments led to complete estrangement from her parents.
Dr. Darwin and the Lunar Brethren ceased to trouble
her by their infidelities and laxities. She kept up her
connection with the Moravian Church, although she

did not become a member till later. She was also in
sympathy with the Bristol Wesleyans, and retained her
old Quaker and Roman Catholic friendships. Mr.
Schimmelpenninck's admiration and amiability made
a comfortable background, but from a desire to save
her pain—or was he somewhat afraid of his superior
wife?—he concealed from her serious financial difficulties, revealing the crisis abruptly just before a large
dinner-party. When their guests had gone she sat up
most of the night, considering details of the necessary
retrenchment. There was no question of real poverty
—they continued to live in one of those beautiful
houses in Berkeley Square—but she had to forgo
luxuries to which she had always been accustomed,
and was glad to supplement their income by her pen.
Hannah More interested her at this time in the Port
Royalists. Her first study on this subject, afterwards
included in *Select Memoirs of Port Royal*, appeared in
1813. The following year she and her husband visited
Port Royal, made friends with a Jansenist bishop, and
with his help procured some rare books, unobtainable
in England, to aid her further work. Her other writings, religious and æsthetic, some of them published
posthumously, make a formidable list, but none of
them proved as popular and influential as the *Port
Royalists*. In 1838 the Schimmelpennincks moved to
Clifton, where he died two years later.

Mrs. Schimmelpenninck's portrait, the frontispiece
of the *Autobiography*, is full of character, but to me,
I confess, rather repellent: a self-willed and arbitrary

old face, with a touch of the poseuse, a likely inheritance from her mother, whose letters suggest an advanced case of exhibitionism. But perhaps I am
prejudiced by her idolatrous biographer, who barely
hints that even she had her human failings. Caroline
Fox's memories of her picture a mellow old woman of
vigorous mind, who had lost all trace of the spiritual
torments of her girlhood. She writes in 1842:

A charming visit from M. A. Schimmelpenninck,
who looks bright, handsome, and active. We soon
got to Roman Catholicism and a book of Miss
Agnew's, *Geraldine*, which sets forth the sunny
side of the doctrine. Mrs. Schimmelpenninck would
define the principle of Roman Catholicism as Belief,
that of Protestantism as Examination, and a just
mixture of these two she conceives to be the true
article. As for any one party getting at the whole
truth, she justly considers this preposterous enough,
and illustrated her view by the account an Indian
missionary gave her of a Christian native, whom he
had been asking, how the diversity of Christian
belief which had come before them from the
settlement of some fresh missionaries, had affected
them. "Why," he said, "it is like a city of the blind,
when an elephant is brought amongst them for the
first time. Each tries to give an account of it. One
says it is like the tail of a thing; another, it is like a
hoof, and so on; and when they begin to quarrel, a
seeing man tells them, 'It's quite true that part is

180

like a tail, part like a hoof, but none of you have any idea how large the elephant is, and how impossible it is for any of you to have felt it all'." Thus she is always anxious that we should not condemn others for their views, however little we can see with them. She talked with a good deal of poetical truth on Quakerism, and she loves the conventual effect of our costumes.

Five years later she saw her old friend at Clifton:

A visit to M. A. Schimmelpenninck: symbolic as ever, and teeming with unimaginative Facts. She is a very genial person, so alive to the beauty of all Religious Faith, however widely diverse. She spoke of having suffered from an indiscriminate theological education; it has made it hard to her to connect herself decidedly with any special body, and this, she thinks, has checked her practical usefulness. But may not her outward vocation have been to introduce opinions to each other, dressed, not in vinegar, but in oil?

Shortly before Mrs. Schimmelpenninck's death, when her health was failing, an attempt was made to convert her to Roman Catholicism. It would seem that she nearly yielded, but afterwards stated without any ambiguity her objections to the practices and dogmas of the Roman Church. She died in 1856 at the age of seventy-eight.

MRS. TONNA'S upbringing was not unlike that of Eliza Fletcher, her senior by twenty years, and as well-calculated to develop her personality, but it is difficult to imagine that even in the most adverse circumstances she would have become a submissive and elegant female.

Charlotte Elizabeth Browne was born in Norwich in 1790. Her father, the Rev. Michael Browne, was a minor canon of the Cathedral and rector of St. Giles. His mother, whom Charlotte must have resembled in character, proudly claimed to be a Percy by descent; she checked any unseemly behaviour by reminding her grandchildren of their ancestry, and taught them to sing *Chevy Chase*. Her diatribes against the Papists, the French and the fashions were buttressed by Biblical support: once, when the folly and vanity of a new sleeve had roused her wrath, she remarked to her granddaughter: "I never wore a gown but of one shape: and because I don't follow the fashion, the fashion is forced to come to me sometimes by way of a change. I can't help that, you know, my dear: but I never was fashionable on purpose."

One of the snares which beset Charlotte's youth, though unrecognized as such till later life, was the extraordinary beauty of the gardens, both of the rectory and of the Bishop's Palace, where she walked at will, peopling them with fairies and goblins from the "wild, unholy fiction" of nursery tales. A precocious child, she began learning French from a young uncle before she was six, putting her lesson book under her pillow, and straining her eyes over it as soon as it was light: the result was some months of total blindness. Her father, an ardent politician, allowed her to sit in his study, listening to the conversation, and, despite occasional visits from the famous Dr. Parr and other Whig disputants, the child became "a thinker, a reasoner, a tory, and a patriot". After her sight was restored the foundations were laid of the vehement Protestantism which distinguished her after-career. Her father used to take her to the Lollard's Pit below Mousehold Heath, and tell her how Queen Mary had burnt good people there because they refused to worship wooden images, and he gave her Foxe's *Book of Martyrs* in blackletter. She pored over it, unable to read the type, but entranced by the woodcuts: "'Papa, may I be a martyr?' 'What do you mean, child?' 'I mean, papa, may I be burned to death for my religion as these were? I want to be a martyr'." "He smiled, and made this answer, which I have never forgotten: 'Why, Charlotte, if the Government ever gives power to the Papists again, as they talk of doing, you may very probably live to be a martyr '."

This ambition was unfulfilled, but in later life she greatly enjoyed abridging Foxe. The family Bible, bound in rich red, and elegantly emblazoned with the royal arms, was, like the Percy descent, a subject of pride: Queen Charlotte had used it at her Coronation: reading in it was a reward of virtue. But another snare, "a net of dangerous fascination", was set for her: when she was seven her brother was taken to see the *Merchant of Venice*: as Charlotte had a cold she was allowed to read the play to herself at home, and, as she says, "I drank a cup of intoxication under which my brain reeled for many a year". The royal Bible was no longer a treat: more and more Shakespeare took its place, and the little prodigy was encouraged by the questions of admiring visitors. Other poisonous poets followed, and "Pope's atrocious *Universal Prayer* would have become my manual of devotion, had not my father denounced it as a most blasphemous outrage upon revelation, and charged me never to repeat what he deeply regretted that I had committed to memory."

Yet another snare was metaphysics: her father asked the reason of a sleepless night: "I was thinking, Papa, of *Cogito, ergo sum,* and I lay awake, trying to find out all about it." "*Cogito, ergo sum,*" repeated my father, laughing and frowning at the same time; "What will you be at twenty, if you dabble in metaphysics before you are ten? Come, I must set you to study Euclid; that will sober your wild head a little."

Meanwhile the delicate, excitable child was being drugged with mercury: to this she ascribes the complete loss of hearing, which came on before she was ten, and lasted the rest of her life. No more music and political controversy: but her mother insisted on her reading aloud the seven mortal volumes of *Sir Charles Grandison*, although she herself could not hear a word of it.

The doctors now ordered an open air life and inhaling the breath of cows. Mr. Browne exchanged his town living for the neighbouring village of Bawburgh, and a still more entrancing garden, sloping down to a mill-stream. Books were abandoned: "all was freedom, mirth, and peace". Mamma objected:

"Mr. B. this will never do; that girl cannot wear a frock twice without spoiling it; nor keep it whole for a week: the expense will ruin us." "Well, my dear, if I am to be ruined by expense, let it come in the shape of the washerwoman's and linendraper's bills; not in those of the apothecary and undertaker."

My dear father was right; and it would be a happy thing for girls in general if somewhat of appearance, and of acquirement too, was sacrificed to what God has so liberally provided and to the enjoyment of which a blessing is undoubtedly annexed. Where, among females, do we find the stamina of constitution and the elasticity of spirit which exist in those of our rural population who follow out-door employment? It positively pains me to see a party of girls, a bonnetted and tippeted double file of humanity,

185

"That like a wounded snake drags its slow length
    along,"

under the keen surveillance of a governess, whose
nerves would never be able to endure the shock of
seeing them bound over a stream, or scramble
through a fence, or even toss their heads and throw
out their limbs as all young animals, except that
oppressed class called young ladies, are privileged
to do. Having ventured, in a fit of my country
daring, to break the ice of this very rigid and frigid
subject, I will recount another instance of the
paternal good sense, to which I owe, under God, the
physical powers without which my little talent
might have lain by in a napkin all my days.

One morning, when his daughter was about eight
years old, my father came in, and found sundry
preparations going on, the chief materials for which
were buckram, whalebone, and other stiff articles;
while the young lady was under measurement by
the hands of a female friend.

"Pray what are you going to do to the child?"

"Going to fit her with a pair of stays."

"For what purpose?"

"To improve her figure; no young lady can grow
up properly without them."

"I beg your pardon; young gentlemen grow up
very well without them, and so may young ladies."

"Oh, you are mistaken. See what a stoop she has
already; depend on it this girl will be both a dwarf
and a cripple if we don't put her into stays."

"My child may be a cripple, Ma'am, if such is God's will; but she shall be one of His making, not our's."

All remonstrance was vain; stays and every species of tight dress were strictly prohibited by the authority of one whose will was, as every man's ought to be, absolute in his own household. He also carefully watched against any evasion of the rule; a ribband drawn tightly round my waist would have been cut without hesitation, by his determined hand; while the little girl of the anxious friend whose operations he had interrupted, enjoyed all the advantages of that system from which I was preserved. She grew up a wand-like figure, graceful and interesting, and died of decline at nineteen, while I, though not able to compare shapes with a wasp, or an hour-glass, yet passed muster very fairly among mere human forms, of God's moulding; and I have enjoyed to this hour a rare exemption from headaches, and other lady-like maladies, which appear the almost exclusive privilege of women in the higher classes.

"Antichrist bestrode our city, firmly planting there his two cloven hoofs of Popery and Socinianism," writes Charlotte. Neither hoof crushed the Brownes: they had no intercourse with the old Catholic families, the Jerninghams and the Petres, and were unaffected by the intellectual unrest which disturbed and stimulated their young neighbours, Sarah Taylor, Harriet

Martineau and Elizabeth Gurney. Norwich, like Edinburgh, was armed for the invasion, and Bonaparte was an ever present terror to Charlotte and her brother. Although not believers in his ubiquity like their village friends, they expected him to attack their tall white house in person, and devised means of slaying him with their own hands.

The other great danger was Catholic Emancipation, and the Brownes regarded the madness of George III as specially arranged by Providence that the Protesters might have time to increase and multiply, and so prevent the ultimate act of national apostacy from being really a national act. Charlotte's deafness did not prevent her from being sound on this fundamental point: she could no longer listen to the conversations in her father's study, but her family kept her abreast of the times by the language of their fingers. She wrote political squibs, and was at sixteen the heroine of a grand election ball. "Alas for the girl who makes such a début." Meanwhile under the influence of Shakespeare and other profane poets she was still enjoying a deplorable phantasy life, the more so that her young brother left home to take a commission in the army. While he was serving in the Peninsula, the father died, leaving only a small annuity to his widow. Charlotte determined to support herself by writing novels, but a devious Providence saved her from this snare by producing Captain George Phelan of the 60th Rifle Corps. Shortly after their marriage he rejoined his regiment at Halifax, Nova Scotia, and summoned his wife: she went out in a troopship. "Although our party was perfectly distinct from those who went out entirely at the charge of Government, consisting of several officers and their wives, yet we too were nearly all military, including the commandant, and were strictly amenable to martial law. Of course, that soul of domestic and social comfort, punctuality, reigned paramount: every meal was proclaimed by beat of drum, subordination carefully preserved, and decorum, to the most minute particular, insisted on. No deshabille could appear, in the cabin or on deck; no litter, not an article of luggage visible. All the sick people, all the cross people, and all the whimsical people, were stowed away in their respective berths; and such drawing-room elegance, combined with the utmost freedom of good-humour, and the unrestrained frankness that results from a consciousness of proper restraint, pervaded our little select coterie, amounting to seventeen gentlemen and two ladies, that it did not need the miserable contrast which I experienced on the homeward passage to assure me that we were among the most favoured of ocean-travellers." The voyage, including a tremendous storm, when the captain abandoned hope, and the romantic Charlotte irritated the company by her unseemly and reckless enjoyment of the mountainous sea with its phosphorescent waves, was one long delight. She spent two adventurous years in Nova Scotia, riding a lovely dappled grey Arab—a link, like the Browne Bible, with the Royal family, as her grandsire had been a gift from George III to the Duke of Kent—an intractable creature who threw the finest equestrians in the regiment, obeying only the voice of her young mistress. Then some months "in a disgusting region of all that is most directly opposed to liberty, civil or religious, to honourable feeling, just conduct, honest principle or practical decency", Portugal in short, and she was in England again.

Captain Phelan was engaged in a lawsuit about some property in Ireland, and soon sent for his wife. She went, full of prejudice, as became a Protester from the cradle, against Ireland and the Irish. But St. John's Eve in King's County was a revelation which charmed and perplexed her: she was restrained with difficulty by "the quality" from joining the peasants in a jig:

But something was to follow that puzzled me not a little: when the fire had burned for some hours, and got low, an indispensable part of the ceremony commenced. Every one present, of the peasantry, passed through it, and several children were thrown across the sparkling embers; while a wooden frame of some eight feet long, with a horse's head fixed to one end, and a large white sheet thrown over it, concealing the wood and the man on whose head it was carried, made its appearance. This was greeted with loud shouts as the "white horse"; and having been safely carried by the skill of its bearer several times through the fire with a bold leap, it pursued the people, who ran screaming and laughing in every direction. I asked what the horse was meant for, and was told it represented all cattle. Here was the old pagan worship of Baal, if not of Moloch too, carried on openly and universally in the heart of a nominally Christian country, and by millions professing the Christian name! I was confounded, for I did not then know that Popery is only a crafty adaptation of pagan idolatries to its own scheme; and while I looked upon the now wildly-excited people, with their children and, in a figure, all their cattle, passing again and again through the fire, I almost questioned in my own mind the lawfulness of the spectacle, considered in the light that the Bible must, even to the natural heart, exhibit it in, to those who confess the true God. There was no one to whom I could breathe such thoughts, and they soon faded from my mind: not so the impression made on it by this fair specimen of a population whom I had long classed with the savage inhabitants of barbarous lands, picturing them as dark, ferocious, discontented and malignant. That such was the reverse of their natural character I now began to feel convinced; and from that evening my heart gradually warmed towards a race whom I found to be frank, warm and affectionate beyond any I had ever met with.

Here I must digress to suggest a question for archæologists. Is there any connection between the ceremony which so much impressed young Mrs. Phelan and the White Horses of Uffington and Westbury?

About Captain Phelan, it is delicately implied, the less said the better: his wife says very little. She does not indicate how soon she discovered his unsatisfactory character as a husband, but it is clear that by this time there was no happiness for her in their married life. As an instrument of Providence the Captain was invaluable; his first function had been to deliver her from the fate of a successful novelist: his second was to bring her to Ireland, the stage chosen for her conversion, and leave her alone in "an aristocratical little town", whose inhabitants considered her beneath calling level. There he required her to ferret out details and copy papers relating to his lawsuit, while he himself lived in Dublin. She shall describe her own state of mind:

My existence was a feverish dream, of vain pleasures first, and then of agitations and horrors. My mind was a chaos of useless information, my character of unapplied energies, my heart a waste of unclaimed affections, and my hope an enigma of confused speculations. I had plenty to do, yet felt that I was doing nothing; and there was a glowing want within my bosom, a craving after I knew not what; a restless, unsatisfied, unhappy feeling, that seemed in quest of some unknown good. How this was awakened, I know not: it was unaccompanied with any conviction of my own sinfulness, or any doubt of my perfect safety as a child of God. In her enforced seclusion she determined:

to become a sort of Protestant nun, and to fancy my garden, with its high stone-walls, and little thicket of apple-trees, a convent-enclosure. I also settled it with myself to pray three or four times every day, instead of twice; and with great alacrity entered upon this new routine of devotion.

Here God met with, and arrested me. When I kneeled down to pray, the strangest alarms took hold of my mind. He to Whom I had been accustomed to prate with flippant volubility in a set form of heartless words, seemed to my startled mind so exceedingly terrible in unapproachable majesty, and so very angry with me in particular, that I became paralyzed with fear. I strove against this, with characteristic pertinacity: I called to mind all the common-place assurances respecting the sufficiency of a good intention, and magnified alike my doings and my sufferings. I persuaded myself it was only a holy awe, the effect of distinguished piety and rare humility, and that I was really an object of the divine complacency in no ordinary degree. Again I essayed to pray, but in vain; I dared not. Then I attributed it to a nervous state of feeling which would wear away by a little abstraction from the subject; but this would not do. To leave off praying was impossible, yet to pray seemed equally so.

It was not in my nature to be driven back easily

from any path I had entered on; and here the Lord wrought upon me to persevere resolutely. I began to examine myself, in order to discover *why* I was afraid, and taking as my rule the ten commandments, I found myself sadly deficient on some points. The tenth affected me as it never had done before. "I had not known lust", because I had not understood the law when it said "Thou shalt not covet". A casual glance at the declaration of St. James, "Whosoever shall keep the whole law, and yet offend in one point, he is guilty of all", alarmed me exceedingly; and on a sudden it occurred to me, that not only the ten commandments, but all the precepts of the New Testament were binding on a Christian; and I trembled more than ever.

What was to be done? To reform myself, certainly, and become obedient to the whole law. Accordingly I went to work, transcribed all the commands that I felt myself most in the habit of neglecting, and pinned up a dozen or two of texts round my room. It required no small effort to enter this apartment and walk round it, reading my mementos. That active schoolmaster, the law, had got me fairly under his rod, and dreadful were the writhings of the convicted culprit! I soon, however, took down my texts, fearing lest any one else might see them, and not knowing they were for myself, be exasperated. I then made a little book, wrote down a list of offences, and commenced making a dot over against each, whenever I de-

194

tected myself in the commission of one. I had become very watchful over my thoughts, and was
honest in recording all evil; so my book became a
mass of black dots; and the reflection that occurred
to me of omissions also being sins, completed the
panic of my mind. I flung my book into the fire,
and sank into an abyss of gloomy despair.

For some weeks she could neither pray nor read
the Bible. The casual loan of a book, the life of a young
man who, overwhelmed like herself by a sense of sin,
had found redemption on his deathbed, brought relief.
She recalled heated family arguments about the doctrine of election, accepted only by her Percy grandmother, and now she too was convinced of its truth.
Then a lucky accident—to speak in the profane tongue
which she herself never employs—at last revealed a
vocation which her conscience could approve. A
stranger sent her a parcel of tracts. How could she
further the good work? Money she had none: why not
write a tract? She sat down forthwith at 7 p.m., and
wrote till 3 a.m. The result pleased her immensely,
but what to do with it? The Bishop of Norwich? How
many franks would it take? Before she had decided
this question, a letter arrived from the sender of the
parcel, asking whether she could not assist with her
pen, and enclosing the address of the Dublin Tract
Society. The manuscript was despatched at once, and
led to congenial friendships and more and more tracts.

Charlotte Elizabeth—one Christian name is not

enough, henceforth she must be called by the two which became a household word—was now a Vital Christian and a literary woman who had dedicated her gifts to the Cause. She declined to cross the Atlantic again with Captain Phelan, and remained in Ireland dependent upon her own exertions. Mrs. Browne, a quiet domestic character, joined her, as amenable to her daughter's religion as she had been to her husband's views on the healthy rearing of girls. They went to live in Kilkenny in 1821, paying a prolonged visit to Dr. Hamilton of Knocktopher. The country, inflamed by the Prophecies of Pastorini, was in a disturbed state. In 1771 Charles Walmesley, the Roman Catholic prelate and mathematician, whose library at Bath was destroyed during the Lord George Gordon riots, had first published his *General History of the Christian Church, from Her Birth to her Final Triumphant State in Heaven, chiefly deduced from the Apocalypse of St. John the Apostle*, under the pseudonym of Signor Pastorini. It ran into numerous editions, and was translated into several languages. According to Charlotte Elizabeth:

He explained the ascent of the locusts out of the bottomless pit to prefigure the rise of Protestantism with Luther at its head; calculating the date of their continuance from 1525, and its termination in 1825: extracts from this impudently mischievous work were disseminated in every possible form among the Romanists; they were translated into

Irish, sent in large numbers to every district to be circulated by careful agents: published in handbills, exhibited on placards, and sung in doggerel rhyme through the streets. There was no article of their faith more devoutly believed by the besotted people than that in 1825 the Protestants of Ireland and of every other country were, by divine appointment, to be put to death, except such as should recant; and while the lower orders prepared with terrible alacrity to execute the will of God, by a general massacre of their unoffending neighbours, those of higher rank and gentler spirits applied themselves to the work of converting their Protestant friends.

Charlotte Elizabeth was herself "the object of a combined attack from the forces of great Babylon". An elegant nun borrowed for her benefit from a Jesuit seminary Milner's *End of Controversy*, reputed to have made innumerable converts: "Never shall I forget the effect it produced on me. I seemed to be holding communion with Satan himself, robed as an angel of light, the transparent drapery revealing his hideous form, but baffling my endeavours to rend it away. Such sophistry, such impudence of unsupported assertion, such distortion of truth, and gilding of gross falsehood, I never met with. I tried in vain to find an answer to things I saw and felt to be anti-scriptural and destructive: but this 'End' was the beginning of my controversy, for I was wholly new to it, and ignorant of the historical and other facts necessary to

197

disprove the reverend author's bold assumptions. At last I burst into tears, and kneeling down, exclaimed, 'O Lord, I cannot unravel this web of iniquity: enable me to cut it in twain'." And so she did, to her own complete satisfaction. Another attack came from a humbler quarter:

One day Pat made his appearance with an important look, his brogues stamping the carpet with unwonted energy, his fine bare throat stiffened into a sort of dignified hauteur, and his very keen hazel eyes sparkling under the bushy luxuriance of chestnut curls that clustered about his face and fell on his neck. The very beau-ideal of a wild Irish youth was my friend Pat. Seating himself, as usual, he began—and here I must observe that my chief knowledge of the phraseology and turn of thought so peculiar to the Irish peasant was derived from this source. Whenever Pat came "to discourse me" I got rich lessons in the very brogue itself from the fidelity with which his spelling followed the pronunciation of his words.—"I wouldn't like," said he, "that you would go to hell."

"Nor I either, Pat."

"But you are out of the thrue church, and you won't be saved, and I must convart ye."

"That is very kind of you, my good lad: if I am wrong you cannot do better than set me right."

"Sure and I will."

"But how?"

"With this," said he, pulling out a small pamphlet, nothing the cleaner for wear. "You must learn my catechism, and it's you that will be the good Catholic."

But Butler's Catechism was also dismissed as "a tissue of falsehood and blasphemy", and it was Pat who became the good Protestant. The activities of Captain Rock increased as 1825, the fatal year of Pastorini's Prophecies, drew near: and Charlotte Elizabeth, who stoutly refused to learn from the gardener's wife the Popish way of signing the Cross, seemed likely to realize her childish ambition of martyrdom, but in 1824 she was obliged to go back to England. Her husband, it is implied, had returned from America in a state of mental derangement, and her only comforts were a deaf and dumb Irish boy whom she had adopted, a flow of tracts, the friendship of Mrs. Hannah More, and her own perfect health and ebullient spirits. A year later her brother, returning from service in the Peninsula, came to her rescue. Captain John Murray Browne, a distinguished soldier, was the author of *View of the Revolutions of Portugal since the close of the Peninsula War*, described by Southey as "a book of great ability, written with full knowledge of the subject on which it treats, in the best spirit, with sound judgment and perfect discretion". John VI of Portugal had wished to retain him as aide-de-camp, but he preferred to keep his British commission and complete a course at Sandhurst. "He was," according to his sister, "of most rare beauty from the cradle, increasing in loveliness as he grew up, and becoming the very model of a splendid man; very tall, large, commanding, with a face of perfect beauty, glowing, animated, mirthful—a gait so essentially military, that it was once remarked by an officer, 'If Browne were disguised as a washerwoman any soldier would give him the salute'."

She went to live with him and his family at Bagshot Heath, and, during a peaceful and happy two years, kept up a flow of religious writing—books, tracts and contributions to periodicals. Unfortunately her consequent prosperity was affected by her husband's claim to some part of her earnings, which could not be legally resisted: it was not till a quarter of a century later that Caroline Norton's case and writings directed public attention to this gross injustice. Her conscience obliged her to refuse a favourable offer from a popular magazine for anonymous tales, as moral as she pleased, but not, in her sense of the word, religious. It was a handsome spiritual compensation that some of her tracts, translated into Italian, were placed on the *Index Expurgatorius*: "I would not exchange for the value of the ten kingdoms ten times trebled, the joy that I feel in this high honour put upon me—this rich blessing of being under the papal curse."

The two shortest years of her life—so she calls them—had a sad sequel. Captain Browne rejoined his regiment in Ireland, and was drowned there. He was Mrs. Woodrooffe's Mr. James incarnate, lacking no charm or virtue, but only the saving grace of Vital Christianity. His sister went through an agony of doubt about his salvation, but persuaded herself that her constant prayers for him since her own conversion could not have been wasted, though he had not lived to recognize or proclaim his rebirth. Next year— "Most hateful year in the annals of England's perfidy to her bounteous Lord"—Charlotte Elizabeth recovered her equilibrium: she distributed tracts and handbills, and organized a petition against Catholic Emancipation from Sandhurst and its neighbourhood: nevertheless Antichrist triumphed. She consoled herself by activities which resulted in opening an Irish Episcopal Church in St. Giles's, and by exposing Irving's errors. For many years she edited *The Christian Lady's Magazine*, and for a short period, anonymously, the *Protestant Magazine*, her crusade against popery now including Tractarianism. In 1837 she paid a short visit to Ireland and found her expectations realized. "Popery rampant, insolent, overbearing, and evidently calculating on soon possessing the land in undisturbed security: Protestantism depressed, discouraged, menaced, and barely enjoying an uncertain toleration." Ulster was more congenial, and her two Orange Songs, *The Maiden City* and *No Surrender*, became very popular.

A verse from each will show their quality:

> Next, crushing all before him
> A Kingly wooer came

(The royal banner o'er him
    Blushed crimson deep for shame);
He showed the Pope's commission
    Nor dreamed to be refused;
She pitied his condition,
    But begged to stand excused.
In short, the fact is known, boys,
    She chased him from the hill,
For the Maiden on the throne, boys,
    Would be a maiden still.

Long may the crimson banner wave,
    A meteor streaming airy,
Portentous of the free and brave
    Who man the walls of Derry:
And Derry's sons alike defy
    Pope, traitor, or pretender;
And peal to heaven their 'prentice cry,
    Their patriot—"No Surrender!"

The same year Captain Phelan died, and in 1841 she married Lewis Hippolytus Tonna, Secretary of the United Service Institution, twenty-two years her junior, but completely sympathetic with her views religious and political.

Charlotte Elizabeth's stories and tracts are interesting only as a sign of her times: they need not be rescued from oblivion. But there is one book, an only less remarkable work for its date than the *Vindication of the Rights of Women*, for which her name should be honoured. Cast in a narrower mould than Mary Wollstonecraft, Mrs. Tonna has a share of her warm democratic sympathies and constructive imagination. *The Perils of the Nation* was hastily compiled at the request of the Christian Influence Society after the Chartist Riots of 1842, and published anonymously in 1843. The secret of its authorship was carefully guarded—it is still unknown to the *Dictionary of National Biography*—for, as her widower justly observes, "it was not to be supposed that legislators and those for whose perusal it was intended, would pay much attention to a work on such a subject, from a woman's pen". Yet it is clearly enough a woman's voice, and rings truer than that of her Socinian fellow-townswoman, Harriet Martineau, whose *laissez-faire* policy she vehemently denounces. She pleads for the whole programme since followed by factory legislation, and lets herself go over the ghastly consequences of unfenced machinery and the fraudulent iniquities of the truck system, and entreats the women of England to rescue their dressmakers and milliners from long hours and appalling sanitary conditions. Appeals to the Bible for support are, of course, frequent—it is Charlotte Elizabeth speaking—but she heroically denounces cheap Bibles as sweated goods. Like the farmer recently invited to join the Anti-Litter Campaign, she did not hold with birth control: "Where God sends mouths He will send meat", and is indignant with the remarks about superfluous brats so freely invented for their poor personages by Miss Martineau and Mrs. Marcet.

The book went rapidly into three editions and was widely read and discussed: it marks, and undoubtedly helped to create, that change of public opinion which resulted in the passing of the Ten Hours Bill and the sanitary legislation which followed it. *The Wrongs of Woman* also deals with the economic exploitation of the workers. She draws vivid pictures of the lives of a dressmaker's apprentice, a country labourer's wife, who went into a screw factory, and children employed as pin-headers and lace-makers.

For the last two years of her life Mrs. Tonna suffered from cancer: indomitable to the last she continued to write by means of a machine invented by herself, and attended the first meeting of the Evangelical Alliance in 1846, a few months before her death: "Sweetly refreshing to the spirit will ever be the remembrance of those five hours enjoyed in Exeter Hall".

Well, had fate decreed that I should choose one of those formidable deaf ladies as friend and companion, it would have been Charlotte Elizabeth Tonna, lovable despite her intolerance, rather than Harriet Martineau.

MARY SOMERVILLE 1780-1872

MARY SOMERVILLE enjoyed in her childhood none of the delights and temptations of an infant prodigy. Her freedom for self-development was the freedom of neglect and disapproval, which must have smothered and stifled ordinary tastes and talents. It was not to an iron will or an indomitable personality but to the sheer, quiet impulsion of genius that she owed her intellectual triumph.

She was born on December 26th, 1780, at the Jedburgh Manse, the house of her mother's sister, Mrs. Thomas Somerville. Her father, William Fairfax, a naval officer, descended from a junior branch of the family of the great Fairfax, was abroad then and for the greater part of her girlhood. In 1797 he was Duncan's flag-captain, and his share in the anxieties of the mutiny at the Nore and the glory of Camperdown was acknowledged by a knighthood. During his brief visits to his home he was a satisfactory father, a handsome hero, ready with stories of his adventures and breezy with his nervous wife, who prepared for a thunderstorm by removing the steel pins from her cap, and reading aloud appropriate descriptive passages from the Psalms to the frightened children. "Drink that, Peg," he would say, fetching her a glass of wine, "it will give you courage, for we are going to have a regular rat-tat-too." Later on Mary spent £20, given for an addition to her meagre trousseau, on a portrait of him painted just after Camperdown by Sir Archer Shee. Mrs. Fairfax was the daughter of Samuel Charters, Solicitor of the Customs for Scotland. After Mary's birth she settled in a house belonging to her father, near Burntisland, where Mary watched flights of goldfinches crowding on the thistles, and clumsy, tame, fat geese trying in vain to follow strings of their wild brethren. Burntisland was a picturesque and primitive spot in those days. The Passing-bell was rung by a crier, who announced the deaths of the townsfolk with a prefatory "Oyez! Oyez! Oyez!" The gaberlunzie man with his blue coat and tin badge was still a familiar figure, and the cripple in a hand-barrow, who was given a meal by one neighbour and then wheeled on to another for his next repast.

Mrs. Fairfax taught her little daughter to read the Bible and say her prayers, and also sent her to the public examinations in the kirk:

This was a severe trial for me; for, besides being timid and shy, I had a bad memory, and did not understand one word of the catechism. These meetings, which began with prayer, were attended by all the children of the town and neighbourhood, with their mothers, and a great many old women, who came to be edified. They were an acute race, and could quote chapter and verse of Scripture as accurately as the minister himself. I remember he said to one of them—"Peggie, what lightened the

206

world before the sun was made?" After thinking for a minute she said—"'Deed, sir, the question is mair curious than edifying".

Besides these public examinations, the minister made an annual visit to each household in his parish. When he came to us, the servants were called in, and we all knelt while he said a prayer; and then he examined each individual as to the state of his soul and conduct. He asked me if I could say my "Questions"—that is, the catechism of the Kirk of Scotland—and asked a question at random to ascertain the fact. He did the same to the servants.

Her mother found the child useful in picking fruit, shelling peas and beans, feeding the poultry, and looking after the dairy, but made no further attempt to educate her. When she was between eight and nine Captain Fairfax came home and was shocked to find her such a little savage:

I had not yet been taught to write, and although I amused myself reading the *Arabian Nights*, *Robinson Crusoe*, and the *Pilgrim's Progress*, I read very badly, and with a strong Scotch accent; so, besides a chapter of the Bible, he made me read a paper of the *Spectator* aloud every morning, after breakfast; the consequence of which discipline is that I have never since opened that book. Hume's *History of England* was also a real penance to me.

Captain Fairfax decided that his daughter must at

least know how to write and keep accounts, so at ten years old she was sent to a boarding-school at Mussel-burgh, where she was supremely miserable:

The change from perfect liberty to perpetual re-straint was in itself a great trial; besides, being naturally shy and timid, I was afraid of strangers and although Miss Primrose was not unkind she had an habitual frown, which even the elder girls dreaded. My future companions, who were all older than I, came round me like a swarm of bees, and asked if my father had a title, what was the name of our estate, if we kept a carriage, and other such questions, which made me feel the difference of station. However, the girls were very kind, and often bathed my eyes to prevent our stern mistress from seeing that I was perpetually in tears. A few days after my arrival, although perfectly straight and well-made, I was enclosed in stiff stays with a steel busk in front, while, above my frock, bands drew my shoulders back till the shoulder-blades met. In this constrained state I, and most of the younger girls, had to prepare our lessons. The chief thing I had to do was to learn by heart a page of Johnson's dictionary, not only to spell the words, give their parts of speech and meaning, but as an exercise of memory to remember their order of succession. Besides I had to learn the first principles of writing, and the rudiments of French and English grammar. The method of teaching was extremely tedious and inefficient. Our religious duties were attended to in a remarkable way. Some of the girls were Presbyterians, others belonged to the Church of England, so Miss Primrose cut the matter short by taking us all to the kirk in the morning and to church in the afternoon.

In our play-hours we amused ourselves with playing at ball, marbles, and especially at "Scotch and English", a game which represented a raid on the debatable land, or Border between Scotland and England, in which each party tried to rob the other of their playthings. The little ones were always compelled to be English, for the bigger ones thought it too degrading.

This purgatory endured for a year. Mrs. Fairfax was disappointed with the results. Mary had not learnt to keep accounts, and her writing was atrocious. She was incapable of composing a polite note to answer inquiries about her mother's health, and her elder brother, who was at the Edinburgh University, jeered when she sent him a bank-*knot*. But at least the little failure could revel in her freedom again. She wandered for hours on the shore alone, watching the sea-anemones and other creatures, collecting shells and fossils, and listening to the sailors' tales of the Kraken, the giant fish which could be mistaken for an island, and of the inevitable sea-serpent. In bad weather she devoured Shakespeare, but an officious maiden aunt, as a household feature, was added to her troubles: "I wonder you let Mary waste her time in reading, she never *shews* (sews) more than if she were a man." Thereupon she was sent to the village school to learn needlework, and care for the house linen became another of her domestic duties. All this disapproval rankled sorely: was it not an injustice to women that they should be given a desire for knowledge which it was so wrong for them to acquire? Still she persisted. Mrs. Chapone's *Letters to Young Women* was in their scant library, and most of the books on history which the young women were advised to read. She might have learnt Latin from the village schoolmaster, but Latin was, of course, suitable for boys only. Mrs. Fairfax, however, considered the use of the globes a not unfeminine, if somewhat superfluous, accomplishment, and he was allowed to give her daughter a few lessons. Mary was beginning to feel her feet. She spent hours at her bedroom window with a small celestial globe.

Religious observances were still a trial.

At Burntisland the sacrament was administered in summer because people came in crowds from the neighbouring parishes to attend the preachings. The service was long and fatiguing. A number of clergymen came to assist, and as the minister's manse could not accommodate them all, we entertained three of them, one of whom was always the Rev. Dr. Campbell, father of Lord Campbell.

Thursday was a day of preparation. The morning

service began by a psalm sung by the congregation,
then a prayer was said by the minister, followed by
a lecture on some chapter of the Bible, generally
lasting an hour, after that another psalm was sung,
followed by a prayer, a sermon which lasted seldom
less than an hour, and the whole ended with a
psalm, a short prayer and a benediction. Everyone
then went home to dinner and returned afterwards
for afternoon service, which lasted more than an
hour and a half. Friday was a day of rest, but I
together with many young people went at this
time to the minister to receive a stamped piece of
lead as a token that we were sufficiently instructed
to be admitted to Christ's table. This ticket was
given to the Elder on the following Sunday: On
Saturday there was a morning service, and on
Sunday such multitudes came to receive the sacrament that the devotions continued till late in the
evening. The ceremony was very strikingly and
solemnly conducted. The communicants sat on each
side of long narrow tables covered with white linen,
in imitation of the last supper of Christ, and the
Elders handed them bread and wine. After a short
exhortation from one of the ministers the first set
retired, and were succeeded by others. When the
weather was fine a sermon, prayers, and psalm-
singing took place either in the churchyard or on a
grassy bank at the Links for such as were waiting to
communicate. On the Monday morning there was
the same long service as on the Thursday. It was

too much for me; I always came home with a head-
ache and took a dislike to sermons.

Our minister was a rigid Calvinist. His sermons
were gloomy, and so long that he occasionally would
startle the congregation by calling out to some culprit, "Sit up there, how daur ye sleep i' the kirk!"
Some sawmills in the neighbourhood were burnt
down, so the following Sunday we had a sermon on
hell-fire. The kirk was very large and quaint: a stair
led to a gallery on each side of the pulpit, which was
intended for the tradespeople, and each division was
marked with a suitable device, and text from Scripture. On the bakers' portion a sheaf of wheat was
painted; a balance and weights on the grocers', and
on the weavers', which was opposite to our pew,
there was a shuttle, and below it the motto, "My
days are swifter than a weaver's shuttle, and are
spent without hop job".

Samuel Fairfax came home for Sundays—Mary's
one chance of companionship—and after a morning
at the kirk they used to escape to the rocks, and watch
whales spouting and porpoises at play. This was another
source of disapproval: the minister, an uncle by marriage, would send to inquire whether Mr. and Miss
Fairfax were ill, as he had not seen them at the afternoon service. In spite of all this they did not take their
religion too seriously. On one occasion, when they were
crossing the Firth in bad weather, Mrs. Fairfax
shouted to the skipper, " 'George, this is an awful

storm, I am sure we are in great danger. Mind how
you steer: remember, I trust in you.' He laughed and
said, 'Dinna trust in me, leddy; trust in God Almighty.'
Our mother, in perfect terror, called out, 'Dear me!
is it come to that?' We burst out laughing, skipper
and all."

When Mary was thirteen Mrs. Fairfax took lodgings
in Edinburgh for the winter and sent her to a writing
school, where at last she acquired a good hand, and
elementary arithmetic, though she objected all her life
to long addition sums. Account-keeping was obviously
not her vocation. An uncle gave her a piano, and she
had some music lessons, practising four or five hours a
day when they returned to Burntisland. She also, for
the sake of occupation, taught herself a little Latin.

That summer the clouds began to break. For the
first time in her life Mary's thirst for knowledge was
approved and encouraged. The friend—he might be
called her discoverer—was her uncle by marriage, Dr.
Thomas Somerville, minister of Jedburgh, in whose
manse she had been born. He was the author of two
historical works, on the Revolution, and on the Reign
of Queen Anne, and left in manuscript *My Own Life
and Times*, 1741-1814, with instructions that it should
not be published till some years after his death. This
can still be read with interest, as he knew many of the
famous people of his day, and traces intelligently the
various social and economic changes which he had
seen. Mrs. Somerville was a woman of far more
education and wider interests than her sister, Mrs.

Fairfax. Her husband records that she always prophesied a brilliant literary career for a certain youth, sometimes their guest, but only lived to enjoy his *Lay of the Last Minstrel* and *Marmion*.

With the Somervilles Mary spent some happy and stimulating months, reading Virgil before breakfast with him, and finding also a congenial companion in her aunt, a fellow-student of Shakespeare. She might have met there another intimate friend of her later life, a son of the village schoolmaster who taught writing to her cousins, but the future Sir David Brewster chanced to be away in Edinburgh.

Her next experience was a winter in Edinburgh with her uncle, William Charters, and his wife. Here she found no sympathy with her aspirations, and, since she could not talk about any of the subjects which interested her, was severely snubbed for her lack of expansiveness, more elegant and forthcoming young ladies being constantly praised at her expense. More writing and arithmetic, and a course at Strange's dancing school:

> Strange himself was exactly like a figure on the stage; tall and thin, he wore a powdered wig, with cannons at the ears, and a pigtail. Ruffles at the breast and wrists, white waistcoat, black silk or velvet shorts, white silk stockings, large silver buckles, and a pale blue coat completed his costume. He had a little fiddle on which he played, called a kit. My first lesson was how to walk and make a

curtsey: "Young lady, if you visit the Queen you must make three curtsies, lower and lower and lower as you approach her, So-o-o", leading me on and making the curtsey, "Now, if the Queen were to ask you to eat a bit of mutton with her, what would you say?" Every Saturday afternoon all the scholars, both boys and girls, met to practise in the public assembly rooms in George's Street. It was a handsome large hall with benches rising like an amphitheatre. Some of the elder girls were very pretty, and danced well, so these practisings became a lounge for officers from the Castle, and other young men. We used always to go in full evening dress. We learnt the *minuet de la cour*, reels and country dances. Our partners used to give us ginger-bread and oranges. Dancing before so many people was quite an exhibition, and I was greatly mortified one day when ready to begin a minuet, by the dancing-master shaking me roughly and making me hold out my frock properly.

She gives a curious sketch of Edinburgh civilization at this time. "In a small society like that of Edinburgh there was a good deal of scandal and gossip; every one's character and conduct were freely criticized, and by none more than by my aunt and her friends. She used to sit at a window embroidering, where she not only could see every one that passed, but with a small tele-scope could look into the dressing-room of a lady of her acquaintance, and watch all she did. A spinster lady of good family, a cousin of ours, carried her gossip so far that she was tried for defamation, and condemned to a month's imprisonment, which she actually underwent in the Tolbooth. She was let out just before the King's birthday, to celebrate which, besides the guns fired at the Castle, the boys let off squibs and crackers in all the streets. As the lady in question was walking up the High Street, some lads in a wynd, or narrow street, fired a small cannon, and one of the slugs with which it was loaded hit her mouth and wounded her tongue. This raised a universal laugh; and no one enjoyed it more than my uncle William, who disliked this somewhat masculine woman."

Political feeling ran high. This, the middle nineties, was, it will be remembered, the period of Lord Cockburn's agitated boyhood, and Eliza Fletcher's early married life. Mrs. Charters was a violent Tory, as, indeed, was Captain Fairfax. "The Liberals were distinguished by wearing their hair short, and when one day I happened to say how becoming a crop was, and that I wished the men would cut off those ugly pigtails, my father exclaimed, 'By G——, when a man cuts off his queue, the head should go with it'." Mary, a silent rebel, already smarting under the disabilities of girls, became a confirmed Liberal, and remained so all her life.

A Burntisland tea-party, with widows and maiden ladies as guests and a pool of commerce for sole entertainment, does not seem a likely source of inspiration for a mathematician. But so it was. Mary, intensely bored, fell into conversation with a girl about her fancy work, and was invited to go and see it:

I went next day, and after admiring her work, and being told how it was done, she showed me a monthly magazine with coloured plates of ladies' dresses, charades and puzzles. At the end of a page I read what appeared to me to be simply an arithmetical question; but on turning the page I was surprised to see strange looking lines mixed with letters, chiefly X's and Y's, and asked "What is that?" "Oh," said Miss Ogilvie, "it is a kind of arithmetic; they call it Algebra; but I can tell you nothing about it." And we talked about other things; but on going home I thought I would look if any of our books could tell me what was meant by Algebra.

In Robertson's *Navigation*, I flattered myself that I had got precisely what I wanted; but I soon found that I was mistaken. I perceived, however, that astronomy did not consist in star-gazing, and as I persevered in studying the book for a time, I certainly got a dim view of several subjects which were useful to me afterwards. Unfortunately not one of our acquaintances or relations knew anything of science or natural history; nor, had they done so, should I have had courage to ask any of them a question, for I should have been laughed at. I was often very sad and forlorn; not a hand held out to help me.

There it rested for the time. When Mrs. Fairfax and

her daughter went again to Edinburgh, Mary had lessons from Nasmyth, the landscape painter, who, it may be noted, afterwards told another pupil that Miss Mary Fairfax was the cleverest young lady he ever taught. She overheard him say in teaching perspective to some other girls:

"You should study Euclid's Elementary Geometry, the foundation not only of perspective, but of astronomy and all mechanical science." Here, in the most unexpected manner, I got the information I wanted, for I at once saw that it would help me to understand some parts of Robertson's *Navigation*; but as to going to a bookseller and asking for Euclid the thing was impossible! Besides I did not yet know anything definite about Algebra, so no more could be done at that time; but I never lost sight of an object which had interested me from the first.

Her opportunity came when they returned to Burntisland. A tutor for her youngest brother was now living with them, a fair classical scholar, but, of course, no mathematician. Fortune was not so lavish in her gifts to Mary. However:

He was a simple, good-natured kind of man and I ventured to ask him about algebra and geometry, and begged him the first time he went to Edinburgh, to buy me something elementary on these subjects, so he soon brought me *Euclid* and Bonnycastle's *Algebra*, which were the books used in the

schools at that time. Now I had got what I so long
and earnestly desired. I asked Mr. Craw to hear me
demonstrate a few problems in the first book of
Euclid, and then I continued the study alone with
courage and assiduity, knowing I was on the right road.

Then came another check. She sat up late reading
Euclid, and the servants reported her extravagant use
of candles to Mrs. Fairfax, who ordered that her light
should be taken away as soon as she was in bed. Then
her father came home on leave and disapproved of her
studies. "Peg," he said to his wife, "we must put a
stop to this, or we shall have Mary in a strait-jacket
one of these days. There was X., who went raving mad
about the longitude!"

That strange woman, Mrs. Fairfax, refused to go
into society during her husband's absence, and, when
Mary grew up, she had to find other chaperones for
winter gaieties in Edinburgh. The Countess of
Buchan, a distant connection, took charge of her at
the first ball, and her first partner was Gilbert Elliot,
afterwards Earl of Minto. In appearance she was the
essence of feminity, tiny with a pretty figure and well-
set head, a lovely complexion and quantities of soft
brown hair; the well-known bust, made in her beautiful old age, speaks for her features. Still, and always,
shy and diffident as the result of constant repression in
her childhood, she was a social success, never lacking
partners and enjoying a little quiet flirtation. She and
her girl friends were not hampered by social conven-

219

tions. They met their young men for a promenade in Princes Street, and invited them to little supper-parties. Though Mary enjoyed her dances and theatres and popularity, she never lost sight of the great object of her life. At daybreak she rose, wrapped herself in a blanket, and read algebra or the classics till breakfast time. She records that she never allowed herself to get tired and muddled, but broke off in time, and rested her brain with needlework or poetry or Mrs. Radcliffe's novels.

When she was twenty-four Mary Fairfax married Samuel Greig, a distant cousin on her mother's side. His father had been sent at Catherine's request to organize the Russian Navy, and the son became Russian consul in London. Neither she nor her daughter explains this marriage, and we are left wondering whether she danced into it lightheartedly, or accepted it as the readiest escape from home limitations. There was no intellectual sympathy. Mr. Greig took as low a view of female intelligence as the rest of her family, and had no knowledge of, or interest in, any science. Luckily he was out all day, and she could pursue her mathematical studies, though without encouragement of any sort. Her chief friend was Countess Catharine Woronzow, afterwards Lady Pembroke. She chaperoned the Countess to the opera, and occasionally dined at the Russian Embassy, but had no general society. Two sons were born. The younger died in childhood; the elder, Woronzow, apparently the one compensation for her marriage, was a constant help and comfort to her till his death, seven years before her own.

After three years of married life, Mr. Greig died, and his widow took her children back to the old home in Burntisland. She had now read plane and spherical trigonometry, conic sections and some astronomy, and had solved an algebraic prize problem set in a mathematical journal, for which she was awarded a silver medal. The editor became Professor of Mathematics at the Edinburgh University, and helped her in the selection of a small library. For the first time, at thirty-three, she had the necessary books at her command. She had also independent means, and faced the disapproval of her family, making no further attempts to conceal her studies. The *Edinburgh Review* was in full swing: she began a lasting friendship with Brougham and Sydney Smith, and the elderly Playfair, susceptible to a little adroit feminine flattery, did not disdain to take an interest in her work, and give her good advice. Her reputation for cleverness and eccentricity was not a protection against suitors: she was too pretty. One of these accompanied his proposal with a volume of sermons, the page ostentatiously turned down at a peculiarly offensive effusion on the duties of a wife. This, as she crisply remarks, was as impertinent as it was premature.

But the right man was on his way, although he had tarried long. William Somerville, eldest son of the minister at Jedburgh, who had been the first to encourage Mary in her thirst for learning, was an army surgeon. He went with Sir James Craig to the Cape of Good Hope in 1795, became Garrison-Surgeon after the capture of Capetown, and was employed on confidential missions to the Kaffir tribes, involving considerable personal danger; and later he held appointments under Sir James Craig in the Mediterranean and in Canada. Somerville's exploits in South Africa, although he was never induced to make a book of his adventures, appealed to Mary's early love of the heroic, and, like her father, he was handsome and had delightful manners. Moreover he was interested in various branches of natural science, was a good classical scholar, a Liberal in politics, and, as she notes, he spoke good English and was emancipated from Scotch prejudices. After all she was half English herself by blood: in disposition perhaps more English than Scotch. William Somerville, like herself, had been disapproved of by the family, except by his broad-minded father and mother. They were enthusiastic about the marriage, but a future sister-in-law wrote that she "hoped I would give up my foolish manner of life and studies, and make a respectable and useful wife to her brother". Peace did not come at once, as some members of this trying family insisted on sharing their honeymoon in the Lakes.

Their first years were spent in Edinburgh, as Somerville became head of the Army Medical Department in Scotland. They often went to merry little suppers at Abbotsford with Adam Ferguson and Willie Clark as fellow guests, singing in chorus before the party broke up:

222

Weel may we a' be,
Ill may we never see;
Health to the King
And the gude companie.

The Waverley novels were still a mystery, but, after the publication of one of them, Woronzow Greig remarked, "I knew all these stories long ago, for Mr. Scott writes on the dinner-table. When he has finished, he puts the green-cloth with the papers in a corner of the dining-room; and when he goes out, Charlie Scott and I read the stories." Years later when they were saying good-bye to Sir Walter before his journey to Italy, he kissed Mrs. Somerville, saying "Farewell, my dear; I am going to die abroad like other British novelists." No doubt he had in mind Fielding and the *Voyage to Lisbon*.

In 1816 Somerville was appointed a member of the Army Medical Board, and they went to live in Hanover Square. An introduction to Sir William Herschel led to a day at Slough, where they examined his telescopes and the records of his discoveries. Unfortunately Caroline Herschel had already gone to live in Germany; Mrs. Somerville and she never met, but the young John Herschel, afterwards one of her closest friends, was of the party. A visit to Paris put her in touch with the leading French savants. Arago, a brilliant talker, showed them all the instruments at the Observatory. They also visited his greater confrère, the Marquis de la Place, who at once accepted Mrs.

Somerville as a fellow student, and pleased her by the gift of an inscribed copy of the *Système du Monde*. Among the rest of this brilliant circle were Baron Humboldt and M. and Madame Cuvier of the Jardin des Plantes. The winter of 1817 was spent in Italy, where she made many new friends and acquaintances. In Venice she saw Byron in the distance at a reception, but he was then ignoring his fellow countrymen. It is interesting that so trained an observer as Mary Somerville failed to notice his lameness: this lends some support to the recent view that the limp was an hysterical symptom.

The life in Hanover Square was in happy contrast to Mrs. Somerville's first lonely experience of London. Dinner parties could be very agreeable when Lord Melbourne and Macaulay, Sidney Smith and Tom Moore, Rogers and Sir James Mackintosh were among the guests. The only drawback was that the men sat so long at the table, and the conversation of the ladies alone in the drawing-room was apt to be boring. Modesty and good manners did not permit her to behave like Mme. de Staël, who, dining with Sir James Mackintosh, flounced about the drawing-room; then, with a *ceci est insupportable!* suddenly rang the bell and said: "Tell your master to come upstairs directly; they have sat long enough at their wine." Not that Mrs. Somerville despised her sex: then and always she had many women friends, but she did require a certain standard of intelligence and width of interests. The Somervilles also came into contact with the leading scientists of the day. Dr. Wollaston, the celebrated chemist and mineralogist, was a constant visitor. They had made a considerable collection of minerals in the course of their travels, and learnt much from him, and were the confidants of some of his many discoveries. Another friend was Babbage, then engaged on perfecting his calculating machines.

Mrs. Somerville's comment following her allusion to Babbage is a self-revelation:

> Nothing has afforded me so convincing a proof of the unity of the Deity as these purely mental conceptions of numerical and mathematical science which have been by slow degrees vouchsafed to man, and are still granted in these latter times by the Differential Calculus, now superseded by the Higher Algebra, all of which must have existed in that sublimely omniscient Mind from eternity.

She notes that neither she nor her husband ever entered into religious controversy with their friends. Perhaps it was as well: some of them might have found the Mind uncomfortably omniscient, while others doubted its existence. Strong in her own personal religious convictions she was never disturbed by any of the subversive scientific discoveries which came thick and fast during her lifetime. Truth could never destroy but only illuminate her conception of the Deity. A letter to her father-in-law, written after the death of their eldest little girl in 1823, shows the depth of her own faith:

I never was so long of writing to you, but when the heart is breaking it is impossible to find words adequate to its relief. We are in deep affliction, for though the first violence of grief has subsided, there has succeeded a calm sorrow not less painful, a feeling of hopelessness in this world which only finds comfort in the prospect of another, which longs for the consummation of all things that we may join those who have gone before. To return to the duties of life is irksome, even to those duties which were a delight when the Candle of the Lord shone upon us. I do not arraign the decrees of Providence, but even in the bitterness of my soul I acknowledge the wisdom and goodness of God, and endeavour to be resigned to His will. It is ungrateful not to remember the many happy years we have enjoyed, but that very remembrance renders our present state more desolate and dreary, presenting a sad contrast. The great source of consolation is in the mercy of God and the virtue of those we lament; the full assurance that no good disposition can be lost but must be brought to perfection in a better world. Our business is to render ourselves fit for that blessed inheritance that we may again be united to those we mourn.

This was not the only misfortune. They lost nearly all their money through misplaced trust in someone responsible, and Dr. Somerville felt obliged to accept the appointment of physician to the Chelsea Hospital. There was, of course, no Embankment: the damp

affected Mrs. Somerville's health, and the distance
from her former friends was a great drawback. She
now made the acquaintance of Lady Byron, who was
living at Esher. Ada studied mathematics by her
advice and often stayed at the Hospital.

Another new friend was Maria Edgeworth, who
describes her thus:

> Mrs. Somerville is the lady who, Laplace says, is
> the only woman who understands his works. She
> draws beautifully, and while her head is among the
> stars her feet are firm upon the earth.

> Mrs. Somerville is little, slightly made, fairish
> hair, pink colour, small, grey, round, intelligent,
> smiling eyes, very pleasing countenance, remarkably
> soft voice, strong, but well-bred Scotch accent;
> timid, not disqualifying timid, but naturally modest,
> yet with a degree of self-possession through it which
> prevents her being in the least awkward, and gives
> her all the advantage of her understanding, at the
> same time that it adds a prepossessing charm to her
> manner and takes off all dread of her superior
> scientific learning.

A tour with Sir James Mackintosh in the Nether-
lands and Germany brought mental refreshment: she
renewed relations with Quetelet, the great statistician,
who never failed to send her his publications, and met
Schlegel for the first time. She notes with amusement
that, at a dinner-party at the Hague, a lady, hearing
the name Abercromby, said in the current language of

the Evangelicals, "Pray, Lord Granville, is that a son of the great captain whom the Lord slew in the land of Egypt?" On one occasion she herself inadvertently figured as one of that persuasion. Invited to dinner by the eccentric Madame de Montalembert, and told to wear high dress, on entering the drawing-room, she found a bishop and several clergymen, "Lady Olivia Sparrow, and some other ladies all in high black satin dresses and white lace caps, precisely the dress I wore, and I thought it a curious coincidence. The party was lively enough, and agreeable, but the conversation was in a style I had never heard before—in fact, it affected the phraseology of the Bible. We all went after dinner to a sort of meeting at Exeter Hall, I quite forget for what purpose, but our party was on a kind of raised platform. I mentioned this to a friend afterwards, and the curious circumstance of our all being dressed alike, 'Do you not know,' she said, 'that dress is assumed as a distinctive mark of the Evangelical party! So you were a wolf in sheep's clothing!' "

Mary Somerville's attainments were now recognized by an inner circle, though she was quite unaware of their unusual nature, regarding herself as a self-educated woman, rather below than above the ordinary university standard. The following letter from Lord Brougham to her husband, written early in 1827, astounded her:

My Dear Sir,
    I fear you will think me very daring for the

design I have formed against Mrs. Somerville, and still more for making you my advocate with her; through whom I have every hope of prevailing. There will be sent to you a prospectus, rules, and a preliminary treatise of our Society for Diffusing Useful Knowledge, and I assure you I speak without any flattery when I say that of the two subjects which I find it most difficult to see the chance of executing there is one, which, unless Mrs. Somerville will undertake, none else can, and it must be left undone, though about the most interesting of of the whole, I mean an account of the Mécanique Céleste; the other is an account of the Principia, which I have some hopes of at Cambridge. The kind of thing wanted is such a description of that divine work as will both explain to the unlearned the sort of thing it is, the plan, the vast merit, the wonderful truths unfolded or methodized, and the Calculus by which all this is accomplished, and will also give a somewhat deeper insight to the uninitiated; two treatises would do this. No one without trying it can conceive how far we may carry ignorant readers into an understanding of the depths of science, and our treatises have about 100 to 800 pages of space each, so that she might give the more popular view, and another the analytical abstracts and illustrations. In England there are now not twenty people who know this great work, except by name; and not a hundred who know it even by name. My firm belief is that Mrs. Somerville could add two cyphers to each of those figures. Will you be my counsel in this suit? Of course our names are concealed, and no one of our council but myself needs to know it.

Yours ever most truly,

H. BROUGHAM.

Brougham followed up his letter by a visit to Chelsea and both he and Dr. Somerville urged her to make an attempt. Her reply may be given in her own words:

Lord Brougham, you must be aware that the work in question never can be popularized, since the student must at least know something of the differential and integral calculi, and as a preliminary step I should have to prove various problems in physical mechanics and astronomy. Besides, La Place never gives diagrams or figures, because they are not necessary to persons versed in the calculus, but they would be indispensable in a work such as you wish me to write. I am afraid I am incapable of such a task: but as you both wish it so much, I shall do my best upon condition of secrecy, and that if I fail the manuscript shall be put into the fire.

Mrs. Somerville attributes her own success to perseverance, but she had another enviable and far rarer power, that of concentration. She wrote in her drawing-room, hiding her papers when the bell rang, like that other writer whose books she loved. It was, she says, like putting a mark in a book she might be reading: when the interruption by visitors or children was over, she could find her place again without difficulty or delay. Once, when she was sitting in the front row at an entertainment in Rome, the improvisatrice turned upon her, and poured out a torrent of panegyric. She remained unmoved. Some problem absorbed her, and she had not heard a word of it.

When the manuscript was ready it was submitted to Sir John Herschel, who had no doubts about publication. His criticisms consisted mainly in suggestions for a fuller treatment of certain points: she did not sufficiently grasp the ignorance of her readers. Dr. Whewell was so much enraptured by his presentation copy that he broke into verse:

Lady, it was the wont in earlier days
When some fair volume from a valued pen,
Long looked for, came at last, the grateful men
Hailed its forthcoming in complacent lays:
As if the Muse would gladly haste to praise
That which her mother, Memory, long should keep
Among her treasures. Shall such usage sleep
With us, who feel too slight the common phrase
For our pleased thoughts of you, when thus we find
That dark to you seems bright, perplexed seems plain,
Seen in the depths of a pellucid mind,
Full of clear thought, pure from the ill and vain
That cloud the inward light! an honoured name
Be yours; and peace of heart grow with your
    growing fame.

It was adopted forthwith as a text book in the

University. This Mrs. Somerville considered the highest honour she ever received. It was indeed remarkable: an honour which Brougham was not allowed to share. He complained that "though the Cambridge men admit my analysis of the 'Principia' to be unexceptionable, and to be well calculated for teaching the work, yet, *not being by a Cambridge man*, it cannot be used!"

A husband is a very useful bit of furniture, as Mary Wollstonecraft remarked to Godwin in one of her happier moments. The "new woman" had not yet appeared, and there was nothing formidable about Mrs. Somerville's personality. Her long struggle had left no touch of defiance, only diffidence and modesty. But, for the nervous male, the adjunct of a husband made her quite "safe" in Henry James's sense of the word. Would Cambridge have arranged a Progress little less royal than Queen Elizabeth's own without Dr. Somerville and the sanctity of a four-poster bed? Here is Professor Sedgwick's letter about the arrangements for their reception:

My Dear Somerville,

Your letter delighted us. I have ordered dinner on Thursday at $6\frac{1}{2}$ and shall have a small party to welcome you and Mrs. Somerville. In order that we may not have to fight for you, we have been entering on the best arrangements we can think of. On Tuesday you will, I hope, dine with Peacock; on Wednesday with Whewell; on Thursday at the

Observatory. For Friday, Dr. Clarke, our Professor of Anatomy, puts in a claim. For the other days of your visit we shall, D.V., find ample employment. A four-poster bed now (a thing utterly out of our regular monastic system) will rear its head for you and Madame in the chambers immediately below my own; and your handmaid may safely rest her bones in a small inner chamber. You will of course drive to the great gate of Trinity College, and my servant will be waiting at the Porter's lodge to show you the way to your academic residence. We have no cannons at Trinity College, otherwise we would fire a salute at your entry; we will however give you the warmest greeting we can.

Other honours followed the publication of the *Mechanism of the Heavens*. Mrs. Somerville was elected an honorary member of various learned societies both British and foreign, and her bust by Chantrey was placed in the hall of the Royal Society. Peel secured for her a Civil List pension of £200, afterwards raised to £300 by Lord John Russell. Under all this limelight the family at last discerned their duckling to be a swan. They became positively proud of her.

Some copies of the preface to the *Mechanism of the Heavens* were printed separately for friends to whom the book itself would have been unintelligible. Maria Edgeworth wrote: "I was long in the state of the boa constrictor after a full meal, and I am but just recovering the powers of motion. My mind was so distended by the magnitude, the immensity of what you put into it!" In her "trade of sentence-monger" she picked out for admiration a passage on the propagation of sound: "So that at a very small height above the surface of the earth, the noise of the tempest ceases and the thunder is heard no more in those boundless regions, where the heavenly bodies accomplish their periods in eternal and sublime silence." Joanna Baillie was "greatly honoured by receiving such a mark of regard from one who has done more to remove the light estimation in which the capacity of women is too often held, than all that has been accomplished by the whole sisterhood of poetical damsels and novel-writing authors." In a later letter Miss Baillie gives an amusing account of scientific talk in London society. "I called upon a lady of rank who has *fashionable* learned folks coming about her, and she informed me that there are new ideas regarding philosophy entertained in the world, and that Sir John Herschel was now considered as a slight, second-rate man, or person. Who are the first-rate she did not say, and, I suppose, you will not be much mortified to hear that your name was not mentioned at all." It must have been at some such gathering that a lady drew the economist aside, saying, "Let you and I have a little talk about Space, Mr. Ricardo."

Before Brougham's proposal Mary Somerville had not dreamt of writing: now she had tasted blood and felt herself at a loose end until she began her book on the *Connexion of the Physical Sciences*. Some of it was written in Paris, where she went, partly for her own health and partly for her daughters' education. There she met old friends, and made many new ones, including the inevitable Lafayette.

Mrs. Somerville often went to the Miss Berrys' receptions, and was much attached to the elder sister, Mary, for whom she felt a special sympathy. "She was a Latin scholar, spoke and wrote French fluently, yet with all these advantages, the consciousness that she might have done something better, had female education been less frivolous, gave her a characteristic melancholy which lasted through life." Miss Berry's acknowledgment of the *Connexion of the Physical Sciences* confirms this impression:

I have just finished reading your book, which has entertained me extremely, and at the same time, I hope, improved my moral character in the Christian virtue of humility. These must appear to you such *odd* results—so little like those produced on the great majority of your readers, that you must allow me to explain them to you. Humbled, I must be, by finding my own intellect unequal to following, beyond a first step, the explanations by which you seek to make easy to comprehension the marvellous phenomena of the universe—humbled, by feeling the intellectual difference between you and me, placing you as much above me in the scale of reasoning beings, as I am above my dog. Still I rejoice with humility at feeling myself in that order of understandings, which, although utterly incapable of following the chain of your reasonings, calculations, and inductions—utterly deprived of the powers necessary *sic itur ad astra*—am yet informed, enlightened, and entertained with the series of sublime truths to which you conduct me.

The new book was published soon after her return to Chelsea. It was dedicated to Queen Adelaide, who thanked the author at a drawing-room. The Duchess of Kent also accepted a copy at a private audience, and Mrs. Somerville had half an hour's conversation with her and the Princess Victoria. Did the youthful Princess feel that this pretty little learned lady was stepping out of Woman's Sphere, about the limitations of which she afterwards held such very definite views? Hallam found a historical error: Mrs. Somerville had made the Egyptian year six hours too long. She gratefully accepted his correction in her second edition, which had a wide circulation. It was translated into German and Italian, and pirated in the United States.

Then came a long gap. Dr. Somerville's health broke down, and he and his wife and their two daughters lived abroad, mainly in Italy, till his death in 1860. She was working intermittently on her *Physical Geography*, although it was not ready for publication till 1859. For this book she was awarded the Victoria Medal by the Royal Geographical Society, and, ten years later, the first gold medal given by the Italian Geographical Society. She was also preached against by name in York Cathedral: such notoriety left her unperturbed. Everywhere the Somervilles enjoyed the best of company, English and foreign, and innumerable learned societies elected Mrs. Somerville to membership. During a winter in Florence the Grand Duke allowed her to take home books from his library in the Pitti Palace, a favour hitherto granted only to the directors.

Dr. Somerville was a remarkable man, and a still more remarkable husband. His own early career had been both adventurous and distinguished, but he had recognized his wife's genius from the first, and ungrudgingly placed all his gifts and knowledge at her disposal. Without his help she must have achieved less, as he often set her free for the higher intellectual work by ransacking libraries and even copying her manuscripts. After his death Mrs. Somerville and her daughters remained in Italy. She was deaf and easily tired, but could still write daily from 8 o'clock in the morning till 12 or 1, her pet mountain sparrow perched on her arm. Her new undertaking was a book on *Molecular and Microscopic Science*, with a motto from St. Augustine, *Deus magnus in magnis, maximus in minimis*. She afterwards regretted having spent so much time on this popular work. "Mathematics are the natural bent of my mind. If I had devoted myself exclusively to that study, I might probably have written something useful, as a new era had begun in that science." In extreme old age she returned again to pure mathematics, studying new books and revising a treatise she had laid aside years before on the *Theory of Differences*. On the very day of her death she was still at work.

Mrs. Somerville never regarded herself as an exceptional woman, or rested content with her own honours. Things had moved since her youth, but there was still a prejudice against a sound literary and scientific education for women. Girls were still suffering from the injustice she herself had suffered and had never forgotten. She signed the rejected petition to the Senate of the London University, praying that degrees should be granted to women, and hailed the foundation of Girton College with delight. Her name headed the Women's Suffrage petition of 1868, and Mill's *Subjection of Women* won her warm approval. She was a true democrat in the great tradition of Mary Wollstonecraft.

Preserved from her one great dread, the decay of her intellectual faculties, Mary Somerville died in her sleep on November 29th, 1872, within a month of her ninety-second birthday.

HARRIET GROTE 1792-1878

HARRIET LEWIN was born in the summer of 1792. Her father had spent ten years in the Madras Civil Service. On the voyage back he fell in with a Madame Grand, once the mistress of Philip Francis in Calcutta. They lived together in Paris for a time, and Lewin drove his four-in-hand to the Royal Meets. The lady continued to receive an annuity from him even after she became the Princess Talleyrand.

This episode never troubled Harriet. Her father was her ideal and from him she inherited her fine physique, her brains and her high spirits. Mrs. Lewin, the eldest of General Hale's twenty children, married at fifteen and became herself the mother of a large family. Her babies were her dolls, and she left the elder children to fight for their liberty with successive governesses. The Lewins had country houses near Southampton and at Torquay, and Harriet had her fill of climbing trees, riding bare-backed, and rowing leaky boats, a forced loan from the fishermen. Her lessons gave her no trouble; thanks to the detested governesses and her own intelligence she was sufficiently well-grounded to profit by more judicious instruction when the time came.

Later on, when the Lewins were living in Kent, near Bexley, Harriet enjoyed all the pleasures of a social girlhood. In appearance she was handsome, with a commanding presence, a delicate complexion, and large luminous eyes, compared by one of her admirers to carriage lamps.

"Perhaps it would have been difficult," she writes, "to find twenty-five couples of dancers wherein beauty, grace, and form were so largely present as in these Kentish meetings of 1814-1820. The Barnards, the Normans, the Edens, the Berens, the Stones, Jenners, and Lewins; the Johnstons, the Wells, the Townshends, the Whitmores, the Cators, and others, furnished forth their attractive contingents; while the parents of the young people, mostly of middle age, and still full of relish for festive enjoyments, amused themselves by looking on, and peradventure scrutinizing the relations growing up among the 'lads and lassies' in the interval of the game."

One neighbour's name is conspicuously absent from this list, with its discreet dichotomy. Andreas Grote, like John Baring before him, came over from North Germany in the middle of the eighteenth century to seek and make his fortune in England. Beginning as a merchant, he afterwards established a banking business with George Prescott in Threadneedle Street. With his house on the Point at Greenwich, his men-servants and carriages, his membership, no doubt, *du Surrey Hunt et de plusieurs autres Hunts*, and his portraits of himself and lady by Sir Joshua Reynolds, Grote became in his own eyes the complete English gentleman, and in those of his neighbours another pushing Dutchman, like Angerstein of Westcombe

Park. His son George married Selina Peckwell, a god-daughter of Selina, Countess of Huntingdon, who brought a strain of French blood into the family, as her maternal forbears, the Blossets, were Huguenots who had settled in Ireland.

The young couple set up house at Clay Hill, near Beckenham, where their eldest son, another George, was born on November 17th, 1794. His mother taught him to read and write adding some instruction in Latin Grammar, but her anxiety about his education induced her to send him to the Sevenoaks Grammar School at the age of five and a half. Four years later he went to his father's old school, Charter-house, where, but for a tendency to wander out of bounds, and a final flogging at the close of his career when he had entertained his friends too well at the Albion Tavern, his record was unblemished.

Mr. Grote obliged his son to enter the banking-house at sixteen. These early years were unhappy. Young Grote, although he forced himself to become an admirable man of business, was a born scholar. His mother had now become absorbed in a narrow Calvinism and withdrew her sympathy from his intellectual pursuits. Grote senior avoided friction by leaving the care of his eleven children mainly to his wife, who insisted on a narrow and secluded home life. His own tastes were entirely those of a country gentleman, and he spent little time in Threadneedle Street. The size of the family made it difficult to secure quiet for study at home, and John, who alone shared George's interests in later life, was nineteen years his junior. Happily he found congenial company in two neighbours of his own age, George Warde Norman and Charles Hay Cameron. Norman became an authority on finance and a Director of the Bank of England. Cameron was called to the Bar, and acted later as Macaulay's adviser in India. He married Julia Pattle, whose photographs still impress us with the distinction and beauty of their friends and contemporaries. Another neighbour was Peter Elmsley, the Porsonian, who became Grote's mentor in his classical studies.

The Normans, it will have been observed, were county, above suspicion, and through them George Grote was admitted to the lively cricket matches and dances, and soon fell in love with Harriet Lewin, who was two years his senior. Unfortunately he made Elmsley his confidant, and was told that Miss Lewin's affections were already engaged. His misery was so obvious that Mr. Grote asked the cause, and extracted a promise that he would propose to no one without his leave. It soon transpired that the Reverend Peter's information was a jealous invention: he had been himself rejected by the fair Harriet. George begged to be released from his pledge, but Mr. Grote, who intended to bestow his son on some suitable city heiress, was adamant.

George gave up all hope of Harriet, and took refuge in writing verse, and in historical and classical studies. His interest in political economy secured him an introduction to Ricardo, at whose house he met James

Mill in 1818. Mill was then an examiner to the East India Company. He had already published his *History of British India* and was engaged upon the *Analysis of the Human Mind*. At first Grote did not find him prepossessing. "His mind has, indeed, all that cynicism and asperity which belong to the Benthamian school, and what I chiefly dislike in him is the readiness and seeming preference with which he dwells on the *faults and defects* of others—even of the greatest men! But it is so very rarely that a man of any depth comes across my path, that I shall most assuredly cultivate his acquaintance a good deal farther." The acquaintance developed into discipleship, and Grote became for a time as intolerant as his master. He was also admitted to the venerable Bentham's *tête à tête* dinners in the top-floor room with the organ at Queen Square Place.

In March, 1818, he saw Harriet Lewin again, and wrote a naïve account of the disturbance of mind produced by the unexpected meeting. "I stood then, and conversed with her for about ten minutes, but something—I know not what it is—kept me during the whole of the time in such a state of indescribable tremor and uneasiness, that I could hardly utter a rational sentence. She looked lovely beyond expression. Her features still retained the same life and soul which once did so magnetize me; I never have seen it, and I never shall see it, on any other face." Mr. Grote now gave his grudging consent to the marriage on condition that it was delayed for two years, and that there should be no intercourse in the meantime between the two families. The Lewins and Harriet herself; who always retained a pleasing sense of her social superiority to the Grotes, resented this attitude. During their engagement they met seldom, but exchanged daily diaries. Grote's were chiefly occupied with his reading. Harriet also worked hard, writing themes at her lover's bidding, and digests of the books he chose for her. Mr. Grote probably raised further objections, as on March 5th, 1820, George Grote and Harriet Lewin were secretly married at Bexley Church. Harriet went back to her father's house, and two days later revealed the truth to him. Mr. Grote was kept in the dark for a month, and his forgiveness was accompanied by a very narrow allowance to the young people.

He insisted that George and his wife should live in one of the houses adjoining the bank. Harriet, who had always been used to fresh air and exercise, hated the Threddle. She was desperately ill early in 1821 after the birth of their only child, a boy who died at a week old. They took a house at Hampstead during her convalescence and there Grote wrote his *Statement of the Question of Parliamentary Reform*. An *Analysis of the Influence of Natural Religion on the Temporal Happiness of Mankind* was compiled from Bentham's papers, and issued the following year under the pseudonym of Philip Beauchamp by Richard Carlile from the security of Dorchester Gaol. They continued to spend part of the week out of the City for the sake of Harriet's health, and acquired a small house at Stoke Newington in 1826. She drove herself in and out in an open chaise, which was also useful for holiday excursions.

James Mill was a frequent visitor in Threadneedle Street, but Harriet disapproved of his influence upon her husband. "Mill, the elder," she said, "had seized him at the most enthusiastic time of life, and narrowed him, under the idea that he was emancipating him." Grote's intolerance was a sore trial at this period of their married life. A democrat in theory, "burning with desire to see all his fellow-creatures equal, yet not able to exchange a word with a common vulgar man without disgust", he could only enjoy the company of men of his own way of thinking, like the Mills and the Austins, Ricardo and John Smith, Romilly and MacCulloch and a few political refugees. Mill had imparted his very definite agnosticism to Grote, and Harriet, who had been brought up in strictly orthodox views, suffered from abandoning her faith as the result of her husband's merciless dialectic. To the end of her life she described herself as a member of the Church of England: it was at any rate respectable; she would have resented an imputation of Unitarianism. Worse than that —she was obliged to give up her "numerous friends and connections among the aristocratic portion of society". Sometimes she enjoyed a lively interlude with her old friends, the Plumers, in Hertfordshire, but Grote would seldom accompany her, and when there "he could not dissemble the indifference he felt for everything that was not associated with books". She hints that but for this lack of adaptability she might have inherited Gilston Park.

In 1822 Grote began work on his *History of Greece*, probably at the instigation of James Mill. His absorption was distressing to Harriet who longed to travel: "all the anticipations fed and cherished by the mutual ardour of commencing happiness, have, on the part of my husband, faded into indifference towards those schemes—schemes which once it afforded us so much delight to construct. Since *he* no longer desires to realize them, they are vanished for me. An absorbing thirst of literary renown now fills up every avenue of his imagination, nor is there left any relish for the contemplation of natural beauty, or works of fancy or art, all of which certainly yield to a sensible mind many enjoyments of an innocent, if not an elevating, character." He retained his interest in psychology and logic, and a few years later invited John Stuart Mill's group of young men, who had originally called themselves *The Utilitarian Society*, to meet twice a week in Threadneedle Street. They assembled at 8.30, and Harriet, who, we may be sure, gave them an excellent breakfast, used to gibe at *The Brangles* and their discussions on "the inconceivability of the opposite".

Grote, in spite of his preoccupation with the bank crises of 1825 and 1828, was also concerned with Brougham and James Mill in the initiation and organization of the new London University. When the foundation stone was laid in April, 1827, Harriet was present in the gallery at the great dinner in the Freemasons' Tavern. There too was Mary Mitford proudly listening when the choir sang:

> The march of armies might be traced
> But not the march of mind.

I see Harriet squeeze her hand, and deftly remove the ticket which reveals the inexpensiveness of her smart turban, but the incident is not elsewhere recorded.

In 1830 the elder Grote died, and George Grote became a wealthy man, and, better still, his own master. Harriet used to quote with approval Sydney Smith's saying—"George Grote is the slave of a pampered conscience." His filial bondage had been heavy: he once confirmed with solemn emphasis the truth of a friend's remark that "parents are generally the most ungrateful people in the world". Politics now became engrossing. The French Revolution of July occurring soon after the first of the Grotes' frequent visits to Paris, George Grote sent £500 for the use of the Committee at the Hotel de Ville. In the spring of 1831 he was asked to stand for the City, and refused in the interests of his *History*. But, like the other philosophical Radicals he expected far-reaching practical results from the passage of the Reform Bill, and next year he yielded. In December Grote headed the poll in the City election, and Harriet wrote exultantly —"He is now the Senior Member for the capital of the

Empire." The Grotes leased Dulwich Wood, "a commodious residence with gardens and some acres of meadow land", where they entertained the philosophic Radicals at the end of the week, lodging in Westminster while the House was sitting. Old Jeremy Bentham, who had enjoyed their turtle soup at an earlier suburban retreat, was to have been one of their first guests, but his visit was postponed by "Wellington Week", and he died soon afterwards. It was agreed that Grote should take over the ballot question from Warburton, and his first motion in its favour was made on April 25th, 1833. He spoke for over an hour: his voice, though not powerful, carried well, and he was quite free from nervousness. The speech was printed and circulated, and was approved by both Liberals and Radicals. Hobhouse coupled it with Macaulay's on Copyright as the two best speeches he had heard in the House.

The session was disappointing: Irish garboils had occupied a disproportionate amount of time, and Grote had offended his constituents by voting against the repeal of the Malt Tax. The Grotes refreshed themselves by a tour in Wales and Wiltshire with their phaeton and a couple of saddle horses, and then returned to Dulwich, Grote riding up to Threadneedle Street three or four times a week. But her husband's state of mind gave Harriet serious cause for anxiety: he was, in short, thoroughly demoralized. "G. did not apply himself"—she writes in her diary—"as I earnestly besought him, to the furtherance of his

History during the winter; but permitted himself to graze about the field of letters—a propensity with which he is not in general reproachable, having usually had distinct objects in view in his studious hours. This winter, he has indulged in all manner of promiscuous reading, and has written fewer memoranda in connection with books than I ever recollect him to have done in the same period. I very much apprehend that he will continue this desultory habit of reading, and feel it painful to resume the old labours to which he once applied himself with fond attention and sustained energy. I see, too, a growing demand in his mind for the acquisition of Physical Science, Geology and Chemistry in particular."

These unwholesome cravings were confined to literature: the only other dissipation during the autumn was a dinner with old Mrs. Grote, now appropriately domiciled on Clapham Common.

The session of 1834 again disappointed the hopes of the philosophic Radicals. Ireland was in the forefront, and it is curious to note that Hansard reports a speech of Grote's supporting a motion for the reduction of the Irish Church revenues, whereas, in fact, Lord Althorpe moved the adjournment, and neither mover nor seconder spoke. Grote again displeased his constituents by his uncompromising support of the Poor Law Amendment Act. He also attacked Macaulay's salary as legal member of the Council of India. As Macaulay received £10,000 a year and saved £30,000 in four years the criticism was not unwarrantable, but

it probably served to increase the mysterious friction
between the two men.

After the dissolution of 1834 Grote was returned at
the bottom of the list. Next year he took an active part
in the Municipal Corporations Reform Bill, opposed
Mr. Gladstone on Irish Disestablishment, and made
his second speech on the ballot. Mrs. Grote records in
her diary: "He spoke for an hour and a quarter in a
very full house, and, from various evidence which I
collected, he was considered to have performed his task
to admiration. Mr. Warburton and Mr. Strutt told me
it was the finest reasoned speech they had ever heard in
the House of Commons. I think it *was* as good as a
second speech on the same topic could be, and George
appears to be content with his success." Charles Buller,
writing to Sarah Austin of the speeches, says: "Grote's
was capital, in his cold, correct style." But William
Wordsworth was of another mind:

Said Secrecy to Cowardice and Fraud,
Falsehood and Treachery, in close council met,
Deep under ground, in Pluto's cabinet,
"The frost of England's pride will soon be thawed;
"Hooded the open brow that overawed
"Our schemes; the faith and honour, never yet
"By us with hope encountered, be upset;——
"For once I burst my bonds, and cry, applaud!"
Then whispered she, "The Bill is carrying out!"
They heard, and, starting up, the Brood of Night
Clapped hands, and shook with glee their matted locks;

All Powers and Places that abhor the light
Joined in the transport, echoed back their shout,
Hurrah for Grote*, hugging his Ballot-box!

During this session the exertions of the philosophic
Radicals made some impression. Sir James Graham
alluded in the House to the threat of "a Grote and
Warburton Administration". This was taken seriously
by Grote who "regretted such a fancy had even been
started, inasmuch as such a situation was as much
above his ambition, as it would be foreign to his taste,
his pursuits, and his interests". In the recess Mrs.
Grote was amused to find an accidental meeting with
"old Joey Hume" at Matlock Bath, regarded as
"*concerted*" between these two *eminent "destructives*".
"Mr. Arkwright (a rich Tory mill-owner, and 'all
that') went down to the shop of a tradesman here
yesterday afternoon, and, in an undertone of voice,
said, 'Mr. Vallance, do you know whom we have got
here at this moment?'—'No, sir.'—'Why, here is
Mr. Grote, and not only he, but Mr. Hume!' as if some
dreadful event must come of so notable a conjunction
of the maleficent planets."

The session of 1836 was disheartening: Harriet notes
that: "Mr. Grote, and about five others, find themselves left to sustain the Radical opinions of the House
of Commons. One evening, after all other guests had
departed, Sir W. Molesworth and Charles Buller re-

* I have inserted the name, of which there can be no
doubt.

251

mained late at our house, talking of the present aspect of affairs. 'I see what we are coming to, Grote,' said Charles Buller; 'in no very long time from this, you and I shall be left to "tell" Molesworth!' " In spite of a flat debate on the ballot the Grotes expended much energy during the autumn in inventing a ballot-box and distributing £50 worth of models.

One of Grote's supporters describes the scene at the Guildhall when candidates were nominated after the dissolution of 1837. "I would have Grote painted as he stood on the rostrum bawling unheard, amid the din and roar, and underneath I would write, 'A Sage and Philosopher, emerged from his closet to enlighten his fellow-citizens upon the topics most deeply allied to their social welfare'." His advocacy of the new Poor Law had gone against him, and he only kept his seat by a narrow margin. During the session he spoke against the proposal for granting an additional £8,000 to the Duchess of Kent, and supported Hume's motion for reducing the vote to the Queen. Both speeches were worded with great tact: an economist who was known to be a republican had to tread delicately.

The philosophic Radicals had lost seats, and the defection of Lord Durham was a blow. The Sage and Philosopher was growing very weary of dissipating his intellectual energy to so little purpose. Harriet wrote that George "has no heart for the coming session, and deplores the loss of old William IV daily". None the less he secured a substantial vote in favour of the ballot in 1838 after a heated debate which lasted seven hours. "I sat up for George," writes Harriet, "and he came home a little before two A.M. (I had posted the carriage for him, by an effort of despotism), old Warburton accompanied him, and Prescott; and Warburton held out his arms to embrace me, and we performed a *dramatical 'accolade'* (strictly dramatic only), *he* in fits of delight at George's speech; I really was half *'toxlicated'*, dead sleepy, but, awakened by his rapturous praises, I seemed in a trance. . . . George, all the while, looking radiant and modest, and to cover his blushes, set to, vigorously attacking a cold capon, which, with other *suitables*, I had caused to be set forth. Well sir, the raptures in due time gave way to *Oysters*, etc., and then came the chorus of contempt from all three, at the figure which the Whig leader and his forty-eight or fifty followers cut, with two hundred Liberals arrayed against him." But next year the ballot debate was "a melancholy contrast with previous occasions, when the whole corps of Radicals were wont to come and pour out their congratulations in Eccleston Street". During the session of 1840 Grote took part in the debate on the Corn Laws but spoke little otherwise.

Meanwhile, in spite of political disappointments, Harriet was the gainer. James Mill was dead, the philosophic Radicals poor company in their disgruntled state, and Grote now allowed her to entertain the sort of society to which she had been accustomed before her marriage. Better still, he actually consented to dine at Holland House with Lord Melbourne

and other distinguished and aristocratic persons. It was
the heyday of the Whig holy of holies. Everybody best
worth meeting, English and foreign, Tories as well as
Whigs, was sure to put in an appearance there sooner
or later. Lord Holland was the most genial and delightful of hosts, Lady Holland, in spite of her auto-
cratic attitude toward her guests, the most successful
mistress of an English salon, then or at any other time.
A letter from Henry Bulwer, who had met her in
Paris, prepared the Hollands for Mrs. Grote's personality: "stiff and gaunt but clever, and tho' laying down
the law on all subjects, commercial, political, literary
and religious, not so disagreeable as I anticipated".
She was accepted and their name appears more than
once in the Holland House dinner-books.

George Grote had been led so far down the primrose
path of sociability that he even went to the Queen's
Ball at Buckingham Palace, and that without a twinge
of his republican conscience. This year also they took
their first journey by rail, to stay with Grote's old
school-fellow, Waddington, now Dean of Durham.
Grote's longing for a life of scholarship was growing,
and he writes to Cornewall Lewis of the pleasures of
literature and philosophy "in this age of steam and
cant". In fact Harriet should have been in the House
of Commons in his stead. As Francis Place said of her,
she *was* the philosophic Radicals. Fanny Kemble,
who met them first early in 1841, remarks that
Grote's speeches were often attributed to Mrs. Grote.
"At that time she was the female centre of the Radical

party in politics—a sort of not-young-or-handsome
feminine oracle, among a set of very clever half
heathenish men, in whose drawing-room Sydney
Smith used to say, he always expected to find an altar
to Zeus. . . . The persons one most frequently met at
her house in Eccleston Street were Roebuck, Leader,
Byron's quondam associate Trelawny, and Sir William
Molesworth; both the first and last mentioned gentlemen were then of an infinitely deeper shade of
Radicalism in their politics than they subsequently
became." The account of their first interview shows
Mrs. Grote's characteristic abruptness. "We did not
say a great deal to each other, but upon my saying
incidentally (I forget about what) 'I, who have always
preserved my liberty, at least the small crumb of it
that a woman can own anywhere', she faced about, in a
most emphatical manner, and said, 'Then you've
struggled for it.' 'No, I have not been obliged to do so.'
'Ah, then, you must, or you'll lose it, you'll lose it,
depend upon it.' I smiled, but did not reply, because I
saw that she was not taking into consideration the fact
of my living in America; and this was the only truly
Grotesque (as Sydney Smith says) passage between us.
Mrs. Grote's appearance," continues Fanny, "was extremely singular; 'striking' is, I think, the most
appropriate word for it. She was very tall, square built,
and high-shouldered, her hands and arms, feet and
legs (the latter she was by no means averse to dis-
playing), were uncommonly handsome and well made.
Her face was rather that of a clever man than a

woman, and I used to think there was some resemblance between herself and our piratical friend, Trelawney. . . . Her taste in dress was, as might have been expected, slightly eccentric, but, for a person with so great a perception of harmony of sound, her passion for discordant colours was singular. The first time I ever saw her she was dressed in a bright brimstone-coloured silk gown, made so short as to show her feet and ankles, having on her head a white satin hat, with a forest of white feathers; and I remember her standing, with her feet wide apart and her arms akimbo, in this costume before me, and challenging me upon some political question, by which, and her appearance, I was much astonished and a little frightened. One evening she came to my sister's house dressed entirely in black, but with scarlet shoes on, with which I suppose she was particularly pleased, for she lay on a sofa with her feet higher than her head, American fashion, the better to display or contemplate them. I remember, at a party, being seated by Sydney Smith, when Mrs. Grote entered with a rose-coloured turban on her head, at which he suddenly exclaimed, 'Now I know the meaning of the word "grotesque"!' The mischievous wit professed his cordial liking for both her and her husband, saying, 'I like them, I like them; I like him, he so ladylike; and I like her, she's such a perfect gentleman'; in which, however, he had been forestalled by a person who certainly *n'y entendait pas malice*, Mrs. Chorley, the meekest and gentlest of human beings, who one evening at a party at her son's house, said to him, pointing out Mrs. Grote, who was dressed in white, 'Henry, my dear, who is the gentleman in the white muslin gown?' "

Mrs. Grote's manners were those of the grande dame, a grande dame who could afford to be as abrupt, if not as rude, as she chose—the Empress had been her nursery name—and casual acquaintance found her formidable: "you feared her till you loved her". She once boasted of her patience with bores. "That may be, dear Grota," answered Sydney Smith, "but you do not conceal your sufferings." But friends could always rely on her understanding and sympathy: she was, as she said of herself, "a good affliction woman". Sydney Smith's first impression was of an ideal wife for a country clergyman, but he should have said squarson. There was more of Lady Catherine de Burgh than of Charlotte Collins in Harriet's composition: she might know—as her friends alleged—if a hoop was off a pail in her back-kitchen, but she never forgot the county.

Mrs. Grote's writings do not do her justice: they are unremarkable for either wit or style. Her own personality and that of her husband may be divined from casual remarks and incidents, but the material is selected with little discrimination, and the gratitude of the reader is constantly claimed for letters and fragments of diaries of no importance. She can never make up her mind whether she is Mrs. George Grote or the first person singular; her use of inverted commas resembles that of the Friendly Society who presented their secretary with a "barometer"—even her "cook" appears so adorned. Always self-possessed and ready, she was at her best in conversation—"she instantly stripped a subject of its false colours or flimsy adornment, walked through a fallacy, or tossed over a half truth".

In 1841 Grote spoke on the Syrian question during the debate on the Address, the most telling of his general speeches: his final effort was a forcible attack on the Sugar Duties. But for the last three years he had been feeling that it was a waste of time to sit in the House of Commons merely sustaining Whig conservatism against Tory conservatism, and after the General Election of 1841 he refused to stand again. A conscientious and respected member of the House, he had brought with him a scholar's standards, and never spoke on any subject which he had not thoroughly mastered. But J. S. Mill, anxiously watching the decline of the philosophic Radicals, recognized that without a heaven-sent leader they could make no headway in the trough of Tory reaction. Grote was not combative enough for such uphill work, though, with his measured judgment, public spirit, and excellent business capacity, he might perhaps have led successfully an established party in times of peace. Many years later when Mrs. Grote was boasting to the Amberleys that Grote would only admit honest, straightforward politicians to their inner circle, and they had never entertained Brougham or O'Connell, or any demagogues, only reasonable Radicals, Mill expressed a doubt whether it was possible to be so particular, and yet keep a party together.

Three months' hard work in Threadneedle Street were followed by the Italian tour of which the Grotes had long dreamed: Verona, Venice, Florence, Siena, and so to Rome. The first night at Verona Grote asked his wife for an Italian grammar: "I want to look up my verbs". When they went next day to the amphitheatre she was astonished to hear him speak Italian with facility. They saw the sights of Rome and the Campagna with characteristic thoroughness; but Paestum was Grote's most absorbing experience, and, curiously enough, he was content to let the Temple of Poseidon remain his nearest approach in the flesh to Greece. As he sat on a fallen column Harriet playfully took off his hat and filled it with acanthus leaves. "Why, bless me!" he remarked in surprise when they had returned to Salerno in the evening, "How could these leaves possibly have got into my hat?" Sydney Smith amused himself and Cornewall Lewis with the idea of Harriet as tourist:

"What shall we do when our friend Mrs. Grote returns from Italy? We must get models of the Antinous and Apollo. Common gestures and human postures will not do. You must look like a dying gladiator, and I must set up in my old age for a Sacerdos Belvedere. I am very sorry she is going; there will be no philosophy but in Pantaloons, till her return."

And again:

"Mrs. Grote is, I presume, abroad, collecting at Rome, for Roebuck and others, anecdotes of Catiline and the Gracchi."

The Grotes were in England again in the spring of 1842. Some years before Mrs. Grote had been captivated by Fanny Elssler, and had entertained Miss Kemble by her belief that she had missed her own true vocation for the ballet, though "she looks like nothing but Trelawney in petticoats". An unfathered Elssler baby was actually born in the Grotes' house, and Harriet undertook to "make an honest woman" of Fanny. She vainly tried to facilitate that enterprise by introducing her into London society. Fanny Kemble was invited to meet her at Burnham Beeches, but Sydney Smith would not allow it: "No, no, my child; that's all very well for Grota, but don't mix yourself up with that sort of thing". Having failed with the mother, Mrs. Grote did her best to save the daughter from peril. When the danseuse was going to America she is reported to have said, "Well, Fanny, send the brat to me; I don't ask you whose child it is, and I don't care so long as it isn't that fool d'Orsay's, and I'll take the best care of it I can." But the world did ask. George Grote and Fanny Elssler! Not, one would think, a promising conjunction, yet with Fanny all things were possible. There was some scandal and much amusement, but Harriet had taken the risks with open eyes, knowing the nature of the witch with whom she was dealing: she was not the woman to be scared by gossip and her heart was almost broken when "the demented Fanny" snatched the child from them à few years later. The little Thérèse was more grateful than her mother. She died soon after her marriage to an Austrian officer, who brought their daughter to see his wife's old friends, and Mrs. Grote left the girl a legacy. Soon after the loss of Thérèse, Harriet took charge of the "Groticles", the three children of Grote's brother, Arthur, who had died in India.

Grote now settled down to his *History* in good earnest. In 1842 he sketched out the first two volumes, and wrote the article on "Grecian Legends and Early History", which excited much interest when published in the *Westminster Review* the following May, and next year he retired from business in order to devote his whole time to it. The diffident scholar assumed that he would have to publish the book at his own expense, but Harriet, knowing better, undertook the negotiations. When she reported on her contract with Murray, Grote remarked—"I only hope that the poor man will not be a loser by me, and then I shall be content, come what may." The first two volumes appeared in 1846. Grote had been much agitated about their reception, and Harriet enjoyed watching the effect of a flood of congratulations and eulogies, among them a long letter of appreciation from Hallam. "Thus I became, for once, witness of a state of feeling on his part approaching to gratified self-love, which at times would pierce through that imperturbable veil of modesty habitually present with him." Her own share in "Our History" was not limited to the publishing arrangements: she was an indefatigable proof corrector and critic, though in the latter capacity she sometimes met with a gentle rebuff. "Now really, George, *are* you obliged to publish all this absurd and incredible stuff?" "Certainly, my love. An Historian is bound to produce the materials upon which he builds, be they never so fantastic, absurd, or incredible." More important than any direct help was Mrs. Grote's determination that nothing should interfere with her husband's work. At Burnham Beeches, as she proudly says, he "enjoyed the leisure of a lodger". She invited and entertained the guests, and Grote, when he emerged from his study in the afternoon, found Lord Lansdowne or Rogers, Nassau Senior, or the young psychologist, Alexander Bain, ready for a walk or a game of billiards. On one occasion Fanny Kemble arrived at Burnham Beeches with Rogers, who was criticizing an addition to the house:

"He had hardly uttered his three first disparaging bitter sentences, of utter scorn and abhorrence of the architectural abortion, which, indeed, it was, when Mrs. Grote herself made her appearance in her usual country costume, box-coat, hat on her head, and stick in her hand. Mr. Rogers turned to her with a very nice smile, and said: 'I was just remarking that in whatever part of the world I had seen this building I should have guessed to whose taste I might attribute its erection.' To which, without an instant's hesitation, she replied: 'Ah, *'tis* a beastly thing, to be sure. The confounded workmen played the devil with the place while I was away.' "

During this visit they were discussing Sydney Smith's letters, and Rogers took a malicious joy in picturing the dismay their publication would create. Mrs. Grote said that those to herself must certainly be expurgated, and showed him one as an example:

"Rogers took the letter from her, and read it with a stony grin of diabolical delight in his countenance and occasional chuckling exclamations of 'Publish it! Publish it! Put an R, dash, or an R and four stars for the name. He'll never know it, though everybody else will.' While Mr. Rogers was thus delecting himself, in anticipation, with R——'s execution, Mrs. Grote, by whose side I was sitting on a low stool, quietly unfolded another letter of Sydney Smith's, and silently held it before my eyes, and the very first words in it ('I never think of death in London but when I meet Rogers') were a most ludicrous allusion to Rogers' cadaverous appearance. As I raised my eyes from this most absurd description of him, and saw him still absorbed in his evil delight, the whole struck me as so like a scene in a farce that I could not refrain from bursting out laughing."

She also records a conversation when Rogers, Nassau

Senior and one of Mrs. Grote's brothers were present, which has the authentic ring of philosophical Radicalism:

"In speaking of Arnold, I was ineffably amused at hearing Mrs. Grote characterize him as a '*very* weak man', which struck me as very funny. The *Esprit Fort*, however, I take it, merely referred to his belief in the immortality of the soul, the existence of a·God, and a few other similar 'superstitions'. They seemed all to agree that he was likely to 'turn out' *only* such men as Lord Sandon and Lord Ashley."

Fanny remarks that they had forgotten Arthur Stanley. Both the Grotes were musical: as a young man Grote himself had played the violoncello. Mrs. Grote took Jenny Lind, a more tractable protégée than Fanny Elssler, under her wing so completely that it was almost impossible to approach the singer except through her formidable patroness. She was often at The Beeches, and Mendelssohn, an intimate friend, and other professional musicians were entertained there. Fanny Kemble describes one of their musical réunions:

"Our party consisted only of my sister and myself; the Viennese composer, Dessauer; and Chorley, the musical critic of the *Athenæum*, who was very intimately acquainted with us all. The eccentricities of our hostess, with which some of us were already tolerably familiar, were a source of unfeigned amazement and awe to Dessauer, who, himself the most curious, quaint, and withal nervously excitable and irritable humourist, was thrown into alternate convulsions of laughter and spasms of terror at the portentous female figure, who, with a stick in her hand, a man's hat on her head, and a coachman's box-coat of drab cloth with manifold capes, over her petticoats . . . stalked about the house and grounds, alternately superintending various matters of the domestic economy, and discussing, with equal knowledge and discrimination, questions of musical criticism and taste.

"One most ludicrous scene which took place on this occasion I shall never forget. She had left us to our own devices, and we were all in the garden. I was sitting on a swing, and my sister, Dessauer, and Chorley were lying on the lawn at my feet, when presently, striding towards us, appeared the extraordinary figure of Mrs. Grote, who, as soon as she was within speaking-trumpet distance, hailed us with a stentorian challenge about some detail of dinner—I think it was whether the majority voted for bacon and peas or bacon and beans. Having duly settled this momentous question, as Mrs. Grote turned and marched away, Dessauer, who had been sitting straight up, listening with his head first on one side and then on the other, like an eagerly intelligent terrier, taking no part in the culinary controversy (indeed, his entire ignorance of English

necessarily disqualified him for even comprehending
it), but staring intently, with open eyes and mouth,
at Mrs. Grote—suddenly began, with his hands and
lips, to imitate the rolling of a drum, and then broke
out aloud with '*Malbrook s'en va-t'en guerre,*' etc.;
whereupon the terrible lady faced right about, like a
soldier, and, planting her stick in the ground, sur-
veyed Dessauer with an awful countenance. The
wretched little man grew red, and then purple, and
then black in the face with fear and shame; and ex-
claiming in his agony, '*Ah! bonté divine! elle m'a
compris!*' rolled over and over on the lawn as if he
had a fit. Mrs. Grote majestically waved her hand,
and with magnanimous disdain of her small adversary turned and departed, and we remained horror-
stricken at the effect of this involuntary tribute of
Dessauer's to her martial air and deportment.''

She bore no malice: when she came back to find
them discussing Glück she shouted for her 'cello, and
played some passages on the lawn "with excellent taste
and expression". Self-consciousness was not one of
Mrs. Grote's failings; she spoke of Audubon dis-
embowelling wild creatures, when he was starving in
the woods, totally oblivious of the shudder which ran
through a Victorian dinner-party at so indelicate a
word on a lady's lips. Fanny Kemble even thought it
necessary to attribute some of the peculiarities of her
demeanour and conversation to her frequent neuralgic
headaches.

The Holland House dinner was dimmed by a greater social triumph. Their neighbour at Windsor sometimes invited them to her private theatricals, and Harriet did not know whether to feel affronted or flattered by the sensation which this distinction created among their friends. Yet she was not altogether satisfied: Fanny Kemble tells how, "after surveying and defining her social position and its various advantages, she exclaimed, 'But I want some lords, Fanny. Can't you help me to some lords?' I told her, laughingly, that I thought the lady who held watch and ward over Mademoiselle Jenny Lind might have as many lords at her feet as she pleased." A snob? certainly—but to me, at least, there is something rather captivating about frank snobbery as there is about frank egotism. Lords are easier to manage with a sociable host: poor Harriet had only a scholarly lodger. In the summer of 1849 she wrote rather petulantly to Nassau Senior: "I no longer feel disposed to pass my life at B.B., seeing that of late years George's learned pursuits have become so absorbing as to render him averse to all country ideas and recreations, as well as to receiving visitors; so that I am checked and cooled in my interest in the place, for want of a congenial partner in the associations which this form of existence generates. Therefore let him have his home in town, and then I shall less hesitate to leave him occasionally, whether in pursuit of health or refreshing society, for my own benefit." It was all very well for her to tell Mme. Alexis de Tocqueville that "both of us have poured our *all* into the more precious *vessel*, and have been content, nay proud, to efface ourselves for the sake of seeing another being shine more brightly". But she was a woman who could not enjoy a sunset without somebody to pinch. Cornewall Lewis, the Fish, as she calls him, and her Historian might be "happy over their learning and their vast doubts of everything", but learning and doubts often palled on Harriet. Her reaction to boredom was acute neuralgia on which the air of Paris and the society of her many French friends had a beneficial effect. Perhaps her absences were sometimes a relief to the precious vessel, though he would never have admitted it even to himself. She was rather an overwhelming wife for a man of retiring disposition. She never saw him with a book, as she complacently observes, without the question "What are you reading, George?" She proudly announced his name to strangers, though he never grew accustomed to his celebrity. "Have I got any dirt on my face, Harriet? Is there anything the matter with my *hat?* What on earth are these people looking at me for?" "Because you are George Grote—that's all."

The Grotes continued to enjoy frequent foreign holidays: both were strenuous travellers, Harriet making notes in her "road books" of anything which interested her, and Grote studying any political conditions which he found suggestive. Both their voices are audible in a letter to Léon Faucher—"I often exclaim as we travel in this enchanting Normandy (we came by Abbeville and Rouen, and by Pont Andemar and

Caen), how I wish we had Léon Faucher with us to explain everything we do not know the reason of. *He* knows everything, from the make of a plough-share to the date of a 'Tourelle'—doesn't he, George?" "Yes, indeed, he has almost universal knowledge of what concerns material existence, as well as intellectual accomplishment." In 1847 Grote, who had been studying Swiss affairs because the dissensions between the cantons struck him as like those between the Greek states, published his *Letters on Switzerland*. Palmerston sent hurriedly for the pamphlet as the Prince Consort had rebuked him for trying to discuss Swiss politics without having read it.

Harriet, by correspondence and frequent visits, had made herself an authority on French affairs. French society suited her better than English: her gifts as a conversationalist were more readily appreciated than in the Grotes' own circle in England, which, after the collapse of philosophic Radicalism, lacked homogeneity and taxed her powers as a hostess. *Esprit clair et pénétrant comme un homme, fin et sensible comme une femme, gai et sérieux à la fois,* she met with a ready response in Paris. Her chief friends were Léon Faucher, editor of the *Courrier Français,* afterwards Minister of the Interior under the Republic, and the Grotes' guest for the Great Exhibition, and Alexis de Tocqueville, who became Foreign Minister in 1849. Tocqueville's remark on one of her articles is a comment on her usefulness as a liaison officer between the two countries. *"C'est le bon sens des économistes anglais,*

*aiguisé seulement et coloré par l'intelligence et l'imagi-
nation d'une femme, ce dont il a souvent grand besoin.*"
Perhaps the English economists, and even George
Grote himself, were insensible to this need. At any rate
there was a peculiar sympathy between Harriet Grote
and Alexis de Tocqueville, and his death in 1859 was a
heavy grief. "There is only *one* left," she wrote,
"whose death could cast me down so low, and God
grant that I may go *myself* before *him*. . . . Whoever
was honoured with the friendship of Alexis might be
regarded as receiving *La croix d'honneur*."

A less congenial acquaintance was George Sand,
whom she described later to Lady Amberley as a bad
woman and the death of Chopin. Once Mrs. Grote asked
her why she did not write to elevate the moral nature,
instead of only romancing; whereupon George Sand
took a pipe out of her mouth and said: "*Voyez, très chère
Mme. Grote, je suis romancière, pas moraliste.*"

Mrs. Grote was in Paris during the *coup d'état* of
1851, and remained there for some weeks as her friends
felt her to be a useful channel of communication with
England. Grote sends Mrs. Austin her news:

> "Mrs. Grote is still at Paris, and talks of remain-
> ing there till the end of the month. She has been in
> no way personally disturbed or alarmed by what
> has been going on. . . . She says generally that
> nothing can be conceived so awful as the state of
> feeling in Paris, the stupefaction and terror which
> reigns there. She has seen shoals of people (she says)

and heard copious details. One paper which I received from her this morning I enclose for your perusal. It is drawn up by some Frenchman whose name she dares not mention, and describes certain feats of the soldiers in the *Blutbad* of December 4. . . .

"I would not be at Paris, as Mrs. Grote is now, for any sum which could be rendered to me. Not because of any personal fear. To an Englishman of common prudence there is no ground for fear, but from the perfect heart-sickening which this tremendous event has given me, and against which I find it hard to bear up, even here, with my books around me. I did not expect to live to see anything so like the brutal setting up of an ancient tyrant in a Grecian City."

And again, a few days later:

"If there be any one portion of France more to be deplored than another in regard to the *régime* now inaugurating, it is the writers and thinkers of the country: men who, above all things, require an atmosphere of freedom. I anticipate an enslavement of speech and thought only paralleled by that of the Empire; and I farther anticipate, what even the Empire did not do, a more complete surrender of all public education into the hands of the priesthood than ever existed before. . . .

"I had a letter from Mrs. Grote yesterday, guarded in its communications, but just in the same melancholy tone as to passing events. She says that Horace Day has received a warning that if he does not mind his doings it will be the worse for him. She says that for a whole day it was fully believed that Léon Faucher, as well as Thiers, had been sent out of the country. She says that she really does not *dare* write all she hears. The quantity of people she sees is greater than her health will sustain; in fact, it seems that the English in Paris are the only persons now exempt from personal terror, and recipients of the breathings of Frenchmen who do not dare to communicate with one another."

Nevertheless there were Frenchwomen who enjoyed the spectacle. Fanny Kemble tells how one of them, showing Mrs. Grote the conveniences of a charming apartment in a central part of Paris, said, "*Voici mon salon, voici ma salle à manger, et voyez comme c'est commode! De cette fenêtre je vois mes révolutions.*"

Sarah Austin, Grote's correspondent, was an intimate friend of Mrs. Grote's from the early days of dinners at the Threddle till her death in 1867. In their letters each is the other's "dearest Cummer". They were drawn together by sympathetic rebellion against the narrow intellectual life which satisfied their learned husbands. For both of them marriage had been a disappointment of their ambitions. After John Austin's death, Mrs. Grote, who had been re-reading letters from Sarah, covering a period of thirty years, describes them as:

> records of a singular series of conflicts, struggles, and chequered fate, such as, if woven into a history,

272

would thrust modern periodical fictions into the shade for interest. Each of our two lives in truth, dear Cummer, if put on paper, would offer a deep and melancholy attraction for thoughtful readers. We both came into the world endowed with the choicest gifts of a "fairy godmother"—personal and mental.

How striking the lesson they (the lives) have both furnished!—that destiny, accident—what you will —mixes the cup of life *for* us, strive as we may. *Your* struggle is over, and you regret your exemption from all care for another. It is well. The evening of *my* course is more serene than the morning and noon thereof, and less agitated by the currents of feeling, and by the torments which every senti- mental and vehement soul *must* be subjected to in the journey through this life.

Her cup did not contain all the spices which Harriet craved, but there was little to sweeten Sarah Austin's bitter draught. The Historian, the Senior Member for the Empire, and the Vice-Chancellor moved in a rut, but Harriet could and did enjoy drawing attention to his illustrious motion, and to her own helpfulness in smoothing his track. Austin's life was a series of failures, followed by supine acceptance of his fate.

Except, perhaps, as a conversationalist, Sarah Austin was an abler woman than Mrs. Grote, a competent translator, journalist and editor of her husband's *Jurisprudence*. Well for him that it was so, as her earnings were at times indispensable. But, even before the shock of her recent biographer's revelations, I had always felt her to be an unpleasant blend of the intellectual woman and the social climber, conventional to the core, and emotionally dependent upon her Platonic flirtations. No. Mrs. Grote I could have loved, if lucky in not boring her, but my relations with Sarah Austin would have been strictly feline.

The Grotes were now established in the last of their London houses, Savile Row, but Harriet found that she must have a country cottage. They built "History Hut" in a small park at East Burnham, where she could fly for health, and entertain the Bunsens and the Milmans in a tent on the lawn. The eleventh volume of the *History* appeared in 1853, and Harriet took special credit for the style, "having pruned and reconstructed without mercy". Two years later the great work was finished, at Christmas, and she celebrated the occasion by brewing punch at History Hut, and carefully noting her husband's reactions:

> Grote himself sipping the delicious mixture with great satisfaction whilst manifesting little emotion outwardly, though I could detect unmistakeable signs of inward complacency as I descanted upon "the happiness of our living to see this day", and so forth.

History Hut was sold in 1858. The Grotes, except for a short break, had been connected with East Burnham for twenty years, but Harriet could no longer endure the position of "a lady residing in the centre of a population dominated by a young servant". The property was in the hands of an elderly and non-resident lady of the manor. The responsible steward lived on another estate, and the charge of East Burnham was left to a deputy whose only concern was to suppress poaching. Cottages were not repaired; the villagers' immemorial rights of turf-cutting were interfered with, their alehouse was tied, with disastrous effects on the beer; ringless pigs routed freely, ditches were unscoured, hedges unlopped, and the roads so neglected that Mrs. Grote could not take proper exercise in the winter. She tried to champion the villagers, but her hands were tied as complainants were threatened with eviction.

Mrs. Grote's views of the relations between rich and poor were a mixture of those of the orthodox squarsoness and of the philosophic Radical. If the gentry began to neglect their duties like the Lady of East Burnham, the principle of centralization, "a symptom of social decline in a free, active, and healthful community" would have to be invoked. "Acts of Parliament will ere long, I expect, establish authority to quicken the activity of rural functionaries on matters involving health, convenience, morality, and decency in village communities." Already the expenditure on the education of the working-classes was excessive, and "an undue proportion of the wealth of this country seems to be, at the present time, employed in teaching the poor to rely on the rich for obtaining

275

many things which they ought properly to aim at obtaining by their own labour and their own virtues". The only alternative to pauperization was birth control, and no one had courage to preach it to the poor. Instead—"A class of writers have betaken themselves to the composition of heart-rending fictions, bearing a resemblance with certain forms of life among our lower classes, and they have succeeded, to a certain extent, in inspiring every eater of daily dinners with something like a sentiment of shame and self-reproach." This only led to almsgiving, and the temporary interference with a great "natural law", the "positive check" of death from poverty. "But the law resumes its march, and the weeping reader of Mrs. Norton's, *Boz's*, Hood's, and other tragical works, must either sacrifice more of his own substance, or let it march." It was monstrous that "humanity-preachers" and "charity-crusaders" should make the existence of poverty a reproach against "the rich and elevated classes", whose possession and enjoyment of property is a fundamental law of civilization. Yet the cottagers of East Burnham lamented that there would be no one left to care for them when "Madam" had gone, and there is reason to suspect that, in spite of her invectives against charity and her belief in the "positive check", Madam's care was not always limited to good advice.

After the disposal of History Hut, Mrs. Grote went to France for the summer leaving Grote, who had begun work on his *Plato* immediately after finishing

the *History*, in Savile Row. He now had social resources of his own as a member of "The Club" *par
excellence*, the club of Johnson and Reynolds and
Goldsmith, where in those days he could enjoy the best
literary talk to be had in London. This was one of
Harriet's triumphs. Grote had pleaded his preference
for dining at home, but she whispered to Lord Overstone, "Slip a shilling into his hand, and enlist him,
in the name of the Club." Lord Overstone accomplished this feat in a farewell hand-shake, and Grote
succumbed. Mrs. Grote complacently prints a letter of
her husband's written during her absence "as attesting
the writer's capacity of cherishing the deepest sentiment of affection, as well as the disposition, to appreciate the blessing granted him in the possession of his
devoted and life-long companion":

"My dearest Harriet, I have received no letter
from you since the letter of the 28th from Fontaine-
bleau. I do not mention this either in the way of
surprise or in that of complaint, but simply to state,
that I have nothing special to reply to, and that the
present letter is a spontaneous effusion. It opens,
therefore, naturally, as a love letter, being the ten-
thousandth of a series which begins in 1818 and
continues still unexhausted in 1858, when you are a
matron, endeared by a long life of delicious companionship. I cannot tell you how I dwell upon you
every hour of the day, and how full my memory is
of our thirty years of married life. The H.G. of the

present has left me, but it is only to give place to the H.G. of the past—the passion of my youth, the tutelary and sympathizing Deity of my mature age, the consolation of my latter years.

"I now enjoy the privilege of passing my old age alone with you, without those family vexations which aggravate so cruelly the burthen of old age. It is with the greatest delight that I reflect that I am not destined to the misery of surviving you, and that the Will I lately executed will be at some future day a reality. I am really unable to conceive what life would be without you.

"Adieu—my dearest and best beloved Harriet—in old age as in youth, in 1818 and in 1858, ever and alike cherished by your tender and affectionate

"GEO. GROTE."

After such a letter it is little wonder that Mrs. Grote was seriously disturbed when, half a dozen years later, her husband embarked on an elderly love-affair. Apart from the shock to her own feelings, she was anxious lest this folly should damage his reputation, and her remonstrances, couched, no doubt, in unvarnished language, caused an estrangement between them. Lady Amberley, one of her two or three women confidantes, writes: "She was so tender on the old Grote and said it was common for old men to have deep passions late in life, she had known several cases of it; two old men had had passions for her and in one case it had hastened the old man's death. She said it was a very eminent man before my time. May be it was Bentham! or de Tocqueville! She said it only belonged to the highest and most refined natures to love at that age, and not to coarse and sensual ones. She was a curious mixture of admiration for his refined nature, and vexation at the trial it had been to her. I cd. not understand talking of it so dispassionately at all." The storm passed over, and the old couple were in complete sympathy again before Grote's death.

In August, 1858, Grote joined his wife at St. Germains. There was nothing of special interest in the political situation: the second empire seemed to be firmly established, but Grote was distressed by the growing ascendancy of the Jesuits, especially in educational matters. He suffered from a severe attack of conjunctivitis, and reflects characteristically on "the justice of that Greek tragic metaphor by which $\beta\lambda\acute{\epsilon}\pi\omega\nu$ is used as equivalent to $\zeta\hat{\omega}\nu$". There is a glimpse of Harriet reading aloud a treatise on physiology—"I remember halting now and then, as I read out passages inconceivably scientific and abstruse, when I would enquire: 'George, do you understand what I am reading to you?' 'Perfectly.' 'Oh! very well, then I will go on; for my part it is quite above *my* comprehension.' A bland smile would be all he had to give in reply to this confession."

For four years the Grotes rented Barrow Green House, near Godstone, where Bentham and the Mills had lived for a time. There Grote wrote much of his *Plato* with the little spitz, Dora, lying helpfully on

279

his lap, and there they entertained Jowett and Dr. William Smith, the Motleys, Bains, Seniors, and other congenial spirits. But the chief success as a visitor was John Stuart Mill, full of recollections of Jeremy Bentham and his own childhood at Barrow Green. Mill was henceforward one of Mrs. Grote's closest friends, and when he died in 1873 she numbered him with Lady Amberley, Felix Mendelssohn and Alexis de Tocqueville as the dearest of her dead. This had not always been so: Grote had maintained his connection with Mill, but for Harriet a Princess de Talleyrand more or less in the family was one thing, and ambiguous relations with the wife of a drysalter quite another.

The Grotes had always rather prided themselves on the admission of Americans to their circle, and Mrs. Grote notes the acceptance of Americans as one of the important social changes of her day. She tells an amusing story of Lord William Bentinck, who had met the jurist, John Duer, at their house—"I thought your *American* very pleasant company, and it was, moreover, a surprise to me, for I never in my life before met an American in society!" "Well, but," I replied, "when you were Governor-General of India you must have seen Americans out there?" "Only ship captains," rejoined Lord William, "whom I now and then thought it right to invite to my great Government House dinners, but I never *spoke* to any of them." But now Grote was antagonized by the American attitude: he strongly approved the neutrality of England during the Civil War, "and the way in

which the Northern Americans have requited such
forbearance is alike silly and disgusting. I never expected to have lived to think of them so unfavourably
as I do at present." His own reputation in America
may be inferred from a sentence in a letter after his
death, preserved with somewhat humourless pride by
his widow. "When the electric cable flashed across the
Atlantic the news of this great loss, the whole of this
vast continent vibrated with sympathy for you."

Grote had received an honorary D.C.L. in 1853,
but, in spite of his cordial reception at Oxford, had not
felt altogether at ease in academic circles. Now, ten
years later, the Grotes paid a radiantly successful visit
to A. P. Stanley at Christchurch, with the Milmans as
fellow guests. Jowett gave a breakfast party in their
honour, and in the evenings the Dean filled his rooms
with a select band of undergraduates. "They clustered
round Grote with eagerness, blending the freedom of
youth with their respectful homage,—even 'elbowing'
one another in order to get close to him and catch every
word that dropped from his lips; while he, resting his
person against the arm of a large chair (not liking to
sit down in the presence of so many *standing* round)
discoursed familiarly with those nearest to him on the
subjects most interesting to their common tastes—
classic lore, of course, the foremost topic." Meanwhile
"gentlemen of the tutorial class" assured Mrs. Grote of
the enthusiasm with which the University youth devoured the works of Grote and J. S. Mill. Even Grote
himself left Oxford convinced of his influence as

scholar and historian. Another gratification was his election in 1864 as Foreign Member of the French Institute in place of Macaulay.

Barrow Green was given up as too far from London, and in 1864 the Grotes bought the last of their country houses, the Ridgeway, so named after the home of Harriet's childhood, near Albury Park in Surrey. *Plato and the other Companions of Sokrates* appeared in 1865: the sale exceeded expectation, and Mark Pattison was among the eulogists. Grote was already at work on his *Aristotle*, the completion of his trilogy. Public work made a heavy call on his strength, meetings sometimes occupying as much as four hours a day. He had succeeded Hallam as a trustee of the British Museum in 1859, and was specially concerned with the removal of the Natural Science department to South Kensington. In 1866 he renewed his effort, which in the first instance had been defeated, to secure a layman for the chair of mental philosophy at University College, and after a prolonged and unpleasant controversy Croome Robertson was appointed instead of the Unitarian minister, James Martineau. Next year Grote became President of the Council. In 1862 he had been elected Vice-Chancellor of the London University, and strongly advocated the claim brought forward by Miss Elizabeth Garrett that women should be allowed to sit for matriculation. This was not conceded till 1868. Mrs. Grote was in full sympathy with her husband's efforts to improve the position of women. She had long worried over the unhappy fate of unmarried women to whom nothing was open but an unbroken course of self-abnegation. Why should they be deprived of happiness except such as they might attain through self-sacrifice? Men were not always expecting self-sacrifice of each other. Although a thorough-paced rationalist, she had even been disposed to look favourably on Protestant Sisterhoods as a means of escape; now better things were in sight. Her eyes had been opened originally to the preposterous state of the law by the theft of her purse, described in the police court, of course, as the property of Mr. Grote. She was a member of the London Society for Women's Suffrage, presiding over a meeting in 1870 when J. S. Mill's young disciple, Sir Charles Dilke, spoke on the recent extension of the municipal franchise.

Her views on another subject have a strangely modern ring. "It is singular," she writes in 1859, "that I have, like . . ., for these ten years past, seen and pointed out to many reflecting friends, the improbability of the world's going on much longer with the old institution of marriage unaltered. The obvious impatience of restraints of all kinds, which characterizes our epoch, will tend to two results: the first marrying, and then unmarrying by legal means to a prodigious extent; second, concubinage becoming less fatal to reputation of women.

"The myriads of spinsters, poor and rich, now fluttering about the world, can never surely accept celibacy for ever, so long as 'heaps of men' are ready to 'make a bargain' with them short of the irrevocable one. The augmented craving for enjoyment now prevailing on the part of young men, reduces the inclination to marry, and thereby circumscribe the *means* of enjoyment.

"I contemplate the coming period of society as fraught with moral evil and difficulty. But society itself never chooses to take note of anything *beforehand*. Wait for the mischief, and then *quack* for it. The tacit agreement to ignore the subject of sex, whilst in reality it occupies the thoughts at least twice as much as any other subject, both in men and women, especially men, is childish folly."

In the 'sixties Mrs. Grote found another protégée, dearer and more congenial than either the bewitching Fanny Elssler or the docile Jenny Lind, Kate Stanley, afterwards Lady Amberley. Her own career as a political *grande dame* had been thwarted: the little salon had never become the social triumph of her dreams. The Amberleys belonged to the aristocracy which she had always adored and envied: an advanced party led by them ought to succeed where the philosophical Radicals had failed. All the aspirations of her own youth might be fulfilled in the person of Lady Amberley. She installed herself as mentor, ready to praise and blame, and to give both the young people the benefit of her own and Grote's experience. They were receptive and affectionate. The death of Lady Amberley in 1872 meant the severing of Mrs. Grote's closest tie with the younger generation.

During 1868, when Grote was in his seventy-fourth year, his wife became very anxious about his health. "Mr. Grote's personal aspect is sensibly changed within the last eight months, whilst I discern a lessening capacity for bodily exertion not fairly referable to his being one year older. His hand shakes worse than it did, his gait has altered to that of an old man, from being remarkably steady and elastic up to a recent date." His mental powers were unimpaired: he says of himself—"as to *quality* (both perspicacity, memory, and suggestive association bringing up new combinations), I am sure that my intellect is as good as ever it was", but he worked less rapidly. For eight months he was wholly absorbed in his essay on Aristotle's *De Anima*, written for publication in Bain's *The Senses and the Intellect*, even talking about it to his wife during their half-hour's walk in Kensington Gardens, the only exercise he could be induced to take. When it was finished he seemed to feel, as she said, that he had hung up his shield in the Temple of Philosophy, content that, if he did not live to complete his work, his fellow students would find there the essence of his Aristotelian studies. But none the less he renewed his unremitting labour on the *Aristotle*, refusing to leave London and join Mrs. Grote at the Ridgeway while any of his "Boards" were sitting. The result was that in the summer of 1869 his doctor diagnosed a serious condition of nervous prostration, and sent him off to Homburg. There they spent a dreary fortnight: Mrs. Grote was also ailing and depressed, and the waters did nothing for Grote. But in Paris his spirits revived: he was exhilarated by the rumour that Thiers himself was converted to republicanism, and by the articles against the Empire in the French Press. Again the two voices can be heard: "Well, my love," said I one morning to the Historian, "you seem to enjoy wading through those sheets of railings about the Emperor, but to my taste the matter is coarse, superficial, and hackneyed." "You say truly," he would reply; "one reads nothing but what has been written again and again about public affairs, and there is, really, no great power in what is here vomited forth. But the pleasure I derive from reading all this flood of abuse arises from the bare fact of its publication, without the writers of it being marched off to the *Bicêtre*. That is the point which touches my sympathies, after eighteen years of suppression of all liberty of speech in the nation."

After their return to the Ridgeway Grote was in better health, and able again to enjoy country walks, and the companionship of a few guests. In November came a letter from Mr. Gladstone with the offer of a peerage. Grote replied with an uncompromising refusal. He was anxious to finish his *Aristotle*, and felt it impossible to add a seat in the House of Lords to his other public work. But the offer cheered and excited the two old people, and some sympathy is due to the loyal wife; the nursery empress was born to the coronet. "To be sure" (Grote would say) "it is one of the most unlooked-for events that could have overtaken me in my old age, to have the offer of a peerage! I am never tired of wondering at the bare notion of *my* passing from the 'Radical' to the House of Lords, at this time of day." "Well, you see, it is because you earned the confidence of the 'Radicals' through your House of Commons period that you would now be regarded as representing the popular interest in the Lords, and so, your voice the more weight with the country when you gave utterance to your sentiments." "Yes, that might be so. But the opinions of the so-called Radicals of the present day do not accurately represent those which I and my friends held thirty years ago, and which I continue to hold, substantively. Indeed, I do not think that, personally, I should have found myself ill-assorted with the members of the Upper House, in which there are many able and well-instructed individuals, moved by the purest impulses towards good legislation; and I daresay I *might* have lent a useful support to a Government disposed to sound views, on many subjects. My insuperable objection really, is to the altering my framework of existence in any way." It will be noticed that he says nothing of his republicanism as an obstacle: to the end he remained a republican in sentiment, but two years earlier he had acknowledged to his wife, who had never shared his views, that—"I have outlived my faith in the efficacy of republican government regarded as a check upon the vulgar passions of a majority in a nation, and I recognize the fact that supreme power lodged in their hands *may* be exercised quite as mischievously as by a despotic ruler like the first Napoleon. The conduct of the Northern States, in the late conflict with the Southern States, has led me to this conclusion, though it costs me much to avow it, even to myself."

Grote was also disillusioned about his favourite panacea, the ballot, now a foregone conclusion. "Remarking to the Historian, at my breakfast," writes Mrs. Grote, "what a change had come about, in relation to this question, since *our* parliamentary days, he replied, 'Yes, certainly, the Ballot seems to me now, not unlikely to be ere long carried.'

" 'Well, then, you will have lived to see your own favourite measure triumph over all obstacles, and you will of course feel great satisfaction thereat?'

" 'I should have done so had it not been for the recent alteration in the suffrage. Since the wide expansion of the voting element, I confess that the value of the Ballot has sunk in my estimation. I do not, in fact, think the elections will be affected by it, one way or another, as far as party interests are concerned.'

" 'Still, you will at all events get at the genuine preference of the constituency in choosing their candidate.'

" 'No doubt; but then, again, I have come to perceive that the choice between one man and another, among the English people, signifies less than I used formerly to think it did. Take a section of society, cut it through from top to bottom, and examine the composition of the successive layers. They are much

288

alike throughout the scale. The opinions, all based upon
the same social instincts: never upon a clear or enlightened perception of *general interests*. Every particular class pursuing its own, the result is, a universal
struggle for the advantages accruing from *party*
supremacy. The English mind is much of one pattern,
take whatsoever class you will. The same favourite
prejudices, amiable and otherwise; the same anti-
pathies, coupled with ill-regulated, though benevolent, efforts to eradicate human evils, are well-nigh
universal: modified, naturally, by instruction, among
the highly educated few; but *they* hardly affect the
course of out-of-doors sentiment. I believe, therefore,
that the actual composition of Parliament represents
with tolerable fidelity the British people. And it will
never be better than it is, for a House of Commons
cannot afford to be above its own constituencies, in
intelligence, knowledge, or patriotism.' "

In May, 1870, the University of London was
opened by the Queen. Mrs. Grote caused the Vice-
Chancellor's gown to be smartened with gold lace, and
herself enjoyed the ceremony, but the Chancellor,
Lord Granville, mischievously inflicted torture on the
modest Grote by a prolonged eulogy. The Members
of Convocation asked him to allow Millais to paint his
portrait. During the last sitting Millais let the studio
fire go out, and Grote, too considerate to complain,
caught a heavy chill, but insisted on attending his
meetings in London and going out in all weathers at
the Ridgeway. He had suffered for some time from

varicose veins, and early in January Mrs. Grote was alarmed by the accidental discovery that his legs were now terribly swollen, a fact which Grote himself had regarded as of no importance. The neglected chill and ill-advised exercise had induced disease of the kidneys, but he was still able to read and write and talk to his friends, and, as spring came on, take an occasional drive. In May, against the doctor's orders, he went to a meeting at the British Museum. A few days later a committee of the senate of the London University met in Savile Row. The chief business concerned the examinations for the M.A. degree, and he went through the Greek and Latin papers in detail. To his wife's inquiry whether he had not found this very fatiguing he replied with his accustomed precision: "It certainly taxed the cerebral faculties severely." This was his last public effort, and on June 18th, 1871, he passed tranquilly away. His old friend Stanley, now Dean of Westminster, granted the formal request of the Club that he should be buried in the Abbey. "I selected"—he wrote to Mrs. Grote— "the spot in the south transept, in what Fuller calls the 'learned side' of Poets' Corner. Camden and Casaubon look down upon the grave, and Macaulay lies a few feet distant."

Mrs. Grote lived on for another seven years. Her marriage had been the happier and her comradeship with her husband the more real because they had wisely agreed not to force their relations. In the early days she had been cramped by the narrowness and intolerance of the James Mill set: later the excitements and wider interests of Grote's parliamentary career brought some relief; then, when, with a temperament and gifts so unlike his, she would have been miserable perpetually chained to his study table, her restlessness and ill-health, effect rather than cause, had led more and more to a life of her own, without weakening in any degree the bond with her husband. This independence of character now stood her in good stead and she became the centre of an admiring circle of friends, young and old: she had mellowed with age and, even to bores, was no longer alarming. There is a pretty story of a small boy, eighty years her junior, who, during a discussion on friendship, piped up— "I have got a friend too; it's Mrs. Grote." She died on December 29th, 1878, at the Ridgeway, the last and best loved of her many homes.

INDEX

293

INDEX

INDEX

303